Militant Acts

SUNY series in New Political Science

Bradley J. Macdonald, editor

Militant Acts

The Role of Investigations in Radical Political Struggles

MARCELO HOFFMAN

Cover image: Tarsila do Amaral, *Workers* (1933). Reprinted with permission.

Published by State University of New York Press, Albany

For information, contact State University of New York Press, Albany, NY
www.sunypress.edu

Library of Congress Cataloging-in-Publication Data

Names: Hoffman, Marcelo, author.
Title: Militant acts : the role of investigations in radical political struggles / Marcelo Hoffman.
Description: Albany : State University of New York Press, [2019] | Series: SUNY series in new political science | Includes bibliographical references and index.
Identifiers: LCCN 2018007502 | ISBN 9781438472614 (hardcover : alk. paper) | ISBN 9781438472621 (pbk. : alk. paper) | ISBN 9781438472638 (ebook)
Subjects: LCSH: Radicalism—History. | Social sciences—Research—Political aspects | Communism—Public opinion.
Classification: LCC HN49.R33 H64 2019 | DDC 303.48/4—dc23
LC record available at https://lccn.loc.gov/2018007502

10 9 8 7 6 5 4 3 2 1

To Caetano

Contents

Acknowledgments ix

1 Introduction 1

2 Sources of the Militant Investigation in Marxism: Marx, Lenin, and Mao 25

3 Workers' Inquiries from Breakaway Trotskyism to Italian Workerism 53

4 Badiou, the Maoist Investigation, and the Party Form 81

5 In the Shadow of Oedipus: *Enquêtes* in Foucault's Theory and Practice 103

6 Conclusion 133

Notes 143

Bibliography 173

Index 183

Acknowledgments

Like any other scholarly undertaking, this book sprang to life from the generosity of others. Perry Zurn and Andrew Dilts provided me with the initial momentum for the book by allowing me to begin to collate my thoughts about the topic of militant investigations in their coedited book, *Michel Foucault, the Prisons Information Group, and the Future of Abolition* (Palgrave Macmillan, 2016). Chad Lavin went out of his way to facilitate a crucial contact for the initiation of the project. Thanasis Lagios provided me with useful materials and supportive words. Stuart Elden went well beyond normal standards of generosity in academe. He discovered and passed on information about an archival source from the Bibliothèque nationale de France in Paris while conducting his own research there. I am grateful to Timophy S. Murphy for reading a draft of one of my chapters and offering helpful feedback on it. Rebecca E. Karl drew my attention to one of Mao Zedong's little-known investigations.

I owe a very special debt of gratitude to the professors who kindly invited me to share portions of my research for this book at their institutions. I thank Dan Smith for inviting me to speak at "The Political Philosophy of Michel Foucault and Gilles Deleuze" conference at Purdue University in November 2015. I thank Thomas Nail for inviting me to present my research to the Philosophy Department of the University of Denver in February 2016. I am deeply indebted to Margareth Rago and Sílvio Gallo for inviting me to present my research in Portuguese at the 10th International Michel Foucault Colloquium, " 'Is It Useless to Revolt?' Foucault and Insurrections," at the State University of Campinas in Brazil in October 2016. I also thank the São Paulo Research Foundation for funding my participation in this wonderful colloquium. The event was quite simply the highlight of my academic life. It has inspired the direction of my future work.

This book has benefited from the comments of Philippe Artières, Çigdem Çidam, Samuel A. Chambers, Kevin Thompson, Todd May, Keith Harris, Jason Read, Darrin Hicks, Robert Urquhart, Karsten Piep, and Diogo Sardinha.

I presented drafts of individual chapters of the book at the following conferences: "Capitalism & Socialism: Utopia, Globalization, and Revolution" in New Harmony, Indiana, in November 2014; "Time Served: *Discipline and Punish* 40 Years On" at the Galleries of Justice in Nottingham, United Kingdom, in September 2015; the Annual Conference of the Association for Political Theory at the University of Colorado in Boulder in October 2015; the Biennial Conference of the Radical Philosophy Association in Lexington, Kentucky, in November 2016; and the Fiftieth Anniversary Conference of the Caucus for a New Political Science in South Padre Island, Texas, in February 2017.

Chapter 4 is an expanded version of my article "Alain Badiou, the Maoist Investigation, and the Party-Form" in *Historical Materialism* (2017), © Koninklijke Brill NV, Leiden, 2017. It is reprinted here with permission from Brill. I thank Tom Weterings for offering me reprint permission. Chapter 5 is an expanded English version of my chapter "*Enquêtes* na teoria e na prática de Foucault" in *Michel Foucault e as insurreições: É inútil revoltar-se?*, edited by Margareth Rago and Sílvio Gallo (São Paulo: Intermeios, 2017). Portions of the latter contribution are reprinted here with permission from Intermeios. I thank the editor of Intermeios, Joaquim Antonio Pereira, for offering me reprint permission. Finally, the image on the cover of this book is of Tarsila do Amaral's famous painting *Workers* (1933). Amaral was one of the great Brazilian painters of the twentieth century. I thank her heirs for granting me permission to use the image of *Workers*. I owe Luciana Freire Rangel a debt of gratitude for helping me obtain permission for the use of the image.

I translate extensively from French and Portuguese sources in this book. Unless otherwise noted, all translations are my own.

I owe a very special debt of gratitude to Bradley Macdonald and Michael Rinella. They gave this book a tremendous amount of momentum by responding enthusiastically to my initial proposal and answering all of my questions as I was preparing the manuscript.

Last but not least, I want to acknowledge the deep and thoroughgoing support that I have received from my family members. I thank my mother and father, Josenilda and Dan, for nurturing certain obsessions, which are reflected in these pages. I thank my sister, Nelia, for tolerating those obsessions. Above all, I need to thank my wife, Dorothy, and my son, Caetano. Without their unyielding support, this book would never have been written. I dedicate the book to Caetano in the hope that he finds something useful in it as he grows.

1

Introduction

The topic of the investigation in radical political struggles takes us into familiar and strange territory. It takes us into familiar territory because the investigation has become a banal practice, especially with the advent of the Internet. Investigations of all types regularly constitute us as objects of knowledge. We are regularly enjoined to offer detailed information about our experiences as consumers through consumer satisfaction surveys. A seconds-long telephone conversation with a customer service representative suffices to prompt the solicitation of information about the quality of our experiences as consumers and the predictable plea for a ranking of these experiences on a nauseatingly familiar numerical scale. State institutions also have a long history of launching investigations to determine the truth of a crime through the painstaking accumulation of facts. One need only remind oneself of the very name of the domestic intelligence agency in the United States, the Federal Bureau of Investigations, to begin to ascertain a sense of the weight of this history. And it is hardly uncommon to hear politicians call for investigations into the activities of other politicians. Yet the investigation also had another rich history, one inscribed in the annals of radical political struggles and theories in the modern era. Intellectuals, students, militants, workers, peasants, prisoners, patients, and feminists forged this history in a multiplicity of institutional and geographical sites, often under conditions of great duress. This history is not well known even among radicals because the investigation simply does not occupy as prominent a place as it once did in radical political struggles. Yves Duroux, a former Maoist militant once described by Louis Althusser as the "cleverest" student in his seminar leading to *Reading Capital*,[1] helps us understand this peculiar state of affairs, albeit in rather exaggerated terms. "Today we know nothing about the world of labor," he laments.[2] Duroux attributes this collective ignorance to the disappearance of the investigation as a militant practice. "There is no longer the investigation," he declares.[3] "There are," he hastily adds, "opinion surveys, consumer surveys."[4]

My immediate aim in this book is to rescue the investigation in radical political struggles and theories from this position of an obscurity reinforced by the predominance of investigations tied to the imperatives of capital and the state. To be more precise, this book explores the constitution of knowledge in radical political struggles and theories by focusing on the concept and practice of the investigation in these struggles and theories. What *was* the investigation in this context? At its most rudimentary, it consisted in acts of publicity in newspapers and pamphlets as well as in physical displacements to other geographical and institutional spaces to gather information about the conditions and struggles of workers, peasants, and other subalterns for explicitly political purposes. Investigations were thus eminently militant acts. They were undertaken before Marxism in the workers' movement in France in the early 1840s, across the history of Marxism in its diverse forms, and beyond Marxism in the form of movements concerned with the struggles of prisoners and women. In terms of method, investigations varied from the use of questionnaires, to one-on-one interviews, to more collective fact-finding meetings with selected informants, to the solicitation of individual narratives and other forms of writing, but they tended to proceed from suspicions about the official representations of subalterns in the party and state, the presumption of not knowing enough about these subalterns and its corollary of learning from them, often in situ. Investigations were also analyzed, initiated, supported, and even personally undertaken in many cases by a wide range of intellectuals. Karl Marx, V. I. Lenin, Mao Zedong, C. L. R. James, Grace Lee Boggs, Raya Dunayevskaya, Raniero Panzieri, Dario Lanzardo, Danielle Rancière, Daniel Defert, Michel Foucault, and Alain Badiou all participated in investigations in some form or other. Yet their names often remained anonymous and pseudonymous to privilege the name of the group or publication undertaking the investigation and to offer protection against political repression. In the following pages, I set out to disclose the diverse histories, underappreciated difficulties, and theoretical import of investigations in radical political struggles. My core argument is that the militant investigation amounts to a highly fluid and adaptable practice whose value resides in the production of forms of collective political subjectivity rather than in the extraction, accumulation, and publication of purely informational contents.

Fragments for a More Comprehensive Analysis

The study of the investigation in radical political struggles and theories compels us to adopt the tirelessly inquisitive posture of an investigator because its history is dispersed across footnotes located in the density of texts, obscure pamphlets, short-lived newspapers and journals, as well as posthumously published questionnaires and reports outside voluminous collected works. In more than one case, researchers have not been able to track down the primary materials for investigations, such as the responses to questionnaires. To further compound matters, some documents authored by titanic thinkers have simply failed to elicit a lot of sustained commentary. Astoundingly but tellingly, the number of English translations of Karl Marx's 1880 questionnaire for French workers, "A Workers' Inquiry," exceeds the number of elaborate interpretations of it in the English language.

Fortunately, there is a recently reinvigorated literature on investigations in radical political struggles, which itself reflects the renewed academic and practical interest in these investigations over the last two decades. The contributions to this literature are invaluable, but they tend to illuminate militant investigations only in bits and pieces, as if the full scope of these practices across time and space eludes a more comprehensive analytical and historical consideration. To be more precise, these contributions tend to focus on one iteration or set of iterations of this practice to the detriment of others. They rarely engage in a critical dialogue with one another, and they tend to leave the much deeper history of the concept and practice of investigations in radical political struggles entirely unaddressed.[5] Even studies of these investigations that manage to achieve a greater degree of breadth across time and space leave a lot to be desired. For instance, Michel J. M. Thiollent devotes a whole chapter of his book *Crítica metodológica, investigação social e enquete operária* to workers' inquiry from its origins in the first half of the nineteenth century through its various articulations in Marx, Lenin,

Mao, Lanzardo, and Panzieri.[6] Yet his remarkably condensed discussion of this practice is dated by more than three decades and limited in some noteworthy respects. It does not deal with the important experience of French Maoism and the experiences of some of the more post-Marxist movements that adopted the investigation. There is therefore a great deal more work to be done in the domain of research into investigations in radical political struggles. One of the immediate costs of not undertaking this research is a significant diminution in the diversity of the experiences of these investigations across time and space. This diversity concerns overarching objectives as well as methods and results.

As a slight difficulty arises from the very terminology used to denote the concept and practice of investigations in radical political struggles, a few words are in order about my terminological choices before proceeding. Alongside "investigation," there is another commonly employed word in English to designate this concept and practice. That word is "inquiry," as in a "workers' inquiry." In everyday usage, there may be subtle shades of difference between these terms. "Investigation" may more forcefully carry the suspicion of wrongdoing, whereas "inquiry" may have more of a formal and official ring about it (at least to American ears), as in a "Commission of Inquiry." An official body, the Canadian government's Panel on Responsible Conduct of Research (PRCR), instructively captures the heightened sense of suspicion in the usage of the term "investigation," as opposed to the term "inquiry." The PRCR defines an "inquiry" as a mere "review" of an "allegation" of a "breach" of policy, whereas it defines an "investigation" as a "process" of "determining" the "validity" of such an "allegation."[7] I opt for "investigation" in the title of this book mainly for the sake of presentational economy. After all, one has to settle on one set of words over others in the limited space of a title. Still, my choice is not arbitrary. "Investigation" has, perhaps, the slight advantage over "inquiry" of lending itself more readily to the study of practices that were overwhelmingly *unofficial* in the hands of radical political movements. However, for all intents and purposes, I do not draw a strident or substantive distinction between the concepts and practices covered by these terms. Moreover, I often shift back and forth between "inquiry" and "investigation," depending on the usages of these terms among the theorists and practitioners under consideration. In this regard, my slippage back and forth between them is in keeping with other languages. Notably, the French word *enquête* translates as "investigation," "inquiry," and "survey."

On the Production of Militant Knowledge

We can more elaborately stress the specificity of the concept and practice of the investigation in radical political struggles by dwelling on another seemingly proximate, if not identical, experience of investigation. Between 1929 and 1931, Erich Fromm initiated an inquiry of German workers on behalf of the Frankfurt Institute for Social Research. Posthumously published as *The Working Class in Weimar Germany: A Psychological and Sociological Study*, the inquiry was undertaken to "determine the social and psychological attitudes of two large groups in Germany—manual and white collar workers."[8] It was carried out on the basis of the distribution of 3,300 copies of a questionnaire consisting of "271 items."[9] The questions themselves consisted of two types, those related to the objective circumstances of the workers and those related to their personality structures.[10] The questionnaires were distributed to workers with the assistance of "doctors, newspaper publishers, teachers in further education and members of co-operative organizations as well as party and trade union officials."[11] Wolfgang Bonss informs us that while 1,100 questionnaires were completed and sent back to the Institute for Social Research, only 584 of them survived the "enforced emigration of the Institute to the United States in 1933."[12] The responses to the inquiry revealed varying degrees of congruence and incongruence between the personality structures of the respondents and their left-wing political commitments. In particular, Fromm identifies one set of workers who did not value freedom and equality at all because "they willingly obeyed every powerful authority they admired; they liked to control others, in so far as they had the power to do so."[13] For Fromm, these workers quite naturally gravitated toward Nazism as it grew in strength.[14]

At first blush, it may indeed seem that Fromm's inquiry should occupy a prominent place in the history of investigations in radical political struggles. After all, his inquiry emanated from a research agenda with a heavily Marxist orientation, and it concerned itself with the conditions and attitudes of workers. Moreover, like other investigations in radical political struggles, Fromm's inquiry was based on an elaborate questionnaire. No doubt for these reasons, Bonss outright describes Fromm's inquiry as an "*enquête ouvrière*," as if it simply belongs to the same tradition going back to Marx's 1880 questionnaire for French workers of the same name.[15] The basic problem with this identification is that Fromm's inquiry *lacks* the manifestly political dimension of Marx's inquiry. As we shall see in greater detail in the next chapter, Marx formulated his questionnaire to enable workers to act politically on their own knowledge of their own conditions and struggles. By contrast, Fromm frames his inquiry as a strictly social-scientific exercise in the accumulation of empirical insights for the purpose of theory building. In the words of the opening paragraph of his inquiry, "[Decisive for this venture] was the conviction that the elaboration of a theory of social development was critically dependent on a general increase in empirical knowledge, in particular on data concerning the group-specific attitudes and personality structure of individuals."[16] Fromm even informs readers that the questionnaires distributed to workers contained a cover letter from the Institute for Social Research stressing "the *purely* scientific nature of the inquiry," as if he and other researchers sought to steer their research endeavor away from any political intonation or reception.[17] Of course, such maneuvers did not necessarily mean that workers could not have taken Fromm's questions in more political directions. Fromm himself reports that at least some workers responded critically to his questionnaire.[18] But Fromm's aversion to a manifestly political purpose in his inquiry *does* put it at odds with the investigations under consideration in this study. These investigations stand out for being *designed* as militant acts rather than as purely social scientific exercises in the accumulation of empirical insights for the purpose of theory building. In other words, the investigations under consideration in this study manifestly serve the broad purpose of facilitating political action and organization among investigators and the investigated. Peter Hallward concisely picks up on this distinctive feature of militancy in his own consideration of the investigation in Badiou. "Investigation," he writes, "is a militant rather than a scholarly process."[19] Thiollent reminds us that the explicit political objectives of this type of investigation dictate its choice of methods. In his deeply illuminating words:

> The launching of a workers' inquiry presupposes a clear political definition of the objectives of the group. Otherwise, the methodological control of the process of investigation is impossible. The political objectives of the group determine the choice of the inquiry as a militant activity and the prioritized targets of the investigation. For example, a political definition is necessary to be able to choose the thematic of the investigation and its recipients. Problems with wages and

> the cost of living? Working conditions in a sector? Broader political problems? Which type of worker is to be privileged as an informant? An "average" worker without class consciousness? A conscious worker? Established militant? Unionized or non-unionized?, etc. Definitive criteria do not exist to answer these questions. Everything depends on the objectives of the group and the evaluation of the conjuncture.[20]

Methods, in other words, cannot be determined in advance of political objectives in the practice of militant investigations. They flow, rather, from the political orientation of the investigation and determine its realization. The more subtle point to be made here is certainly not that this political orientation implies a pure and simple rupture with or exclusion of sociological methods. Debates about the utility of these methods for workers' inquiries raged in the pages of the Italian journal *Quaderni Rossi* in the early 1960s. Sociology also inflected investigations in radical political struggles in far less obvious ways. The Prisons Information Group (GIP), founded by Foucault and others in 1971, emphatically distinguished its own investigations from sociological investigations, yet the sociologist Jean-Claude Passeron had reviewed what became the first questionnaire of the GIP for its authors.[21] It would therefore be more precise to suggest that investigations in radical political struggles were employed to constitute knowledge for explicitly political purposes *even when* they relied on sociological methods. Or, rather, these investigations employed and modulated sociological methods for their own unique political purposes.

Militant investigations can also be distinguished from certain iterations of the much more diffuse notion of "militant research." In one such iteration, militant research amounts to "research that is carried [out] in a fashion in keeping with the aims and values of radical militants."[22] This gloss on militant research, taken from a glossary entry in a whole edited book on the topic, offers a much looser and even incidental relationship between research and militant political goals than what can be found in the militant investigation as portrayed here. This incidental relationship also comes through in the same book in the very wording of its presentation of the nuances of the translation of the Spanish phrase "*militancia de investigación*" from the Argentine group Colectivo Situaciones. The translators of the contribution from this group ask: "Does the Spanish phrase refer to knowledge production that *happens* to be radical in some way (militant research)?"[23] The investigation as it is portrayed in this book does not just *happen* to be radical. It is not *merely* "in keeping" with radical political "aims" and "values."[24] A professor sitting in his or her office could easily and very effectively realize that kind of endeavor. The militant investigation is, once again, *designed* to *fulfill* radical political aims and values *through* solicitations of knowledge in some form or other from subalterns.

Why should militant investigations retain our attention? Why not leave them buried in long-forgotten and elusive documents as well as in the recesses of the living memory of the *soixante-huitards* and others? Let us clear up one point straightaway: the purpose of revisiting investigations in radical political struggles is certainly not to conjure up nostalgia for a revolutionary or insurrectional past. Such nostalgia would be especially misplaced because these investigations resulted more often than not in stark failures by conventional measures. The value of revisiting investigations in radical political struggles as an object of study resides elsewhere. First of all, the militant investigation has undergone something of a rebirth in the last two decades, as we shall see in greater detail in the conclusion. Now therefore seems like an especially germane and propitious time to revisit the details of its history and draw lessons from it. As a second approximation, we can say that the little-known but rich history of the militant investigation vividly illustrates that political struggles concern the constitution of knowledge as well as the exercise of power. We can be even more precise about the character of this knowledge. Alongside (and as an intrinsic part of) the well-known and repeatedly staged drama of sabotages, occupations, protests, strikes, rallies, revolts, and revolutions, there were perhaps less dramatic but no less ambitious efforts to constitute a popular knowledge in radical political movements. Broadly speaking, these efforts sprang from a profound skepticism with regard to official and theoretical representations of workers, peasants, and other subalterns. It was deemed necessary to appeal directly to these others to find out what *they* thought about *their own* conditions and struggles. These efforts involved the deployment of a wide range of tools: questionnaires, individual interviews, fact-finding meetings, and the solicitation of individual narratives as well as other forms of writing. These tools reached their intended recipients (and plenty of others) through acts of publicity in newspapers and pamphlets as well as through the physical displacements of the investigators themselves to other geographical and institutional sites, often for prolonged periods of time. The knowledge sought through these manifold activities was "popular" in the straightforward sense of emanating from popular strata. Questions about what exactly these strata thought as well as how their thoughts might have palpable political consequences figured centrally in the minds of militant investigators. And these investigators tended to put this popular knowledge to distinct but interrelated (and potentially incompatible) uses. One was to enable militants to formulate effective political strategies and tactics. The other was to furnish popular strata themselves with a basis for their own political activities. In other words, the history of investigations in radical political struggles shows us that radical political movements turned *directly* to workers, peasants, prisoners, and other subalterns for processes of knowledge production. Ideally, these strata would be the bearers and/or agents of a knowledge that would serve to facilitate a process of thoroughgoing social and political transformations culminating in their own emancipation as well as the emancipation of society as a whole. However, given that bearers of a more theoretical knowledge, such as militants, intellectuals, and students, tended to *initiate* the solicitation of knowledge in the practice of investigations, we need to exercise some caution in our references to "popular" knowledge. Indeed, it would be more accurate to suggest that investigations in radical political struggles sprang to life from the immensely complicated and fraught intersection of the aspiration to constitute a popular knowledge, on the one hand, and the recourse to more scholarly or erudite forms of knowledge, on the other hand.[25]

Investigations from Marxism to Post-Marxism (and Pre-Marxism)

This book interlaces historical and theoretical threads of argument. The historical thread begins with the Marxist tradition of investigations, though we shall see that the practice of workers' inquiries predates Marxism. This starting point is not arbitrary. Among radical political traditions, Marxism stands out for its elaborate practices and theorizations of the investigation. Marx's 1880 questionnaire inaugurated the tradition of investigations in Marxism. His questionnaire offered a methodological matrix for the practice. It also spelled out one of the main objectives of the investigation, namely, to enable the working class to constitute its own knowledge for the sake of its own political activity. Yet Marx's questionnaire failed to generate enough responses from workers in spite of its mass distribution. One of the many possible reasons for this failure is that workers were asked to respond to a lengthy questionnaire consisting of demanding questions at a time when they experienced acute constraints in their literacy, time, access to information, and political organization.

Lenin and Mao also made very important though often overlooked contributions to the Marxist tradition of investigations. In the mid-1890s, Lenin formulated his own questionnaire for workers and engaged in a series of interviews with a factory worker from St. Petersburg. Yet his disappointing experiences with these interviews led him to disavow workers' inquiry in favor of a critical recourse to official and legal sources of knowledge. In the 1920s and 1930s, Mao framed his investigation as a collective experience centered on the fact-finding meeting. The purpose of this experience was to align the subjective orientation of militants with objective conditions for the sake of formulating successful revolutionary tactics and strategies. Mao obtained a modicum of success in his investigations and therefore retained an overall emphasis on the investigation in his oeuvre.

Notably, each of these contributions to the investigation made no reference to the preceding one or ones. The contributions of Marx, Lenin, and Mao also shared markedly different historical and political fates. Lenin's practice of the investigation did not have *any* political afterlife, owing to the remarkably belated publication of his questionnaire (roughly sixty years after his death) and his own harsh judgments about his interviews with a worker. Marx and Mao's articulations of the investigation, on the other hand, flourished in radical political movements into the late twentieth century in large part because they spoke readily to the aspiration in these movements to ground critique and political practice in popular knowledge rather than simply defer to the representations of subalterns in official and theoretical forms of knowledge.

In the 1940s and 1950s, breakaway Trotskyist and post-Trotskyist groups, such as the Johnson-Forest Tendency and Correspondence in the United States as well as Socialisme ou Barbarie in France, latched onto Marx's effort to enable workers to write about their own experiences to facilitate their own self-activity. Yet, in a sharp break with Marx, these groups based their versions of workers' inquiry on the solicitation of individual narratives rather than on the questionnaire. In the early 1960s, Italian workerist currents affiliated with *Quaderni Rossi* resuscitated the practice of workers' inquiry in the form of the questionnaire after its eclipse in the hands of oppositional Trotskyist and post-Trotskyist groups.

Italian workerists used questionnaires to gauge the political implications of the emergence of a new working class consisting of deskilled old workers and unskilled young workers. They also formulated groundbreaking interpretations of Marx's questionnaire that framed workers' inquiry as a means of spurring a process of consciousness-raising to transform the working class into an antagonistic class.

French Maoists adopted Mao's investigation before and after the tumultuous events of May 1968. Unsurprisingly, they followed Mao in directing their investigations toward poor peasants in the countryside as well as toward workers in the factories. Perhaps surprisingly, however, French Maoists stretched the bounds of the investigation beyond these classical revolutionary figures to include prisoners and former psychiatric hospital patients. They also framed the investigation in varying degrees of relation to *établissement* as the practice of taking up working positions alongside others to radicalize them. Finally, French Maoists launched their investigations to explore possible instantiations of collective political subjectivity inside and outside the party form.

Here again, however, the original divisions in the birth of the investigation in Marxism cast a long shadow over its subsequent history. Remarkably, the contributions of Marx and Mao each spurred largely independent experiences of the investigation. Most notably, Italian workerists drew explicitly from Marx's questionnaire, rather than the Maoist investigation, whereas French Maoists built on Mao's investigation rather than Marx's questionnaire. The investigations in these different currents nonetheless had some noteworthy features in common, such as the channeling of doubts about the capacities of parties to represent workers and an overall emphasis on the physical displacements of the investigators to factories and other spaces of labor. And yet there was very little obvious influence of the experiences of workers' inquiry in Italian workerist currents on the experiences of investigations in French Maoism, as if they belonged to mutually exclusive spaces. Tellingly, Duroux admits that the French Maoists with whom he circulated simply did not know about the nearly contemporaneous experience of workers' inquiries in Italy. "At the time," he rather candidly informs Andrea Cavazzini, "we did not know all that. And I still don't know it today."[26]

Perhaps paradoxically, then, it took a group that was more transversal in composition and orientation than Marxist to fuse together different sources of the investigation in Marxism. That group was the aforementioned GIP, which lasted from 1971 to 1972. The GIP drew its own practice of investigation into prisons from Marx's questionnaire *and* Mao's investigation. To be more precise, it used these sources of the investigation in early Marxism to enable prisoners to express themselves about the intricacies of the materiality of the prison. But the novelty of the investigations of the GIP hardly ended with this fusion of otherwise disparate sources. The Marxist self-presentation of investigations does not appear to have even hinted at the experience of workers' inquiries *outside* Marxism, as if Marxism possessed sole ownership of these inquiries. By contrast, the declarations of the GIP authored by Foucault sought to build on a whole tradition of nineteenth-century workers' inquiries *prior* to the birth of Marxism. The GIP and Foucault thus help us redraw the historical parameters for the study of investigations in radical political struggles. They gesture to the significance of these practices in an earlier period of industrialization in nineteenth-century France. However, as they get no further than mere gestures, it is incumbent upon us to supplement their remarks with a greater degree of content. We turn to Hilde Rigaudias-Weiss's account of early nineteenth-century workers' inquiries for that content.

There is one more feature to the investigations of the GIP that makes them stand out against the backdrop of so many Marxist experiences: they were successful in generating and publishing written responses. The GIP solicited, received, selected, and then published the written responses of prisoners to an amalgam of detailed questions about what makes the prison intolerable. I suggest that the success of the GIP in obtaining these responses had to do with the simplicity of its questionnaires, the availability of time in the prison, and the reliance on a ramified network of confidants.

While I address very recent experiments in militant investigations from remarkably diverse groups in the conclusion, the core historical thread of the argument in the main body of this book culminates in the early 1970s. This cutoff point is no more arbitrary than our starting point in Marx's questionnaire. Deployments of the investigation among radical political movements peaked right around 1970 to 1971 simply in terms of acquiring a greater breadth. During these years, the framework for conducting investigations exploded to suddenly encompass women, prisoners, and former psychiatric hospital patients *in addition* to the standard revolutionary figures of the worker and the peasant. Afterward, many of the groups and publications that had undertaken investigations retreated, if they did not cease to exist, under a variety of pressures, including outright state repression. More generally, the more restricted notion of a *workers'* inquiry, which remained at the root of the practices of the investigation in radical political struggles and informed so many of these practices well beyond the space of the factory, went into precipitous decline. Cavazzini helps us understand this decline. He suggests that neoliberal policies in the mid-1970s began to undercut the notion of the working class as the embodiment of an alternative organization of modern society. In his deeply sobering words:

> The working class ceased to exist as an antagonistic force to the existing economic and political system; it ceased, above all, to represent the possibility of an alternative organization of society. The moment of irreducible negativity upon which it had been possible to found both a critical theory of society and a political strategy in which worker centrality was the bedrock disappeared. The demands of philosophical or political critique no longer had a structural link with active historical forces; and the workers once again became the passive objects of sociology and economics, even of a morbid or hypocritical pity directed at the consequences of deindustrialization and liberalization. Fatal accidents and plans for mass layoffs became the only occasions for public visibility of a social stratum which now exists only as the recipient of a humanitarian morality, and which now only asks to be helped to bear an increasingly difficult life, without opportunities and hopes.[27]

This transformation of the working class into an object of humanitarian pity undermined the core rationale in workers' inquiry of enabling the working class to emancipate itself and, in the process, emancipate the whole of society. As this transformation began in the mid-1970s, this period marks an appropriate cutoff point for the main historical thread of the argument in this book.

Rethinking the "Failure" of Militant Investigations

The theoretical thread of the argument in this book cuts across the historical thread. It flows from the strident emphasis on the militant character of the investigation outlined above. In the following pages, I treat investigations as a means of producing collective political subjectivity rather than purely informational contents. This point is worth stressing because there is a strong tendency to judge even militant investigations from the standpoint of the quantity and quality of the written responses to them, as if these responses exhaust their effects. Interpreters of militant investigations and former practitioners use this standpoint to arrive steadfastly at the following resounding and sobering conclusion: *these investigations failed.* Weiss, for instance, writes of the "failure" of Marx's questionnaire to elicit enough responses.[28] Lenin ultimately deemed his own interviews with a factory worker a failure because the responses of his interviewee did not disclose a comprehensive enough view of working conditions. Duroux stunningly describes the investigation as "one of the gigantic failures of French Maoism" on account of its lack of any practical realization.[29] One can also find such conclusions in some of the more broadly construed experiences of the investigation in the following pages. Stephen Hastings-King refers repeatedly to the "failure" of a worker newspaper supported by Socialisme ou Barbarie to elicit the writings of nonmilitant workers.[30] He attributes this failure in large part to the social function of literacy in French society during the postwar period.[31]

As we can see from this mere sampling, "failure" figures as a central and powerful leitmotif in the literature on militant investigations. This leitmotif understandably spurs efforts to come to grips with the reasons for the failure of this type of investigation. Interpreters ask how and why these investigations failed, and they come up with a wide range of reasons. There is thus a problematic of failure in the literature on militant investigations that tends to revolve around the failure of worker writing in particular.

To be resolutely clear, I should add that I do not fully escape this problematic in the preceding and succeeding pages. Obviously, the publication of written and spoken responses to militant investigations can be quite important in drawing persons not involved in them into their political objectives. The act of reading these responses can politicize or further politicize the non-investigated and the non-investigators. Written and spoken responses also enable investigators to generate larger findings. They offer a clear standard by which to evaluate the success or failure of an investigation.

Yet judgments about the failure or success of investigations in radical political struggles should not hinge entirely on their written, spoken, and published responses because these investigations are *first and foremost* about realizing political objectives, rather than generating informational contents, and there are other far less obvious ways in which they can still facilitate these objectives. The exchange of questions and answers tends to be at the heart of the practice of the investigation, at least outside its iteration as a narrative form (and even in that iteration there is still a demand for and expectation about information from the narrating individuals). Determining the political effects of questions can be a very tricky matter because questions in themselves are neither inherently liberating nor inherently constraining or oppressive. Their political effects depend to a large extent on their framing, ordering, context, and resonance. But the simple act of posing a carefully crafted and ordered question or set of questions in certain institutional or geographical contexts (*without* even eliciting an immediate and recorded response) *can* invite others to appraise their political situations differently. It can instill doubt, spur unanticipated reflections, incite the imagination, and foster conversations between the investigator and the investigated as well as between the investigated and others belonging to their situations. What goes missing in the often hasty and resolute judgments about the failure of investigations in radical political struggles is any sense of the political potentialities involved in the mere process of exchanging questions and answers.

More than any other interpreter of militant investigations, Dario Lanzardo helps us see this point through his deeply innovative interpretation of Marx's questionnaire. For Lanzardo, whether or not workers actually responded to the questions in Marx's meticulous and lengthy questionnaire is an entirely secondary matter. What matters for Lanzardo is that the questions in Marx's questionnaire stimulate workers to generate their own politically impactful knowledge of capitalist exploitation by provoking forms of reflection and communication among them.[32] Lanzardo thus shifts the center of gravity in his interpretation of Marx's questionnaire away from the paucity of *written* responses, which underpins the problematic of failure, and toward the less obvious resonance of the questions among the workers themselves. Of course, none of the foregoing means that we cannot speak of the failure or success of militant investigations. What it does suggest, however, is that what we say about the failure or success of militant investigations should be framed in more careful and expansive terms with a view to their political objectives and effects.

Collective Political Subjectivity

If, however, we should be attuned to these political objectives and effects of militant investigations, how are we to understand them? And what is the larger value of these investigations in radical political struggles? As indicated above, I suggest that the value of investigations in these political struggles resides in their potential to instantiate forms of collective political subjectivity. The investigation is not an activity between two ready-made subjects who simply exchange questions and answers (or information more generally) with no further consequences. It is an act that harbors the potential to *produce* a collective political subject, a new "we" among the various participants in the investigations, not to mention many others. Writing from the Argentine context, Colectivo Situaciones makes a similar point in its rendition of research militancy. In its words, "research militancy is not the name of the experience of someone who does research but that of the production of (an) encounter(s) without subject(s) or, if you prefer, (an) encounter(s) that produce(s) subject(s)."[33] For our purposes, the exchange of questions and answers in an investigation can compel participants to envision their conditions, positions, and struggles in the world differently. On the side of the investigated, carefully framed and ordered questions can serve to enable persons to locate the particularities of their individual circumstances within more general parameters. For instance, they can compel workers to view themselves as an exploited and potentially self-emancipating class rather than just as employees vying for greater compensation for the sale of their labor-power. On the side of the investigators, the answers to the questions can yield (sometimes shocking) revelations about the investigated that serve as political learning opportunities. More precisely, they can disclose previously unaccounted or even discounted social forces as suddenly integral to any definition of a more general political subject. The case of Mao's practice of investigation is instructive in this regard. Shortly before his investigation of peasants in Hunan province in 1927, Mao did not attribute a great deal of importance to peasants in general and poor peasants in particular. He tended to abide by a more orthodox Marxist view of a revolution led by the industrial proletariat. After his investigations in Hunan, Mao concluded that the entire prospect of revolution in China suddenly depends on poor peasants. What changed his views were the process and results of the investigation. Something similar happened through the workers' inquiries of *Quaderni Rossi* at the massive FIAT factory in Turin in the early 1960s. These inquiries revealed unskilled young factory workers and deskilled old workers as suddenly integral to the definition of a new working class. *Quaderni Rossi* members then faced the question of whether this new working class might be oriented toward a rupture with the prevailing system of capitalist social relations rather than simply bargaining for more compensation within it. Investigators in both of these historical instances were confronted with the question of how to relate to and identify with newly revealed social forces for the sake of generating a more general political subject. What is more, investigations can enact a collective political subject by blurring the distinction between those belonging on the inside and outside of certain geographical spaces and institutional sites. Some French Maoists at least aspired to this kind of blurring by placing investigating militants in working positions alongside poor peasants in the countryside for lengthy periods of time. This placement was known as the aforementioned practice of établissement. Other groups sought to foster a collective subject of political knowledge by destabilizing hierarchies in the production of knowledge. The GIP, for instance, engaged in a destabilization of these hierarchies when it involved former prisoners in the formulation of questions for its first questionnaire. If it had fully respected hierarchies in the production of knowledge, the GIP would have left the articulation of such questions entirely in the hands of the eminent sociologists whom it also consulted. Finally, as indicated above, investigations can stimulate the production of a collective political subject in less tangible ways by merely disseminating questions and answers that can serve as occasions for reflection and communication within, between, and beyond communities of subalterns.

Yet, if the value of investigations in radical political struggles resides in the potential to instantiate forms of collective political subjectivity, how are we to understand these forms? Duroux provides one answer to this question in his own provocative consideration of the French Maoist experience. He suggests that the investigation raised the question of what it means to "consolidate knowledge in a non-party form."[34] There is a lot of merit to this view. Investigations were used to channel and affirm suspicions about the capacities of parties to represent workers. Groups and movements that eschewed the party form in their internal organization also rather unsurprisingly used investigations to facilitate forms of collective political subjectivity beyond the party. And yet investigations were not so unequivocally indexed to "knowledge in a non-party form" even in the French Maoist experience. After all, one of the first Maoist groups to practice the investigation in France, the Union of Marxist-Leninist Communist Youth (UJCML), did so to build a genuinely revolutionary party. Another group, the Group for the Foundation of the Union of Marxist-Leninist Communists of France (UCFML), more modestly launched investigations to *explore* the possibilities for the constitution of a new kind of party. My point here is not just that Duroux diminishes the historical complexity of the investigation in French Maoism. My point is, rather, that his identification of the investigation with this form grates against the whole emphasis on the polyvalence of the investigation in this book. In other words, the "we" generated through militant investigations can bear many names: an antagonistic working class, a party of a new type, a public intolerant of intolerable conditions in prisons. From a different and somewhat opposed perspective, this point seems all the more important to stress today because there is a concerted effort in some currents of radical political theory to index collective political subjectivity to the party form, albeit without any reference to militant investigations.[35]

Once we definitively index the practice of the investigation to the non-party form (or the party form), we run the risk losing sight of its fluidity and adaptability, as evidenced by its much larger history within radical political struggles. We open ourselves up to the perhaps comforting view that the investigation can be possessed definitively for one purpose or another. We locate it outside the dynamic space of political struggles, with its seemingly incessant play of investments and counterinvestments. If Lanzardo is instructive in getting us to understand the wide range of potential political effects generated through questions in militant investigations, Foucault attunes us to this other point about the fluidity and reversibility of these investigations. Indeed, a consideration of Foucault's deployment of the investigation on behalf of the GIP against the backdrop of his rich genealogy of the inquiry suggests that radical political movements had taken over and modulated a practice of the *official* inquiry that goes all the way back to Greek antiquity and the birth of the medieval state.

Perhaps the most dramatic, immediate, and humorous (but also serious) case of a reversal of an investigation took place shortly before the creation of the GIP and Foucault's public presentation of his genealogy of the inquiry. In November 1970, the French magazine *Elle* convened a conference on women's issues with a predominantly male list of speakers.

The organizers of the conference distributed a questionnaire in advance of the event to solicit the preferences of women on a wide range of issues.[36] Militants from the Women's Liberation Movement (MLF) objected to these efforts "to assume the right to represent all women through a questionnaire."[37] They deemed the questionnaire "a manipulation for channeling and taking back the rebellion of all women; for nipping in the bud any attempt at grouping together and for defusing the inevitable collective revolt of women."[38] However, rather than simply denounce the questionnaire for posing questions that address women's issues from within a patriarchal framework, MLF militants reformulated the questions in the original questionnaire in their own *counter*-questionnaire, which they proceeded to distribute at the event.[39] To take one of the many questions they reframed, MLF militants turned the question posed by *Elle* " 'Do you think that women are more, equally or less able than men to drive a car?' " into " 'In your opinion, do double X chromosomes contain the genes of double declutching?' "[40] Through such comedic but damning maneuvers, the MLF provided a condensed and highly dramatic instance of a questionnaire suddenly being used for a different and totally opposed purpose, namely, to compel the public to suddenly see the sheer vacuity and sexism of the questions in the original questionnaire.

Overview of the Chapters

Each of the chapters is organized around distinct experiences of the militant investigation. The chapters also proceed along roughly chronological lines, though not without returning us to earlier moments in the history of militant and official investigations or briefly projecting us forward in anticipation of other moments in this history. In the second chapter, I set out to engage the intricacies of the sources of the investigation in early Marxism in order to set up the larger historical and theoretical account in this book. The bulk of the chapter is divided into three parts: a section on Marx's questionnaire, a section on Lenin's version of workers' inquiry, and a section on Mao's investigation. I take on three main tasks that correspond to each of these sections. One is to lay the groundwork for rethinking the problematic of failure by suggesting other ways of assessing the much-discussed failure of Marx's questionnaire. I suggest that if we keep in mind the eminently political purpose of Marx's questionnaire and expand our historical horizons about its uses, then it is far from clear that his questionnaire resulted in an unambiguous failure. I then turn to Lenin's little-known experiences with workers' inquiry through his questionnaire and lengthy interviews with a factory worker. Like Marx's questionnaire, Lenin's questionnaire prompted workers to recognize general patterns of class struggle in the fine details of their own circumstances. However, Lenin ultimately disparaged workers' inquiry because it failed to generate sufficiently comprehensive information about working conditions in the factories. He not only endorsed the recourse to legal and official sources of knowledge for information about these conditions, but he also plunged headlong into a critical deployment of these sources. In so doing, Lenin ended up eclipsing the more didactic political logic of his own questionnaire. Lastly, I suggest that Mao's investigations in China in the late 1920s and early 1930s succeeded in generating politically consequential results because they were based on comparatively immersive experiences. Mao's success with these investigations spurred him to offer more elaborate theoretical reflections on the practice of the investigation itself. He cast the investigation as a practice that mediates political subjectivity through a moment of objectivity. The result is that Mao easily stands apart from Marx and Lenin in having made the greatest strides toward practicing and theorizing the investigation in early Marxism.

What leaps out at us from chapter 2 is not only the compartmentalized formulation of the investigation in early Marxism (relative to the preceding contributions to the investigation in this tradition) but also the sheer heterogeneity of this practice in early Marxism. Yet common patterns cut across this heterogeneity. We can see that Marx, Lenin, and Mao turned to militant investigations out of an explicit or implicit skepticism about official representations of workers and peasants. We can also explain why Lenin's version of workers' inquiry never appears to have experienced *any* afterlife in radical political movements. His questionnaire for factory workers only appeared in print more than half a century after his death in altogether disadvantageous circumstances for its usage among these movements. Finally, we can see that the broad import of the investigations of Marx, Lenin, and Mao resided in challenging vanguard traditions of political practice by privileging the knowledge of workers and peasants about their own conditions and struggles.

In the third chapter, I turn to the resuscitation of Marx's project for a workers' inquiry among oppositional Trotskyists, post-Trotskyists, and Italian workerists between the late 1940s and early 1960s. This chapter compares the workers' inquiries of the Johnson-Forest Tendency, Correspondence, and Socialisme ou Barbarie, on the one hand, with the workers' inquiries of *Quaderni Rossi*, on the other hand. My main point here is that while all of these groups shared a view of workers' inquiry as a means of raising the political consciousness of the working class, they differed radically on their views of the *form* of this inquiry. The Johnson-Forest Tendency knew about Marx's questionnaire but avoided any recourse to it. Socialisme ou Babarie went further. It explicitly rejected the form of the questionnaire. Writing on behalf of the latter group, Claude Lefort objected to the questionnaire on grounds that it lends itself to artificial responses from workers. The questionnaire prompts these responses, he reasoned, because its questions emanate from the concerns of interviewers outside the proletarian frame of experience. Breakaway Trotskyist and post-Trotskyist groups gravitated toward the more open-ended form of the narrative as a way of overcoming these perceived shortcomings of the questionnaire and facilitating the creative self-expression of workers. Yet the Johnson-Forest Tendency in particular remained caught up in an acute contradiction in its presentation of the narrative of an autoworker in its 1947 pamphlet *The American Worker*: the group set out to overcome the division between manual and mental labor, but it reproduced this division in the organization and presentation of the pamphlet. Beyond this contradiction, oppositional Trotskyist and post-Trotskyist currents failed, on the whole, to solicit the writings of nonmilitant workers. In marked contrast to these currents, members of the *Quaderni Rossi* collective *returned* to workers' inquiry in the more traditional guise of the questionnaire out of a concern that the narrative form only registers individual opinions without disclosing the larger dynamics of working-class behavior. Marx's questionnaire in particular provided a framework for accessing this behavior and fostering the political self-activity of the working class. Writing on behalf of *Quaderni Rossi*, Lanzardo theorized the questionnaire as a means of transforming the working class into an antagonistic class. His approach enables us to see beyond the problematic of failure in the literature on workers' inquiry because it shifts the focus *away* from worker writing.

The fourth chapter explores the deployments of Mao's investigation in the French Maoist experience of the late 1960s and early 1970s. French Maoism now seems to be back in academic vogue, thanks in no small part to the rise to global prominence of Badiou as a French philosopher with a long and controversial history of Maoist thought and practice.

The resurgence of scholarly interest in French Maoism has resulted in an expansive literature in the Anglophone world. This literature seems to almost unanimously recognize the importance of the practice of the investigation in French Maoism. It was, after all, French Maoists who further popularized Mao's injunction "No investigation, no right to speak." It was also these Maoists who earned a reputation for going to factories and the countryside to conduct their investigations among workers and peasants. Yet it does not take much more than a scratch on the surface of the literature on French Maoism to realize that discussions of these investigations (or better yet, the mere references to them) tend to occupy an obligatory but fleeting presence. One effect of such treatments of French Maoist investigations is to leave us without an elaborate sense of their specificity in the experience of French Maoism or the broader history of investigations in radical political struggles. I redress this limitation by probing the UCFML's *Le livre des paysans pauvres: 5 années de travail maoïste dans une campagne française*. This little-known book consists mainly of narratives written by UCFML militants about their investigations and other activities among poor peasants in the French countryside between 1971 and 1975. These investigations were launched to test whether UCFML militants were prepared to found a mass-based, revolutionary party. The narratives of these militants reveal important modulations in the scope, target, form, and purpose of the militant investigation. Apart from disclosing these modulations, the narratives of UCFML militants caution us against romanticizing this practice by conveying the practical difficulties of undertaking investigations among peasants in the countryside over a prolonged period of time. They also reveal an antinomy between the goals of *poor-peasant autonomy* and *proletarian political leadership over poor peasants*. Finally, the narratives of UCFML militants illuminate Badiou's subsequent abandonment of any aspiration toward social representation through the party form by highlighting the difficulties of enacting the representation of poor peasants in particular.

Chapter 5 shifts the focus of the analysis once again, albeit within the parameters of the French national context in the early 1970s. This chapter addresses the investigations of Foucault and the GIP. To broach this topic, we have to remind ourselves that Foucault's use of the word enquête tends to be translated as "inquiry" in the context of his genealogies and as "investigation" in the context of his political interventions on behalf of the GIP. To avoid potential confusion among English readers, I therefore retain the French word enquête in many instances while discussing Foucault's contributions. The substantive starting point for the analysis in chapter 5 is the *simultaneity* of Foucault's explorations of the official inquiry in his lectures at the Collège de France and elsewhere, on the one hand, and his participation in militant investigations into the prison system on behalf of the GIP, on the other hand. In his lectures, Foucault construed the inquiry as a technique for establishing the truth as fact going all the way back to tyranny in Greek antiquity and the birth of the medieval state, yet he barely grappled with its uses as an instrument of resistance in popular political struggles. In his political activities on behalf of the GIP, Foucault used the investigation as an instrument of resistance in struggles over the prison system, yet he did not even hint at its much broader history in Western political power. These simultaneous but contrasting moves (between 1971 and 1972) raise the question of how we should understand the relationship between his enquêtes in theory and practice, and what exactly we should take away from this relationship for our larger study. I suggest that a gap separates Foucault's analyses of inquiries from his practical deployment of investigations on behalf of the GIP. However, this gap is not absolute. It can be crossed if we attend to Foucault's disparate references to nineteenth-century workers' inquiries in France. He refers to these inquiries as a source of inspiration for the practices of the GIP and as a historical instance of popular resistance to the production of an administrative knowledge. Nineteenth-century workers' inquiries thus provide a point of articulation between Foucault's practices and analyses of the investigation. These inquiries also have the benefit of suddenly expanding the historical parameters of our study by disclosing the uses of the investigation among workers *prior* to the birth of Marxism. As indicated above, I dwell on the content of these uses by drawing extensively from Rigaudias-Weiss's seminal account of nineteenth-century workers' inquiries in France. However, I have no intention of simply closing the gap between the enquêtes in Foucault's theory and practice because this gap harbors an important lesson for students of militant investigations. Simply put, this lesson is that the practice of the investigation is adaptable, fluid, and reversible in political struggles. In elaborating this main point, I also distinguish between the knowledge *contents* of an investigation and the unpredictable effects of the *process* of producing these contents. This distinction is important in once again getting us away from a facile and narrowly construed problematic of failure in the practice of militant investigations.

Chapter 6 concludes this study less by restating the argument than by critically engaging recent experiences of the militant investigation in light of the history explored in the preceding chapters. As in the case of the larger history of militant investigations, these experiences cut across an impressive array of spaces, from the streets of Madrid to the cocktail lounges of Manhattan. It is not easy to sum them up in a few words, but they tend to concern the shift toward the precarious employment of workers and the greater reliance on the service economy in particular. The recent experiences of militant investigations also deal much more extensively with the roles of affective labor and gender than preceding investigations. The history of investigations in radical political struggles had one foot in Marx and another foot in Mao. It seems fair to say that more recent experiences in militant investigations have largely moved on from these classical sources. They have left aside Mao and critically retained Marx. Many of them even draw inspiration from the Situationist notion of drifting. Some of the criticisms of workers' inquiry in particular in the recent experiences of militant investigations seem especially pertinent for our purposes. They serve to caution us against the suggestion that the exchange of questions and answers at the heart of an investigation is somehow intrinsically oppositional or liberating. Yet some strands of this argument simply go too far. They divest questions and answers in investigations of *any* oppositional or liberating potential. I suggest that overall context, especially the relationship between the militant investigator and the investigated, provides one way of understanding the promises and hazards of questions in a militant investigation.

This book thus ends up in a much more contemporary space than where it started. It started by attempting to rescue the militant investigation from the weight of an obscurity reinforced by the predominance of investigations driven by the imperatives of capital and the state. It ends by (rather appropriately) reminding us that this task is not simply a matter of scholarly erudition concerning historical materials. Radical movements *are* currently pursuing investigations to try to answer the all-important questions: "Who are we?" and "What do we want?" And these investigations offer the possibility of producing a new "we."

2

Sources of the Militant Investigation in Marxism

Marx, Lenin, and Mao

Investigations did not originate or remain in Marxism, but they cut across its rich and complicated history. This chapter explores the sources of the investigation in Marxism through the writings and experiences of Karl Marx, V. I. Lenin, and Mao Zedong. Their contributions to the investigation warrant scrupulous attention individually and comparatively because they weigh heavily enough to frame theories and practices of the investigation within and beyond Marxism.

The first thing to note about the formulation of the investigation in early Marxism is that it abounds with peculiarities. It took place in a highly compartmentalized manner. Lenin forged his approach to workers' inquiry without any apparent knowledge of Marx's inquiry. Mao in turn articulated his own approach to the investigation without any apparent knowledge of either Marx's inquiry or Lenin's inquiry. And, at the risk of getting ahead of ourselves, we could add that Marx himself articulated his version of workers' inquiry without explicitly acknowledging the history of such inquiries among French workers in the early nineteenth century. In other words, Marx, Lenin, and Mao each formulated his own investigation *as if* starting from scratch.

These investigations yielded a mixture of success and failure by conventional measures. Marx's inquiry did not result in any published findings because it failed to generate enough written responses from workers. Lenin interviewed a factory worker at great length, but he ultimately deemed the responses of the worker limited in comparison to the more comprehensive information about working conditions available in legal and official sources of knowledge. Mao, by contrast, succeeded in generating a great deal of politically impactful information through his various investigations. He also continued to offer theoretical reflections on the practice of the investigation throughout his lifetime. The compartmentalized and widely differing results of the experiences of these investigations facilitated a striking unevenness in their influence on contributions to the concept and practice of the militant investigation in posterity. As we shall see in great detail throughout the remainder of this book, Marx's inquiry and Mao's investigation had prodigious afterlives in radical political struggles of various stripes well into the late twentieth century, whereas Lenin's inquiry never gained any traction beyond its original uses in St. Petersburg at the end of the nineteenth century.

How are we to make sense of this tremendous disparity in influence? Why did some investigations succeed while others failed? How do we understand success and failure in this context? How did Marx, Lenin, and Mao come to perceive the need for investigations in the first place, especially given their apparent lack of knowledge of preceding investigations in Marxism and workers' struggles? And, more generally, what are the broader implications of the appearance of the practice of the investigation in these thinkers?

These questions have not been formulated, much less answered, because the literature on investigations does not even account for some of the most important contributions to the investigation among Marx, Lenin, and Mao. It thus tends to mirror the compartmentalized articulations of the investigation in early Marxism. In the following pages, I attempt to overcome this shortcoming through a detailed exploration of the contributions of Marx, Lenin, and Mao. In this context, I take on several intricate tasks that lay the groundwork for more general observations. The first concerns the much-discussed failure of Marx's questionnaire. This failure confronts us with the first of many instances of failure in the practice of investigations in radical political struggles. Yet the seeming obviousness of the failure raises deeper questions about the measure and meaning of failure (and success) in this practice. If we keep in mind the eminently political purpose of Marx's questionnaire and expand our measures of success and failure to include less tangible features beyond written responses, then it is far from clear that the first experience of militant investigations in Marxism resulted in an unequivocal failure. If we expand our historical horizons, it is even less clear that Marx's questionnaire simply failed. After all, it appeared as an altogether crucial reference point in various kinds of radical political experiences in the late twentieth century. The succeeding unevenness in the afterlives of the militant investigations of Marx, Lenin, and Mao therefore cannot simply be chalked up to their original successes or failures (by conventional measures). I then turn to Lenin's little-known contributions to workers' inquiry. He formulated a questionnaire that echoed many of Marx's questions. Like Marx's questionnaire, Lenin's questionnaire prompted workers to recognize the more general dynamics of class struggle in the fine details of their own individual circumstances. Lenin also interviewed a worker about working conditions at a factory for a prolonged period of time. Yet he ultimately dismissed workers' inquiry on grounds that it results in a fragmentary view of working conditions. In other words, *unlike* Marx, Lenin explicitly and forcefully disavowed workers' inquiry after his own tremendously disappointing experiences with it. He relied instead on a highly critical usage of legal and official sources to obtain a more comprehensive view of working conditions for revolutionary purposes. In so doing, Lenin eclipsed the more didactic logic implicit in his own questionnaire. Finally, I submit that Mao's investigations in China in the late 1920s and early 1930s were successful in generating political consequential information because they were based on comparatively immersive experiences. These successes spurred Mao to theorize the investigation as a practice that mediates political subjectivity through a moment of objectivity. Mao thus occupies a unique position in the history of militant investigations in early Marxism. He went much further than Marx and Lenin in practicing and theorizing the investigation.

What stands out from the consideration of the contributions of Marx, Lenin, and Mao is the remarkable heterogeneity of the militant investigation in the formative stages of the Marxist tradition. This heterogeneity concerns methods, immediate objectives, results, and subsequent influence. Yet, as we stand back from this heterogeneity, we are able to discern broad patterns that enable us to answer the questions above. We see that Marx, Lenin, and Mao engaged in militant investigations out of an implicit or explicit skepticism with regard to official representations of workers and peasants. We can also answer the question of why there was an unevenness in the afterlives of their investigations. This unevenness stemmed from a combination of Lenin's own highly critical approach to workers' inquiry and the disadvantageous circumstances behind the publication of his main contribution to it. Lastly, we can discern the broad import of the investigation in Marx, Lenin, and Mao. The investigation grates against vanguard traditions of political practice to the extent that it privileges the knowledge of workers and peasants about their conditions and struggles.

Marx's Questionnaire: An Unambiguous Failure?

The Marxist tradition of investigations goes back to one widely translated but underappreciated text: Marx's "A Workers' Inquiry."[1] This text consists of a lengthy questionnaire and brief introduction anonymously published on April 20, 1880, in Benoît Malon's newspaper *La Revue socialiste*. A footnote informed readers of the text that twenty-five thousand copies of the questionnaire had been "sent to all workers' societies, socialist and democratic groups or circles, French newspapers, and persons who requested it."[2] News of the questionnaire appears to have spread quickly. Only eight days later, Jules Guesde's newspaper *L'Égalité* praised the workers' inquiry for seeking to create the will to end capitalist exploitation by publicizing information about it. His newspaper went on to encourage its readers to support the workers' inquiry, and it even promised to reproduce the questionnaire as an insert in a future issue.[3]

Michel J. M. Thiollent reminds us that "A Workers' Inquiry" belonged to Marx's long-standing effort to ground his critique of the capitalist mode of production in a concrete knowledge of the working class. This knowledge implied a critique of existing theoretical knowledge and official knowledge.[4] Yet, as is well known, Marx himself did not hesitate to critically mobilize these forms of knowledge. In his preface to the first edition of volume one of *Capital*, Marx even praised official inquiries into the working class in England for laying bare the horrors of capitalist exploitation. He simultaneously blamed the absence of such investigations in Continental Europe for obscuring these horrors. In his reprimanding words to the publics of Continental Europe:

> We should be appalled at our own circumstances if, as in England, our governments and parliaments periodically appointed commissions of inquiry into economic conditions; if these commissions were armed with the same plenary powers to get

> at the truth; if it were possible to find for this purpose men as competent, as free from partisanship and respect of persons as are England's factory inspectors, her medical reporters on public health, her commissioners of inquiry into the exploitation of women and children, into conditions of housing and nourishment, and so on. Perseus wore a magic cap so that the monsters he hunted down might not see him. We draw the magic cap down over our eyes and ears so as to deny that there are any monsters.[5]

David Harvey helpfully situates the rise of the factory inspectors praised in this rich passage in the peculiar dynamics of class struggle in England in the 1840s. He points out that a coalition made up of the working-class movement and the landed aristocracy supported the factory inspectors to limit the growing power of the industrial bourgeoisie.[6] The British Parliament commissioned the factory inspectors to enforce the limits on the length of working day in the various Factory Acts. Marx considered the reports of these inspectors so illuminating that he relied extensively on them throughout *Capital* to the point of simply deferring to the words (in lengthy block quotes) of the factory inspectors themselves.[7] In Marx's judgment, the availability of a knowledge sanctioned by the British state provided a deeply useful and politically impactful level of information about working conditions that was lamentably absent in Continental Europe.

Writing more than a decade later, Marx lambasted the absence of inquiries in France in particular from the opening sentence of the introduction to his questionnaire. "Not a single government," he wrote, "whether monarchy or bourgeois republic, has yet ventured to undertake a serious inquiry into the position of the French working class. But what a number of investigations have been undertaken into crises—agricultural, financial, industrial, commercial, political!"[8] His opening declaration pointed to an absence in state-based political practices, the absence of an inquiry into the working class relative to the presence of so many inquiries into various types of crises. By highlighting this absence, Marx's opening statement to his questionnaire set out to motivate his readers to participate in the collective enactment of the practice of workers' inquiry.

However, taken as a historical point, Marx's claim that no government had undertaken a "serious inquiry" into the French working class requires a bit of clarification because the French state had a history of sponsoring and directly undertaking inquiries into the working class long before 1880. As early as 1834, a newly reestablished institution of this state, the Academy of Moral and Political Sciences, had initiated an inquiry into the condition of textile workers during a time of heightened working-class militancy.[9] This inquiry was published in a report authored by the hygienist Louis Villermé in 1840.[10] In the same year, the Academy of Moral and Political Sciences sponsored an inquiry into the causes of poverty authored by Eugène Buret.[11] Both inquiries resulted in findings that appealed to the resolution of the problem of poverty through state intervention. Yet, as Andrew Aisenberg observes, the eruption of conflict between workers and the state in the revolution of 1848 signaled the failure of these inquiries to fulfill this deeper purpose.[12] After the 1848 revolution, the French government succumbed to popular pressure to initiate an inquiry into the working class.[13] It undertook this inquiry to placate an increasingly militant working class and counter the spread of socialism in particular.[14] However, as Hilde Rigaudias-Weiss hastens to elaborate, this negative motivation rendered the French government indifferent to the substantive realization of the inquiry, turning its execution into little more than a form of lip service to working-class militancy.[15] It thus condemned the official inquiry of 1848 to a colossal failure. This inquiry failed to elicit the mass participation of workers.[16] It even failed in the far more elementary task of simply retaining some of its own documentation. Rigaudias-Weiss notes that eight hundred documents expressing grievances from areas known for worker militancy and socialist activities went missing, and she does not consider their disappearance a mere coincidence.[17] Rather than inducing legally binding transformations in the everyday lives of workers, the 1848 inquiry found an entirely different fate. Back in 1936, Rigaudias-Weiss vividly described this fate. "The documents of the 1848 inquiry," she wrote, "lie covered in dust in the cardboard boxes of the National Archives without ever having been used."[18]

If we take Marx's reference to the absence of a "serious inquiry" on the part of the French government to mean the absence of a *legally and politically impactful inquiry* into the French working class, then we can go some distance in salvaging his opening declaration in "A Workers' Inquiry" from the standpoint of a historical claim. The absence of such an inquiry served as the immediate reason for the production and distribution of Marx's questionnaire. In this regard, Marx even revisited the inquiries in England that he had praised in volume one of *Capital*. He suggested that the success of these inquiries in legally curbing the length of the working day had induced the "French bourgeoisie to tremble even more before the dangers which an impartial and systematic investigation might represent."[19] The immediate purpose of his questionnaire was to compel the government in France to follow the lead of the government in England in conducting an official investigation into the working class.[20] Yet, in pursuing this goal, Marx put the accent squarely on the *self-activity* of workers. He solicited the support of workers and insisted that *only they* are capable of describing *and* remedying their own exploitation. It was, in other words, up to the workers themselves to constitute their own knowledge of their exploitation and to act politically on this knowledge. In a passage that would circulate as an epigraph to future theorizations of workers' inquiry, Marx communicated this point in no uncertain terms:

> We hope to meet in this work with the support of all workers in town and country who understand that they alone can describe with full knowledge the misfortunes from which they suffer, and that only they, and not saviors sent by Providence, can energetically apply the healing remedies for the social ills to which they are a prey.[21]

From this perspective, the succeeding list of questions was intended to act as a stimulus to raise the consciousness of workers about their exploitation so as to equip them to resist and eventually overcome this exploitation. The basic idea was that in reading and answering the questions, the worker would ultimately hold up what Ken Lawrence aptly describes as a "mirror" to "his or her own exploitation."[22] This "mirror" would then enable the worker to situate the circumstances of his or her own employment within the broader dynamics of exploitation and class struggle in capitalist society. The worker would thus "become aware," as Weiss puts it, "of the social determination of his conditions of life; he would gain an insight into the nature of the capitalist economy and the state, and would learn the means of abolishing wage labor and attaining his freedom."[23]

Alongside his appeals to the support of workers, Marx solicited the support of socialists who sought "an *exact and positive* knowledge of the conditions in which the working class—the class to whom the future belongs—works and moves."[24] The remainder of the introduction to his questionnaire offered instructions on the more mundane matters of how to fill out the questionnaire and where to send it upon completion. Marx insisted that not all of the questions had to be answered but only that the answers be "as detailed and comprehensive as possible."[25] He assured respondents that their names would "not be published without special permission."[26] Marx also asked that the answers be sent to the address of the office of the secretary of *La Revue socialiste* in Paris.[27]

The questionnaire portion of his text consists of 101 numbered questions divided into four thematically distinct sections without any subheadings. Andrew Rothstein instructively detects something of a movement from particularity to universality in the organization of these questions and their anticipated effects. "These questions," he writes, "gradually widen the worker's horizon, until he is forced to consider his own problems *as part of the general problems of the working class, in its struggle against the capitalist class, whose organ is the capitalist State*."[28] The first section opens with questions about the number and types of workers employed at the workplace. It then turns to questions about the locus and spatial organization of work as well as the health and safety of workers.[29] Broadly speaking, these questions are designed to get workers to think about the health hazards they encounter in the workplace as well as the governmental measures in place to both diminish these hazards and compensate for any accidents. For instance, the twenty-sixth item contains the following question: "Is the employer *legally* bound to compensate the worker or his family in case of accident?"[30] Confronted with such a question, the worker is already compelled to reflect on the role of the state in relations between workers and employers. The second section addresses the length and regimentation of the working day.[31] In particular, the questions in this section encourage workers to reflect on both the extraction of their time in the workplace and the loss of their time in commutes to and from the workplace. A subset of the questions even focuses on the extraction of the time of children and the young in particular. The fortieth question asks about the existence of schools for employed children and the young as well as the duration and content of their education at these schools. This question clearly invites workers to reflect critically on the much larger developmental implications of the extraction of the time of children and the young at the workplace. The questions in the third section broach the intricacies of contractual relations, the payment of wages, and living expenses. Several questions stand out in this section for prompting workers to arrive at predetermined conclusions. The fifty-sixth item asks the following questions: "If you receive piece-rates, how are they fixed? If you are employed in industries in which the work done is measured by quantity or weight, as in the mines, don't your employers or their clerks resort to trickery, in order to swindle you out of a part of your wages?"[32] Other questions in the third section reframe the conventional terms in the relationship between employers and employees to spur workers to think about this relationship differently. In this regard, the fifty-eighth question identifies work as "credit" provided to employers to be paid back in wages.[33] This question suddenly challenges the more conventional view of employers as sources of credit for needy employees. The leading questions in the following item drive the point even further home by depicting the employer as an unreliable debtor who turns his worker-creditors themselves into debtors. In its words:

> Have you noticed that delay in the payment of your wages forces you often to resort to the pawnshops, paying high rates of interest there, and depriving yourself of things you need: or incurring debts with shopkeepers, and becoming their victim because you are their debtor? Do you know of cases where workers have lost their wages owing to the ruin or bankruptcy of their employers?[34]

The questions in the fourth section deal with changes in wages and technological improvements before gravitating toward the topics of strikes, organizational forms on both sides of the class conflict, and the role of government in this conflict.[35] Questions ninety-two and ninety-three seek to ascertain this role by respectively asking workers if they know of any instances of government intervention on behalf of employers against workers or on behalf of workers against employers.[36] As part of this final section, the very last item in the questionnaire opens up entirely to invite observations unanticipated by the preceding questions in the questionnaire. It reads: "General remarks."[37] Marx's own introduction to the questionnaire downplays the importance of this item. It informs readers that the first "hundred questions are the most important," no doubt on account of their far less open-ended character and corresponding ability to generate precise and comparable data across a selection of responses for the purpose of amassing a comprehensive view of working-class conditions and struggles.[38]

Taken together, the majority of the questions in Marx's questionnaire solicit facts, and many of them are fairly straightforward in the solicitation of these facts.[39] For instance, the first question is quite simply "What is your trade?"[40] There is nothing complicated or excessively demanding about this question. Rothstein is therefore quite right to point out that the questions in Marx's questionnaire "start from the simplest facts of factory life, intended to bring home to the worker under capitalism how the very conditions of employment mean that he is exploited by the capitalist."[41] Similarly, the editors of the *New International* are equally right to stress the "simplicity and directness of Marx's approach to the actual problems confronted by the workers."[42] Yet, in a complication of these affirmations of straightforwardness in Marx's questionnaire, we can add that at least some of his questions even in the beginning seem to presuppose information that may have been out of the immediate reach of workers. The second question instructs workers to list the "names" of "the directors of the company" for which they work.[43] Whether workers would have known the names of all of these directors in addition to the names of their immediate superiors is not clear. The fourth question asks workers to "state" the number of employees at their workplace according to "age and sex."[44] The answer to this question may have been easy for workers in small enterprises, but it would have been taxing for workers in large enterprises who lacked access to employee data. Then again, the more didactic purpose of such questions was precisely to demonstrate that workers lacked important factual details about their working conditions so as to spur them to ascertain these details. It was in this sense that Marx's questionnaire amounted to an exercise in consciousness-raising.

Asad Haider and Salar Mohandesi have recently criticized Marx's questionnaire for foreclosing the "creative expression" of workers by posing "prefabricated questions" to them that demand "mechanical answers."[45] We address this criticism in much greater detail in the following chapter. For now, it suffices to note that Haider and Mohandesi's criticism does not acknowledge the presence of the far more open-ended questions at the end of Marx's questionnaire. The hundredth question asks workers to comment on "the general physical, intellectual and moral conditions of life of the working men and women" in their trades.[46] This question is general enough to facilitate a wide variety of responses. The succeeding item goes even further in its open-endedness. It elicits "General remarks," as indicated above.[47] This item is certainly minimal enough to leave plenty of space for the creative expression of workers. And while Marx diminished its importance relative to the preceding one hundred questions in his questionnaire, workers were under no obligation to follow his advice.

However, judged from the perspective of simply generating written responses from workers, Marx's workers' inquiry *was* an abysmal failure. For reasons that are somewhat unclear, the questionnaire did not succeed in eliciting enough responses from workers in spite of its widespread distribution. Dario Lanzardo puts the number of completed questionnaires sent to the address of *La Revue socialiste* in Paris at around one hundred.[48] Haider and Mohandesi more stunningly claim that Marx himself "never" received "a single response" to his questionnaire.[49] Obviously, these conclusions are far from incompatible: perhaps the responses received at the address of *La Revue socialiste* never made it to Marx. Whatever the precise number of completed and returned questionnaires, the best proof that the inquiry fell short of meeting the expectations of its own organizers came in the form of an anonymous plea for more responses published just three months later in a July 1880 issue of *La Revue socialiste*. The plea reads as follows:

> A certain number of our friends already sent back a response to our questionnaire for the workers' inquiry; we thank them for it, and we encourage those among our friends and readers who have not yet responded to kindly hurry up. We only want to start our work when we have the most monographs possible so that it is the most complete. We ask our proletarian friends to consider that the elaboration of these "Work Notebooks" is of the greatest importance, and that in helping us in the difficult work that we have undertaken they work directly for their emancipation.[50]

Weiss speculates about the authorship of this plea. For her, "the style" of the plea "suggests that it may have been written by Marx."[51] The contention in the passage that workers contribute to their own emancipation by participating in the inquiry certainly chimes with the overall emphasis on generating the self-activity of workers in Marx's questionnaire. If Weiss is right in her speculation, then the plea demonstrates the depth of Marx's concern with successfully carrying out the inquiry rather than simply initiating it and letting others handle the details of its execution. However, one possible problem with Weiss's speculation is that the plea for more responses appears in a bibliographic and short news item section signed by Lecluse.[52]

Whatever the case with regard to authorship, the message in the plea above was perfectly clear: too few responses were submitted to the office of *La Revue socialiste* for the inquiry to move forward, and many more were needed immediately. Yet, owing to the ongoing lack of adequate responses from workers to the questionnaire even after the publication of the plea, the inquiry was eventually discontinued, and its findings were never published in the projected "Work Notebooks" mentioned above.[53] From this strict standpoint, Marx's project for a workers' inquiry could be considered an even greater failure than the official inquiry of 1848 because, as Rigaudias-Weiss tells us, the latter at least generated *some* information on the overall state of the French economy and on opinions across different strata of French society.[54] To compound matters from a research perspective, we do not even know the contents of the meager number of responses that *were* dutifully returned to *La Revue socialiste* because researchers have never succeeded in tracking them down. As Weiss conceded as far back as 1936: "It has proved impossible to find even the few replies that did arrive, in spite of the active search for them."[55]

Here we come across the first instance in Marxism of a practical problem that would pervade the practice of workers' inquiry in its divergent forms: workers very often did not respond to the solicitations of their writings. Weiss rather cautiously offers two reasons for this failure. She suggests that the demand that workers answer all of the questions in the questionnaire may have asked too much of them at a time when they confronted acute limitations in the availability of their time, widespread illiteracy, and a limited access to newspapers compounded all the more by censorship. Weiss also points to a political conjuncture in France marked by a labor movement and working class still reeling from the defeat of the Paris Commune.[56] Weiss's caution in offering these reasons for the failure of Marx's questionnaire is fully justified. The paucity of historical documentation concerning Marx's questionnaire leaves us in rather speculative territory about the precise reasons for its failure. To Weiss's reasons, we may add other possible and related explanations for this failure: a fear of reprisals from employers, inadequate organizational bonds between the organizers of the inquiry and workers, and, finally, the highly demanding and potentially painful nature of some of the questions themselves. The questions may have been a source of emotional pain, rather than enlightenment, to the extent that they asked workers to revisit the details of their own exploitative conditions. It even seems conceivable that the placement of some of the highly demanding questions at the very beginning of the questionnaire may have had the effect of turning workers away from any further engagement with it. Another possibility is that some *completed* questionnaires may not have reached their destination. After all, *L'Égalité*, which reproduced the questionnaire as an insert, asked its readers to send their responses to the address of *its* offices rather than to the address of the offices of *La Revue socialiste*.[57] Such divergent instructions may have created problems in the collection of responses.

Overall, there seem to have been so many possible reasons for the failure of Marx's questionnaire to elicit responses from workers that maybe the more pertinent question is how it *could not* have failed rather than *why* it failed. Be that as it may, in searching for the reasons for the limited number of responses to Marx's questionnaire, it is too easy to lose sight of other measures of its success or failure. The questionnaire, it should be remembered, brought together various aspirations: the aspiration to nudge the French government to undertake an inquiry; the aspiration to raise the consciousness of the working class to enable it to act on its own; and, finally, the aspiration to make knowledge of the working class available to socialists. If the overarching purpose of the questionnaire was to raise the consciousness of workers, its success did not necessarily hinge on *written* responses from them so much as the far more diffuse reception of the questions *among* them. Lanzardo points us in the direction of this interpretation, as we shall see in much greater detail in the next chapter.[58] Thiollent, who also takes his cues from Lanzardo's reading of Marx's questionnaire, nicely emphasizes the element of collective discussion in the reception of the questionnaire. In his illuminating words, "Marx's questionnaire implies thought, the faculty of observation, the reasoning of those involved and, eventually, collective discussion in each factory."[59] If the questionnaire could lend itself to verbal processes as potentially untidy and unpredictable as collective discussions, why should we restrict our measure of its historical success to *written* responses? The obvious answer is that these responses provide easy measures, but they are too easy in some sense because all kinds of verbal and reflective processes escape them. Of course, the absence of written responses from the workers *was* no doubt disappointing, if not profoundly dispiriting, to organizers of the inquiry, but this absence did not necessarily mean that the questionnaire had simply failed or that it was invariably doomed to failure. The questionnaire could have served to raise the consciousness of workers in far less tangible ways with far from self-evident results.

Moreover, what *is* clear from the subsequent history of Marx's questionnaire is that it did not share the same dust-covered, archival fate as the 1848 inquiry of the French government. His questionnaire was translated and reprinted various times in numerous pamphlets, anthologies, and other publications. Marx's questionnaire was translated into

English alone at least half a dozen times beginning with a translation by the Communist Party of Great Britain in 1933.[60] Of course, the mere translation of his questionnaire did not necessarily guarantee its practical enactment or theorization. In fact, there were noteworthy delays from the former to the latter moves, and sometimes this shift appears to have never materialized. Yet the numerous translations of Marx's questionnaire put it in the air of Marxist organizations, so to speak. It circulated among varieties of these organizations in the following century. Marx's questionnaire also served as a source of inspiration for *other* types of radical movements. These movements found the meticulous focus on materiality in the questionnaire helpful even as they concerned themselves with conditions of oppression and struggle beyond the space of the factory.

Lenin's Critique of Workers' Inquiries

Unlike Marx, Lenin receives almost no attention in the literature on workers' inquiries. Indeed, as far as I can surmise, only Thiollent attempts to draw out Lenin's contributions to the theory and practice of workers' inquiry.[61] He suggests that Lenin affords a critique of workers' inquiry based on the purported economism of the practice. This economism, Thiollent tells us, derives from the privilege accorded to the conditions of workers in the space of the factory. He speculates, "Along the lines of *What Is to Be Done?*, we could even think that workers' inquiry would be open to criticism for limiting itself to a description of work and therefore remaining subject to economism."[62] There are some grounds for this kind of extrapolation. After all, as Thiollent stresses, Lenin criticized the use of leaflets that relied on the contributions of writings from workers to expose factory conditions in Russia.[63] While acknowledging the importance of these leaflets in channeling and stimulating working-class struggles, Lenin claimed that their usage by Social Democrats did not succeed in facilitating a broadening of these struggles beyond demands for greater compensation for the sale of labor-power within particular trades.[64] Put differently, the uses of these leaflets did not disrupt or challenge capitalist relations of production. If Lenin could level the charge of economism against pamphleteering based on the writings of workers about their own conditions, *why not* simply extend these charges to another practice based on the writing and speaking of workers, namely, workers' inquiry? The problem is that Thiollent does not attend to the specific instances in which Lenin actually practiced and subsequently criticized workers' inquiry. In other words, we do not need to extrapolate from Lenin to understand his attitude toward workers' inquiry because there are moments in which he forthrightly addresses the practice.

In this section, I want to tease out these moments in order to better understand and situate his critique of workers' inquiry. What we get from them is something far more precise (and lively) than an extrapolation. We get Lenin's arduous *process* of *arriving* at a critique of workers' inquiry based on disappointing experiences. We also see that the substance of his critique focuses more precisely on the production of limited knowledge contents through the practice of workers' inquiries. Lenin sought to rectify this problem through recourse to official and legal sources of knowledge. In so doing, he ultimately cast aside the didactic possibilities opened up by the exchange of questions and answers in his own practice of workers' inquiry.

Remarkably, Lenin engaged in his own little-known workers' inquiries without any apparent stimulus from or even knowledge of the experience of Marx's questionnaire. Lenin drew up a questionnaire for workers and personally interviewed them during his period of Social Democratic activism in St. Petersburg from 1894 to 1896.[65] Unfortunately, only a shortened version of Lenin's questionnaire remains available in English,[66] and even it exists in the relative obscurity of a short text outside his forty-five-volume *Collected Works*. In marked contrast to Marx's questionnaire, Lenin's questionnaire does not consist of an introduction laying out the rationale behind its formulation and providing instructions for its completion. It also does not contain an address for the delivery of the completed questionnaires. The questionnaire leaps straight into pleas for information organized around sixteen items.[67] The content of these pleas nonetheless echoes the content of many of the items in Marx's questionnaire. Lenin's questionnaire concerns the intricacies of the conditions of exploitation in factories and the struggles against this exploitation. It deals with the following topics (in the order of their appearance): the number of workers in enterprises both in total and divided into gender and age groups; the terms of employment and the fidelity to these terms among employers and workers; the length of the working day and attenuations to time devoted to labor through holiday and overtime hours; the monthly output of workers; the extent to which payments for holiday and overtime work exceed payments for regular work; the frequency and form of the payment of wages; increases and decreases in wages as well as deductions; fines and the execution of penalties; the treatment of workers by employers; the dissatisfaction among workers over working conditions and the channeling of this dissatisfaction through revolts; factory laws and factory inspectors; the cost of items at factory shops and consumer cooperatives; and, finally, the overall costs of living for workers.[68] These topics clearly suggest that Lenin took an acute interest both in the details of the conditions of workers and in their forms of struggle against these conditions. However, owing to a paucity of historical documentation, the fate of Lenin's questionnaire remains shrouded in even more mystery than Marx's questionnaire. We do not know how many copies of his questionnaire were produced and distributed. We do not know if they were intended for workers to fill out on their own or if they were more exclusively intended for use among revolutionaries interviewing workers. And we do not know how many questionnaires were filled out, what the contents of the responses were, and how the responses were ultimately put to use.

We can nevertheless glimpse something of the rationale behind Lenin's questionnaire from his overall political strategy in the mid- to late 1890s. As Lars T. Lih demonstrates, Lenin subscribed fully to the well-established view of Social Democracy as a merger of socialist doctrine and the worker movement. Among other things, this merger implied that socialists would bring insight and organization to workers about their historical mission to establish socialism. It also implied that workers would respond positively to the socialists by acting on this insight and organization.[69] Lenin's questionnaire clearly fit into this overall strategy. Its questions even lend themselves to a didactic function. They seek to foster the awareness of workers about their conditions of exploitation and their means of resisting this exploitation. Noteworthy in this regard is the thirteenth item in Lenin's questionnaire. It poses the following lengthy question:

> Is it possible to give more details of all the strikes in this institution or in others in which [the workers] have participated, or about which they have known: when, for what reason, how many people took part, how it went—peacefully or violently, were the army called in, how did it end—whether it was a success or a failure and why it ended as it did?[70]

This densely detailed question deals rather straightforwardly with facts, but it also solicits an explanation of the reasons for strikes and their efficacy (or lack thereof). In so doing, the question lends itself to the stimulation of more general reflections on the need for and the dangers of collective action and organization. It encourages workers to reflect on why strikes of different types ended in successes or failures and what role a repressive state institution, the army, played in generating these results. The question thus pushes workers to evaluate strikes as modes of collective action, and, depending on their responses, it incites them to envisage alternative modes of collective action and organization. The question also compels workers to consider the role of the state in the class struggle and what interests it serves as this struggle erupts into strikes. Like Marx's questionnaire, Lenin's questionnaire prompts workers to recognize the more general dynamics of class struggle *in* the fine details of their own individual circumstances. It thus equips them to begin to organize in these struggles.

Lenin's retrospective comments on his actual experience of interviewing a worker nonetheless eclipse the more didactic logic in his questionnaire by disclosing a far more immediate or mundane methodological rationale behind his efforts to interview workers. These comments appear tucked away in a lengthy footnote to his 1902 classic *What Is to Be Done?* In the footnote, Lenin "vividly" recalls his experience of interviewing one worker over the course of weeks about "every aspect" of working conditions at a factory.[71] Lenin conducted his interviews with the unnamed worker to gather illegal materials about working conditions. Notably, Lenin does not tell us anything about the professional and political status of the worker or why he interviewed him over other workers. Lenin also does not clarify whether the worker approached him for the interviews or whether he approached the worker for the interviews. He mentions only that the worker "would often visit" him.[72] Just as notably, Lenin's commentary leaves unclear whether he used his questionnaire as the basis for the interviews.

What *is* overwhelmingly clear is his negative assessment of the experience. Lenin recounts with evident frustration that his interviews yielded altogether paltry results. They resulted, he complains, in material for a description of working conditions in only "one single factory!"[73] He also points out that his steady stream of questions left the worker exasperated. As Lenin describes it, the worker half-jokingly told him, "'I find it easier to work overtime than to answer your questions.'"[74]

What lesson did Lenin draw from this tremendously disappointing experience? He concluded that interviewing workers to obtain illegal materials from them makes for a poor use of the time of revolutionaries. Lenin reasoned that workers tend to have a fragmentary view of working conditions in their factories because of the division of labor. In his words:

> A worker who very often knows only a single department of a large factory and almost always the economic results, but not the general conditions and standards of his work, cannot acquire the knowledge which is possessed by the office staff of a factory, by inspectors, doctors, etc., and which is scattered in petty newspaper reports and in special industrial, medical, Zemstvo, and other publications.[75]

His overall point was clear: revolutionaries seeking to obtain a knowledge of working conditions in factories should consult legally available sources and make extensive use of these sources rather than waste precious time on interviewing workers. Lenin's seemingly harsh point here suddenly dispenses with the didactic logic in his own questionnaire. There is no need to instigate a process of consciousness-raising among workers through questions directed toward them because the answers to these questions already reside elsewhere. The possibilities opened up by the mere exchange of questions and answers in questionnaires and interviews get swept aside in favor of a recourse to legal sources of knowledge.

Be that as it may, Lenin cannot be faulted for failing to stick to the insights generated through his disappointing experience of interviewing workers. In fact, he had already demonstrated his staunch adherence to these insights in his magnum opus, *The Development of Capitalism in Russia*, published in 1899.[76] He relied on a dizzying array of official statistics to demonstrate the formation of the home market in Russia. In particular, Lenin marshaled the statistical returns from house-to-house censuses undertaken by rural governing bodies known as the Zemstvo.[77] As indicated in the quote above, he later recommended these very bodies as sources of comprehensive information about working conditions. The immediate purpose of his usage of Zemstvo statistical returns was to demonstrate the differentiation of the peasantry into a rural bourgeoisie, a middle peasantry, and a rural proletariat through data on peasant households classified (in the main) according to the number of draught animals and the extent of cultivated land. The realization of this immediate purpose belonged to Lenin's larger polemic against Narodnik economists who identified the ruin of small producers with the shrinkage of the home market and the corresponding need to realize surplus value in foreign markets.[78] Contra these economists, Lenin deemed the differentiation of the peasantry the very basis for the creation of the home market: the rural bourgeoisie created a market for productive consumption by transforming its newly acquired means of production into capital, and the rural proletariat created a market for personal consumption through the transformation of its labor-powers into commodities.[79]

Lenin nonetheless harnessed the Zemstvo statistical returns in a highly critical fashion to make his point about differentiation. What he found problematic about these returns was their classification of peasant households according to allotment land holdings and their summarizations of findings through average figures. Classifications according to allotment land holdings simply failed to differentiate between categories of peasants because allotments were a legal requirement for all peasants in Russia.[80] Summaries based on average figures also obscured acute differences in economic strength between categories of peasants.[81] These averages even lent themselves to romanticized conceptions among Narodnik economists of a homogeneous and integral peasant community intrinsically averse to capitalist development. As Lenin sarcastically quipped, "In Russia, one-horse farm laborers are combined with wealthy peasants, 'averages' are struck, and sentimental talk is indulged about the 'community spirit.'"[82]

Beyond his critical deployment of Zemstvo statistical returns, Lenin subjected factory statistics to a critique as he turned his attention to the development of large-scale industry in Russia.[83] His basic critique of these statistics was that they lead to a distorted view of the growth of large-scale machine industry in Russia because they include small establishments in the category of "factories" and even confuse home workers from domestic industry with factory workers. Factory statistics therefore understate the growth of factories in Russia by exaggerating their numbers as one goes back in time.[84] Lenin sought to remedy this problem by proposing a more restricted criterion for "factories" as establishments "employing not fewer than 16 workers."[85] His adherence to this criterion led him to the conclusion that "*the number of factories in Russia in the post-Reform period is growing, and growing fairly rapidly*."[86]

Thus, even as Lenin affirmed the superiority of legal and official sources of knowledge over the knowledge obtained through workers' inquiries, he engaged in a highly critical usage of these sources. Moreover, it would be deeply misleading to suggest that Lenin's analyses had no repercussions in the history of investigations in Marxism. *The*

Development of Capitalism in Russia served as a model of scientific rigor for French Maoists aspiring to initiate their own investigations into the French social formation of the late 1960s.[87]

Stepping back from all of these details, we can also see that Lenin and Marx moved in somewhat opposite directions with regard to the relationship between their appeals to and uses of workers' inquiries, on the one hand, and their reliance on official sources of knowledge about working conditions, on the other hand. Marx turned to workers' inquiries *in light* of the failure of the French state to replicate the British model of producing a politically and legally impactful knowledge about the working class. Lenin turned resolutely to official sources of knowledge about working conditions *only after* experiencing the failure of his version of workers' inquiry to generate a comprehensive knowledge about working conditions.

Between Subjectivity and Objectivity: Mao's Investigation

Mao reproduced the broader pattern of compartmentalized articulations of the investigation in early Marxism. He formulated his own approach to the investigation without any apparent knowledge of Marx and Lenin's formulations of workers' inquiry. However, Mao's investigations succeeded in generating politically consequential information because they were based on comparatively immersive experiences. This information revealed poor peasants in particular as suddenly indispensable to revolutionary ambitions. Mao's successful experiences with the investigation also spurred him to theorize it as a practice that mediates political subjectivity through a moment of objectivity. He thus stands apart from Marx and Lenin in having made the greatest strides in practicing and theorizing the investigation in early Marxism. Indeed, Mao transformed the investigation from a practice that had not gained much traction at all in Marxism into a carefully reflected guide for revolutionary knowledge and action with major political ramifications in his own lifetime.

Mao's initial articulation of the investigation took place through two distinct but intimately related steps. As if in anticipation of his own affirmation of the primacy of practice, Mao first practiced the investigation before theorizing it. Roger R. Thompson traces this practice all the way back to Mao's journeys as a student through Hunan Province in 1916.[88]

Of course, Mao's most famous investigation was of the peasant movement in Hunan in 1927. He undertook this investigation in January and February 1927 to appraise the political import of the peasant movement in Hunan for the leadership of the Chinese Communist Party (CCP).[89] Mao then wrote a deeply influential report of his investigation, "Report on an Investigation of the Peasant Movement in Hunan," published in March 1927. He used the findings of the report to persuade the CCP leadership of the crucial role of the peasantry in the revolution. The CCP leadership needed persuading because it adhered to a more orthodox Marxist view of revolution based on the leadership of the urban proletariat.[90]

Mao proceeded in his labor of persuasion by depicting the peasant movement as a torrential force that would soon sweep away the entire feudal order in the countryside. Through this movement, peasants had transformed themselves into subjects of history. They had shattered the long-standing power of landlords and suddenly inverted social hierarchies in the countryside. Peasants now issued orders to landlords, and landlords now feared peasant associations. Mao suggested that the sheer scale and momentum of the peasant movement would speedily test the commitments of revolutionaries by forcing them to adopt one of three positions: to lead the peasant movement, to fall behind and criticize it, or to outright oppose it.[91] As Rebecca E. Karl incisively observes, Mao's very framing of these options made it clear that there was really only *one* option, namely, to lead the peasant movement.[92] Indeed, Mao devoted a considerable portion of his report to defending the actions of peasant associations against charges from fellow revolutionaries of excessive violence and irresponsibility. For Mao, these charges simply failed to take into account the long history of the violence of landlords against peasants. They also emanated from the fantasy of a peaceful revolution that played into the hands of landlords. Beyond fending off the charges of excessive violence and irresponsibility, Mao offered more refined reflections on precisely what strata of the peasantry would be most likely to assume the role of the avant-garde in the revolution. He arrived at the audacious conclusion that the *entire* prospect of revolution in China would depend on *poor* peasants in particular. These peasants enjoyed a numerical superiority in the population. Their material destitution also left them far less ambiguous about the revolution than upper strata of peasants.[93]

These bold conclusions had their roots in fact-finding meetings convened by Mao. "I called together," he recalled, "fact-finding conferences in villages and county towns, which were attended by experienced peasants and by comrades working in the peasant movement, and I listened attentively to their reports and collected a great deal of material."[94] Apart from this recollection, however, Mao disclosed few details about how exactly he conducted his famous investigation in Hunan. To further muddy the waters from a research standpoint, Mao subsequently lost the materials for the investigation containing these details.[95] Yet he left no doubt as to the overall importance of the fact-finding meetings for his outlook because he registered their didactic effects on his own subjectivity. As if utterly bewildered, Mao told his readers, "I saw and heard of many things of which I had hitherto been unaware."[96]

Three years later, Mao revisited the practice of the investigation in more theoretical terms, though not without conducting yet another investigation. He conducted this lesser-known investigation in the rural county of Xunwu over a two-week period in May 1930.[97] Thompson describes the Xunwu investigation as "the most detailed investigation of local society" that Mao "would ever make."[98] He even suggests that it "represents the crystallization of a method of inquiry that Mao had been developing for almost fifteen years."[99] Mao himself opened his *Report from Xunwu* by describing his investigation there as the "largest" in "scale" he had ever undertaken.[100] As in the case of his investigations in the province of Hunan, Mao's investigation in the county of Xunwu centered on the experience of fact-finding meetings. Yet he offered far more details about these meetings. Mao disclosed that he relied on eleven persons to serve as informants during his meetings in Xunwu.[101] These persons ranged in age from the young to the elderly. They also varied in their social and professional backgrounds, from poor peasants to a general store owner.[102] Mao conducted his investigation by questioning these informants about their life experiences to obtain a comprehensive knowledge about social conditions in Xunwu.[103] The result of his labor was a lengthy report on the fine details of administration, transportation, communication, commerce, land relationships, and land struggles in Xunwu. These details can make for very tedious reading, and their relationship to the larger political thrust of the investigation may not be clear. For instance, Mao devoted page after page of his report to the granular details of the products at the stalls of the market in Xunwu City. He elaborated these rather dry details to distill the vicissitudes wrought by the fierce "competition" between "handicraft products and capitalist products."[104] Yet Mao seems at times to have been far more fascinated by the flatly technical aspects of producing these products than by their relationship to a larger economic and political context, as in the case of a whole paragraph that he devoted to elaborating the instructions for making soy sauce. Such moments suggest that an excess of knowledge presented in an improperly focused manner can digress from the political goals of an investigation.

Thankfully, Mao's May 1930 article "Oppose Book Worship," which also was written in Xunwu, serves as a counterpoint to this lack of focus. It elaborates a much more theoretical rationale for his investigation and offers a step-by-step exposition of the practice.[105] At its most abstract, Mao's rationale for the investigation is fairly straightforward: the purpose of the investigation is to ward off idealism among revolutionaries by mediating their subjectivity through objectivity. The realization of this task entails an appraisal of the totality of class forces and the identification of leading classes in the revolutionary struggle.[106] In more general terms, the investigation involves searching for solutions to problems through the study of social and economic conditions. Obviously, Mao had undertaken precisely this task in his investigation of the peasant movement in Hunan and his investigation in Xunwu. The goal of aligning the subjectivity of revolutionaries with objective conditions (so as to avoid errors in the revolutionary struggle) dictates that the investigation proceeds along far more experientially immersive lines than anything in the workers' inquiries of Marx and Lenin. For Mao, it is not enough to distribute questionnaires en masse through newspapers and pamphlets or even to interview an individual worker. It *is* absolutely imperative to personally undertake an investigation in a collective setting. Only this deep commitment and careful involvement with others can yield the effects at the level of subjectivity that Mao himself had experienced in Hunan.

The demand for this commitment and involvement appears readily in his step-by-step elaboration of the investigation as a technique. From the very first step, Mao stresses the collective character of the investigation. He emphasizes that investigators should "hold fact-finding meetings and undertake [an] investigation through discussions."[107] In formulating this demand, Mao manifestly disqualifies individual interviews and casually formulated questions.[108] The former capture only partial experiences at odds with the comprehensive thrust of the investigation, and the latter lack precision. Here we should note that Mao's critique of individual interviews renders his own position proximate to the position that Lenin would *eventually* adopt. Yet, in marked contradistinction to Lenin, Mao's position is bound up with an affirmation of the deepening of the experience of the investigation rather than with a critical endorsement of official and legal sources of knowledge about workers. Mao affirms this deepening as well as a more methodical approach to questions in the context of his elaboration of the fine details of commerce in Xunwu. In his metaphorical words, "If one rides a horse to view the flowers, like a certain comrade's so-called 'going to a place and asking questions randomly,' then one cannot understand a problem even after a lifetime of effort."[109] Mao further suggests that the subject matter should dictate who exactly attends a fact-finding meeting. Not every subject matter requires universal participation. In keeping with his own practice of investigation in Xunwu, Mao appeals to the participation of those knowledgeable about "social and economic conditions" from a range of age groups, social backgrounds, and professions.[110] His insistence on the participation of the elderly in particular was rooted in the view that their memory of past experiences could offer an interpretive lens to illuminate "*why* things were the way they were," as Thompson puts it.[111] Mao then recommends that the competence of the investigator should determine the size of the fact-finding meeting. Only investigators skillful at managing meetings should hold meetings with more than a dozen persons.[112] Mao advises investigators to base their questions on outlines formulated in advance of the meeting.[113] He urges persons in leadership positions to personally undertake investigations rather than rely on the reports of others. Mao also encourages budding investigators to "probe deeply" into "a particular place or problem" to streamline the task of their future investigations.[114] Finally, he stresses the importance of personal note taking during meetings rather than relying on others to take notes.[115]

We should note that in offering all of this rather intricate advice, Mao clearly diverges from the concept of workers' inquiry in the strict sense of a practice of knowledge production directed toward and emanating from workers. His investigation strives toward an examination of *all* classes. As indicated above, Mao considers even the dry and tedious details of this examination absolutely imperative for the formulation of revolutionary tactics and strategies. As he observed of commerce in Xunwu, "A person who is completely ignorant of the inside story of the world of commerce is bound to fail in choosing proper tactics to deal with the mercantile bourgeoisie and in attempting to gain the support of the poor urban masses."[116] Yet his investigation shares a manifestly political goal with strict iterations of workers' inquiry, and the realization of this goal depends to no small degree on the solicitation of the knowledge of subaltern classes in particular. Mao's investigation thus covers (and exceeds) what had been previously practiced and theorized in Marxism as workers' inquiry. And, at the risk of once again getting ahead of ourselves, let us simply note that this more wide-ranging orientation in Mao's approach to the investigation may have lent itself more readily to the focus on figures outside a classically revolutionary repertoire, such as prisoners and former psychiatric hospital patients, in the experiences of investigations among French Maoists roughly four decades later.

Mao deems the knowledge of class forces generated through the investigation so important the he straightforwardly ties the investigation to the right to speech in his pithy and provocative injunction "No investigation, no right to speak."[117] This injunction, which would have a rich afterlife among Maoist and non-Maoist groups in late twentieth-century France, is intended to remind revolutionaries of the grave dangers of speaking about a problem without first undertaking an investigation of it. Without an investigation, speech can become disconnected from a moment of objectivity. It can therefore lend itself to grave errors in the formulation of revolutionary tactics and strategies. More precisely, speech without the objective pull of an investigation can lead revolutionaries to overestimate or underestimate their own strengths with perilous consequences.

From the foregoing, it is easy to see that the investigation acquired the status of a deeply reflected practice in Mao's oeuvre as early as 1930. He would revisit this practice many times in the succeeding decades. It would implicitly complement his strident emphasis on particularity (as a bearer of universality) in his philosophical reflections on dialectics to the extent that it would aspire to disclose the more general dynamics of a local situation.[118] From this perspective, Mao's investigation is perfectly in keeping with the movement from particularity to universality in the organization and intended effects of the questionnaires of Marx and Lenin. Mao would also continue to uphold the fact-finding meeting as the matrix of the investigation. He would even convey the need for an attitude of zeal and humility on the part of the investigators. In his 1941 "Preface to *Rural Surveys*," Mao wrote, "One certainly cannot make an investigation or do it well, without zeal, a determination to direct one's eyes downward and a thirst for knowledge, and without shedding the ugly mantle of pretentiousness and becoming a willing pupil."[119] This modest attitude implies a destabilization, if not inversion, of more traditional hierarchies in the production of knowledge. Investigators have to *learn* from the investigated rather than simply extract knowledge from them in order to verify their preexisting theoretical schemas. Mao's explicit focus on cultivating this attitude is simply nowhere to be found in the workers' inquiries of Marx and Lenin for the simple reason that their inquiries do not demand such an immersive and unsettling experience from the militant investigator.

Mao induced a major shift in the theory and practice of the investigation in early Marxism. Quite apart from his success in yielding politically consequential information through his investigations as well as his elaborate theorization of the practice of the investigation, Mao stands out for having focused on the subjectivity of revolutionaries as the principal object of the investigation. Mao thus offers a somewhat different measure of the success of the militant investigation: investigations are successful to the extent that they align the subjective orientations of revolutionaries with objective conditions. The pursuit of revolutionary tactics and strategies confirms whether such an alignment has transpired. Ultimately, then, practice itself tells us whether investigations are truly successful.

On the Political Afterlives of Investigations

We have seen that the militant investigation differed in terms of its immediate objectives, methods, and results in its initial formulations in early Marxism. Its immediate objectives gravitated between fomenting the self-activity of workers for revolutionary purposes to empowering militants with an objective knowledge for these same purposes. The investigation depended on the formulation and communication of questions and answers, but the methods employed for the formulation and communication of these questions and answers varied from the mass distribution of the questionnaire, to one-on-one interviews, to more collective fact-finding meetings between the investigator and selected informants. The results also ranged from an outright failure to generate satisfactory responses to a successful reorientation of militant subjectivity. It should be abundantly obvious from this variegation that the investigation in early Marxism was not a homogeneous or static procedure. It was subjected to various modulations as it traveled through time and space even within the parameters of the formative stages of Marxism.

With the bulk of the historical details of our analysis in this chapter in hindsight, one question now impresses itself upon us more than ever before: how exactly did Marx, Lenin, and Mao *each* arrive at formulations of the militant investigation, given their apparent lack of knowledge of preceding formulations of this practice? How, in other words, did they perceive the need for militant investigations in the first place independently of a familiarity with preceding experiments in these investigations? It is difficult to answer these questions in broad strokes owing to the heterogeneity in the elaboration of the rationales for the practices and theories of the investigation in early Marxism. As we have seen, Lenin in particular did not spell out the precise motivation for his questionnaire. Still, we can say that investigations in early Marxism responded implicitly or explicitly to a lacuna in the official representations (of the state or party) and construed this lacuna in productive terms. After all, if official representations of the conditions and struggles of workers and peasants *were* sufficient, *why* launch an investigation in the first place? It was deemed necessary to produce a concrete knowledge of the lives of these subalterns for the sake of their own political self-activity and/or for the sake of providing militants with an objective basis for the formulation of political strategies and tactics.

In the succeeding chapters, we shall see that the investigations of Marx and Mao in particular took off in radical political struggles and theories throughout the twentieth century. They were mobilized, theorized, and modified by a wide range of organizations and movements in a wide range of settings. Lenin's version of workers' inquiry, on the other hand, appears to have *never* had an afterlife in radical political struggles. The history of the investigation in these struggles therefore poses a straightforward problem: why did the investigations of Marx and Mao circulate widely in these struggles, whereas Lenin's investigation never extended beyond its original uses? As indicated in the introduction to this chapter, failure is not a compelling enough answer because Marx's workers' inquiry also failed by standard measures. The preceding analysis of Lenin's workers' inquiry furnishes us with some more compelling answers. The most obvious one is that his version of workers' inquiry occupied the margins of his own oeuvre. Lenin's questionnaire, it should be recalled, was discovered in the mid-1980s and published outside his *Collected Works*. The timing of the appearance of his questionnaire, long after a crescendo in the use of investigations in radical political struggles from around 1970 to 1971, was not at all favorable to its widespread circulation. What is more, Lenin appears to have devoted no more than a footnote to reflections on his own experience of interviewing a worker. And the content of the footnote clearly disparages the experience. It is therefore entirely unsurprising that Lenin's version of workers' inquiry never gained any traction beyond its original use. Quite apart from the belated discovery and publication of his questionnaire, Lenin's own few words about interviewing a worker ultimately discouraged any future deployment of his own version of workers' inquiry.

This version of workers' inquiry nonetheless belongs to a set of investigations in early Marxism with broad implications. These investigations sit uneasily with vanguard political orientations often associated with Lenin to the extent that they manifestly privilege the knowledge of workers and peasants about their working conditions and struggles rather than the knowledge of professional revolutionaries about these conditions and struggles. Investigations privilege this popular knowledge in two ways. First, they enable workers and peasants to learn from themselves through the stimulus of externally formulated questions. Second, investigations orient militants to learn directly from workers and peasants through questionnaires, individual interviews, and fact-finding meetings. Either way, workers and peasants appear as the active subject-objects of knowledge for the arduous task of social and political reconstruction. Put in more synthetic terms, they learn about their conditions and struggles *as* they enable others to learn about these conditions and struggles. Indeed, it would be more accurate to say that workers and peasants retain the possibility of learning from their conditions and struggles *even when* the ostensible purpose of an investigation is to principally enable *others* to learn about these conditions and struggles. Why? Once formulated and communicated in print or speech, questions and answers can always take on lives of their own beyond any prescribed (and circumscribing) purpose. If that is the case, then we need to broaden the horizons of our thinking about the political effects of the investigation. We need to consider the less tangible domain of the potential afterlives of questions after the investigators have cleared the scene and after their probing questions have received initial outbursts of publicity. To be more precise, we need to consider the potential political effects of questions or mere demands for information beyond those reflected in an extraction, accumulation, and publication of written or spoken responses. In other words, we need to refine and expand our horizons of thought about what basically *counts* as a success or failure in the practice of militant investigations. We will pursue this task in greater detail as we explore the dissemination of the investigation in radical political struggles in the twentieth century.

3

Workers' Inquiries from Breakaway Trotskyism to Italian Workerism

The most extensive resuscitation of Karl Marx's "A Workers' Inquiry" took place in Italy in the early 1960s. This resuscitation transpired through workerism as an unorthodox current of Marxism that stretched from the contributions of the journal *Quaderni Rossi* in the early 1960s all the way up to Workers' Autonomy in the 1970s. Workers' inquiries in Italy also had important antecedents in breakaway Trotskyist and post-Trotskyist currents outside Italy. These currents were the Johnson-Forest Tendency and its successor, Correspondence, in the United States as well as Socialisme ou Barbarie in France. Indeed, there is a budding but remarkably rich literature that ties the workers' inquiries of *Quaderni Rossi* to the workers' inquiries of these groups.[1]

In the following pages, I engage this literature at length to shed light on what separates and binds together these inquiries. What distinguishes the workers' inquiries of the aforementioned Trotskyist and post-Trotskyist groups from the workers' inquiries of the *Quaderni Rossi* collective is their form, whereas what binds them together is a strident, if at times implicit, focus on consciousness-raising. This chapter introduces a remarkable and deliberate transformation in the *form* of the militant investigation itself. In striking contradistinction to Marx, the Johnson-Forest Tendency eschewed the use of the questionnaire. Socialisme ou Barbarie went a bit further. It outright rejected to the form of the questionnaire. Writing on behalf of the latter group, Claude Lefort suggested that the reliance on questions formulated by outsiders yields inauthentic responses from the working class. The Johnson-Forest Tendency, Correspondence, and Socialisme ou Babarie sought to facilitate the creative self-expression of the working class by publishing individual narratives and other writings by workers about their experiences at the point of production. Ideally, the publication of these writings would serve to raise the consciousness of a working-class readership by provoking processes of identification among its readers. Yet, in pursuing this task, the Johnson-Forest Tendency in particular got caught up in an acute contradiction. The group set out to overcome the division between mental and manual labor, but it ended up reproducing this division in the organization and presentation of its most famous worker narrative, *The American Worker*. More generally, the Trotskyist and post-Trotskyist groups above rarely succeeded in getting workers outside a militant milieu to write about their experiences on the shop floor.

The *Quaderni Rossi* collective was deeply influenced by the contributions of these groups, but it returned to the form of the questionnaire in its inquiries out of a concern that the narrative form fails to register broad patterns of working-class behavior. Marx's questionnaire in particular provided a model for accessing these patterns while also generating the political self-activity of the working class. Writing for *Quaderni Rossi*, Dario Lanzardo and Raniero Panzieri theorized the questionnaire as a means of raising the consciousness of the working class to transform this class into an antagonistic class. While consciousness-raising *has* elicited attention in the literature on the workers' inquiries of all of the groups above, it has *not* necessarily been seen as an element that cuts right through the experience of the *Quaderni Rossi* collective.[2] The focus on consciousness-raising in the latter group in particular should be given its proper interpretive due because it helps frame workers' inquiry as a *process* (of producing an antagonistic political subjectivity) whose success depends on the initial stimulus provided by questions in a questionnaire rather than on an aggregation of written responses. The theorizations of workers' inquiry in *Quaderni Rossi* thus shift the focus away from the problematic of the failure of worker writings. They open new ways for us to assess the political efficacy of workers' inquiries and enable us to appreciate the form of the questionnaire in a whole new light.

only offering a remarkably similar history of workers' inquiry but also in casting *The American Worker* in particular as an iteration of Marx's project for a workers' inquiry.[17] Unlike Haider and Mohandesi, however, Woodcock frames his analysis in more forthrightly cautious terms. He repeatedly stresses that his analysis addresses only "particular moments" in the history of workers' inquiry.[18] In other words, Woodcock's analysis does not purport to be anything akin to an exhaustive account of this practice. Striking omissions and lapses therefore mark the recent histories of workers' inquiry, but the preponderance of references to and discussions of *The American Worker* suggests that this little-known pamphlet deserves serious consideration.

In the remaining space of this section, I interrogate and assess the claim that *The American Worker* embodies an effort at workers' inquiry. I suggest that it is indeed a form of workers' inquiry that occupies an altogether singular standing in the history of this practice. But *The American Worker* is also a problematic form owing to a disjuncture between its divided self-presentation into distinct practical and theoretical components, on the one hand, and the commitment of the Johnson-Forest Tendency to overcoming the social basis of this division, on the other hand. In pursuing this tack, I attempt to offer something other than the prevailing (and perfectly compelling) criticism of the pamphlet in the literature on workers' inquiry. That criticism is that its narrative form blurs the *particular* experience of the narrating worker with the *general* experience of workers.[19]

From his opening paragraphs, Romano identifies his audience as other "rank and file workers" rather than as "intellectuals who are detached from the working class."[20] His immediate objective is to record the "day-to-day reactions" of workers "to factory life" in order to disclose the reasons for their "deep dissatisfaction" to other worker readers.[21] This immediate and straightforward objective has the much broader purpose of enabling workers to see that the impetus for socialist transformation resides *in them*. As Romano declares in his concluding paragraphs, "It is from the workers that will come the men and women who will lead and guide the tremendous upheavals to come."[22] His narrative thus sets out to raise the consciousness of workers by demonstrating the underlying reasons for their dissatisfaction with factory life. For Romano, the proof that workers recognize these reasons resides in the fact that they have already approvingly and enthusiastically read drafts of his pamphlet after long and tiring hours at the factory.[23] Romano thus inscribes the very process of consciousness-raising he seeks to obtain *in* the very text of the pamphlet itself.

In the contents of his contribution to the pamphlet, Romano details *so many* of the reasons for the dissatisfaction of workers with factory life that enumerating all of them can be a challenge. He describes the deleterious effects of the material conditions in the factories on the bodies and minds of workers; the stresses of the temporal pressures of work on family life; anger over the speed-up of machines; the exhaustion induced by the incentive system; the resentment against time-study men, checkers, foremen, and plant superintendents; the hostility toward the introduction of new technologies; the frustration over the inaction of unions; the resentment among African-American workers over the racism at the hands of other workers; the anger over the rigidity of the classifications system; the boredom over routine work tasks; and the dislike of fellow workers who complain about shared miseries. As his narrative develops, however, readers learn that a core reason for the dissatisfaction among workers concerns the gap between their creative abilities, on the one hand, and the utter inefficiency of the factory system, on the other hand. Romano suggests that the former phenomenon is rooted in the experiential knowledge of workers, whereas the latter phenomenon derives from bureaucracy. In his words, "the bureaucratic supervision of work results in inefficiency on a tremendous scale in view of the effort involved."[24] Bureaucracy results in inefficiency because it sacrifices greater productivity for "the subjugation and control of the laborer."[25] Romano captures the sheer exasperation of workers with this inefficiency in the following passage:

> Inefficiency and red tape on the part of the company often drive the worker to the point of a combination of tears and anger. A shortage of tools at a critical moment, an improperly ground tool, a faulty machine left unrepaired and endangering a worker, help not around when needed, stock for the machines left not at the machine for which it is needed but ten machines down where it is not needed; passing the buck down the line when something goes wrong all contribute to the aggravating situation.[26]

For Romano, workers *would be* more efficient and therefore more productive if they had more opportunities to express their creativity in the execution of work tasks. He acknowledges that, to some extent, workers *can* express this creativity. They can do so through experimentation with machines for the purposes of illicitly creating their own personal devices as well as through testing the speed of the machines.[27] But the division between manual and mental labor in the factory limits such expression, ultimately compelling workers to channel their creativity elsewhere. As Romano explains, "Since the workers are unable, in the shop, to express fully their creative instincts, outside the factory and in the home, they seek to give free rein to these instincts" through hobbies and home projects.[28] Romano nonetheless acknowledges that even these activities ultimately leave workers unfulfilled. Something is clearly missing even outside the space of the factory.

Enter Stone, who illuminates the lack of fulfillment among workers through a discussion of alienated labor. She picks up on the problem of fettered productivity from the outset of her theoretical commentary. Stone suggests that the value of Romano's narrative resides in enabling readers to understand the widely discussed problem of harnessing productivity "by penetrating into what the workers are doing and thinking as they work at their benches and at their machines."[29] She claims that Romano's narrative more specifically enables readers to grasp the contradiction between the alienated character of labor in the factory and the productive forces of the worker. In her words, "To read Romano's description of life in the factory is to realize with shocking clarity how deeply the alienation of labor pervades the very foundations of our society."[30] Stone explains that this labor is alienated because it is abstract rather than concrete. In other words, it serves the purpose of value production rather than the fulfillment of the needs of workers. And this labor becomes all the more abstract as it is objectified in machinery.[31] But Stone follows Romano in emphasizing the efforts of workers to escape the alienation of their labor by experimenting with machinery inside the factory and by tinkering with the products of their labor outside the factory. As Stone observes, "The workers described by Romano who wander about the plant, hungrily eyeing different machines and different operations, are seeking to make this appropriation and create this new human and natural relation."[32] Yet the culmination of capitalist social relations in a division between intellectual and manual labor limits these pursuits with the overall effect of hampering the forces of production. As Stone notes, "The class relations of bourgeois production, by being a fetter upon the productive powers of the workers, are also a fetter upon the development of the means of production."[33] On the basis of this conclusion, she appeals to the construction of socialist relations of production through a proletarian revolution. But her appeal contains an all-important proviso: these relations can *only* emerge from the workers themselves.[34] The theme of the reconstruction of society in Stone's contribution thus flows organically from the preceding theme of factory life in Romano's contribution.

Stone also recognizes the intertwining of these broad themes in Marx. In her words, "Marx never took his eyes off the workers' activity in production because he never lost sight of the revolution which would transform labor into a human activity. Conversely, because he always had this revolution in mind, his main concern was always the actual life of the workers."[35] It is in a footnote at the end of this passage that Stone recognizes the importance of Marx's questionnaire. She refers her readers to "'A Workers' Inquiry' by Karl Marx in which one hundred and one questions are asked of the workers themselves, dealing with everything from lavatories, soap, wine, strikes and unions to 'the general physical, intellectual, and moral conditions of life of the working men and women in your trade.'"[36] Here Stone cites the aforementioned translation of Marx's questionnaire in the *New International* from December 1938.[37] Her remark is noteworthy first and foremost because it confirms that she was fully aware of Marx's questionnaire at the very moment she drew out the theoretical import of Romano's narrative. The importance of this detail will become apparent below. As far as interpretations of Marx's questionnaire go, the sheer brevity of Stone's commentary leaves a lot to be desired. She refers to the questionnaire to quite correctly demonstrate Marx's concern with the concrete lives of workers, but she offers nothing more.

Haider and Mohandesi make a powerful and sophisticated, if highly counterintuitive, case for treating *The American Worker* as version of workers' inquiry. This case pivots on their idiosyncratic framing of the pamphlet as a belated realization of Marx's workers' inquiry to the extent that it entails a worker recounting his own experiences to other workers for the purpose of realizing their consciousness as a revolutionary class. Haider and Mohandesi write that Romano "provided Marx with the first, comprehensive response to his questionnaire—it was just several decades late."[38]

They nevertheless disclose two complications with their own argument. The first is relatively minor: *The American Worker* was *never called* a workers' inquiry, even though Stone had a knowledge of Marx's questionnaire and cited it in a footnote in her portion of the pamphlet.[39] As this problem is purely formal, Haider and Mohandesi do nothing more than acknowledge it and move on. Yet it does leave us with a nagging query: why *didn't* the Johnson-Forest Tendency simply adopt a variant of Marx's questionnaire? One possible answer to this question is that the questionnaire was seen as reproducing a division of labor by deriving the very formulation of questions from intellectuals. Another possible and related answer is that the questionnaire was seen as less equipped to facilitate the creativity and self-expression of workers, which were, after all, so central to the overall standpoint of the Johnson-Forest Tendency. Yet, as I argue below, the presentation of the narrative form in *The American Worker also* reproduces the division between intellectual and manual labor. Moreover, as we shall see below, the demand for whole narratives can be far too open-ended to be successful. It did not succeed in eliciting the writings of *nonmilitant* workers in the experiences of other post-Trotskyist groups.

Haider and Mohandesi acknowledge another complication with their own identification of *The American Worker* as an iteration of Marx's "A Workers' Inquiry": the pamphlet assumes a narrative form *rather* than the form of responses to line-by-line questions in a questionnaire. However, they do not construe this recourse to a narrative form of workers' inquiry as an unambiguous drawback because it simply throws into relief a limit in *Marx's* questionnaire. In their illuminating words, "Although Marx made it clear that knowledge of the working class could only be produced by workers themselves, his original project seemed to foreclose the space for any kind of creative expression, demanding mechanical answers to prefabricated questions."[40]

Yet this criticism exaggerates the distance between the narrative form and Marx's questionnaire. As indicated in the previous chapter, the very final item in Marx's lengthy questionnaire was not so much a question as an open-ended plea for information. It simply read "General remarks."[41] This plea with a minimal content opens up a space in which workers can at least theoretically elaborate a narrative about their working conditions, albeit at the very end of a long list of questions. The narrative form in *The American Worker* therefore does not present an abrupt departure from the numbered questions in Marx's questionnaire so much as the fulfillment of a possibility in the latter. More generally, we should be extremely cautious about even hinting at a hard and fast opposition between the narrative and questionnaire because some of the inquiries explored in subsequent chapters intertwine these forms.

Still, *The American Worker* occupies a singular position in the history of workers' inquiries. No other inquiry explored in this book entails a narrative account by a worker complemented by an immediately adjacent and nearly proportional theoretical reflection by an intellectual. Yet this form poses a vexing problem for a straightforward reason: it *reproduces* the division between manual and mental labor that the Johnson-Forest Tendency sought to overcome. In his introduction to the 1972 edition of *The American Worker*, Martin Glaberman nicely picks up on this problem. He insists that while the formal division between the two parts of the pamphlet testifies to the manifest failure of Marxist groups to fuse together intellectuals and workers, the side-by-side presentation of these parts in *one* document at least expresses the aspiration to overcome this division.[42] Glaberman's incisive view of this matter nevertheless appears to be too generous because it tends to gloss over the tension he so incisively draws out. Indeed, it is difficult to overstate the significance of the problem of the division between intellectuals and workers for the Johnson-Forest Tendency. Stone saw this division as an expression of the underlying alienation of manual and mental labor in capitalism. As she succinctly observed, "To the degrading alienation of the manual worker from the intellectual processes of his production, there corresponds the debilitating alienation of the brain worker from the manual application of his ideas."[43] For Stone, as we have seen, this alienation accounted for the immensely fettered character of productivity under capitalism. But if Romano's narrative of his own experiences in the factory *enacts* an overcoming of the alienation of mental and intellectual labor, Stone's part suddenly *reintroduces* the division between intellectuals and workers. The separation of *The American Worker* into distinct experiential and theoretical components therefore *reproduces* a division that the Johnson-Forest Tendency found so objectionable. Glaberman tries to gloss over this problem by suggesting that these parts enter into a dialectical relationship with one another: Stone's part offers "a theoretical framework to free the worker to express his deepest needs" whereas Romano's part provides "the basis for the continuing expansion and development of theory."[44] Yet his rendering of this relationship reinforces the division between intellectuals and workers because it seems to assume that only a theoretical capstone offered by an intellectual would enable workers to fully articulate their underlying needs, as if Romano could not adequately articulate these needs in his own voice. Thus, even as it productively elicits the voice of a worker, *The American Worker* ends up reproducing the division between workers and intellectuals.

For its part, the successor to the Johnson-Forest Tendency, Correspondence, built on this broadly construed tradition of workers' inquiry. It solicited writings from workers for its publications. Like its predecessor, Correspondence also identified the division of workers and intellectuals as a pervasive problem in modern society. And it did not exempt itself from this problem.[45] Indeed, Correspondence did not eliminate the division of workers and intellectuals in its version of workers' inquiry so much as *aspire to invert it*. The collective sought to invert this division through a radical diminution in the space in its publications accorded to theorizing by intellectuals. This diminution was quite pronounced in the contents and editorial organization of its newspaper, *Correspondence*, founded in October 1953.[46] Correspondence cast its newspaper as a workers' newspaper in the precise sense of a periodical that publicizes the contributions of workers for workers through the combined editorship of workers and intellectuals. *Correspondence* was, in other words, an effort to enable workers to speak for themselves through writing.[47] Somewhat paradoxically, an intellectual, Dunayevskaya, articulated this overarching objective in an anonymous article for her regular column, "Two Worlds: Notes from a Diary," in *Correspondence*.[48] In her words:

> If the workers themselves and only they know what is wrong and how to change it, then what they say is what really matters. Let them say it and say it in their own words. Anyone who can talk can write. Let them. We practiced putting out a mimeographed paper, written not at a center by a few intellectuals, but written and edited by the local committees themselves. . . . The unique combination of workers and intellectuals that got together to produce a workers' paper, the first of its kind in America, or for that matter the world, is what distinguishes our paper.[49]

In keeping with this objective, the editorial organization of *Correspondence* reflected a very deliberate privileging of workers *over* intellectuals. The editorial cells of the newspaper subjected intellectuals and even worker-intellectuals to the editorial authority of workers.[50] The rationale behind this subjection was that intellectuals are bearers of a theoretical orientation that stifles a purportedly natural style of writing among workers.[51] The actual contents of *Correspondence* were distributed across four sections, each devoted to one of the following themes: labor, African-Americans, women, and youth.[52] Within these sections, *Correspondence* certainly accommodated space for writings by intellectuals such as Dunayevskaya. Her column addressed topics as diverse as the conditions and struggles of workers in Russia, the European reception of *The American Worker*, youth in communist countries, the finances of *Correspondence*, and the importance of listening to workers in struggles for a new society.[53] However, *Correspondence*'s manifest privileging of the voices of workers over the voices of intellectuals facilitated an episode that was something of the *inverse* of Stone's theoretical commentary on Romano's text: a worker subjected one of Dunayevskaya's articles to a scathing "line-by-line critique."[54]

Still, as Stephen Hastings-King cautions, "the fact was that very few workers actually participated in the production of this 'worker newspaper,'"[55] in spite of their numerical superiority in the editorial cells.[56] He attributes this low level of participation to a variety of reasons, ranging from the insularity of the Correspondence collective to conflicts between its layers of editorial authority.[57] We thus once again encounter the now increasingly familiar theme in the history of workers' inquiry of the reluctance of workers to write about their own experiences, albeit with regard to contributions to a newspaper rather than answers to a questionnaire.

Socialisme ou Barbarie and the (Failed) Solicitation of Worker Narratives

Socialisme ou Barbarie shared many similarities with the Johnson-Forest Tendency and Correspondence. It started out as an oppositional Trotskyist tendency, the Chaulieu-Montal Tendency, in the late 1940s. The name of the Tendency combined the pseudonyms of its two principal theorists, Pierre Chaulieu for Cornelius Castoriadis and Claude Montal for Claude Lefort. By 1949, the Chaulieu-Montal Tendency broke with Trotskyism over issues related to the interpretation of Stalinism.[58] Socialisme ou Barbarie was born in this rupture. It was a small group devoted mainly to the production of a journal by the same name up until its dissolution in 1967.[59]

Like the Johnson-Forest Tendency, Socialisme ou Barbarie took bureaucracy seriously, to the point of elaborating a whole theory of bureaucratic capitalism. This theory identifies bureaucracy as a process that separates those who issue commands from those who execute them, or, in the parlance of the group, the *dirigeants* from the *exécutants*.[60] While bureaucracy in this rendering is abstract enough to encompass various forms, including the party, Socialisme ou Barbarie contended that it generates "a fundamental contradiction" in the context of Fordist production in Western countries.[61] Management seeks to impose a production design on workers, but the actual implementation of this design generates all kinds of problems that require improvised solutions from workers. To further compound matters, the division of labor in bureaucratic capitalism forecloses the possibility of even acknowledging this creativity, thereby fueling conflicts between management and informal worker collectives.[62]

Socialisme ou Barbarie appealed to socialism based on worker self-management against the alienating effects of bureaucratic capitalism. Its solicitation of worker writings for the journal *Socialisme ou Barbarie* grew out of this appeal and its corresponding rejection of the Leninist party. The animating supposition behind the effort to get workers to write about their experiences on the shop floor was that *only they* could represent themselves.[63] As in the case of the Johnson-Forest Tendency and Correspondence, Socialisme ou Barbarie saw worker narratives as a potent means of raising class-consciousness by drawing out common experiences recognizable to other workers.[64] These narratives would have the additional advantage of enabling theorists hailing from other classes to access the "germinal form of socialist rationality that was developing through conflicts on the factory floor."[65]

What is the connection between Socialisme ou Barbarie's solicitation of individual narratives from workers and the broader tradition of workers' inquiries? How can the former even be construed as an extension of the latter? As in the case of the Johnson-Forest Tendency, Socialisme ou Barbarie certainly did not pursue workers' inquiries in the sense of producing and distributing questionnaires for workers. A former member of Socialisme ou Barbarie, Henri Simon, even goes so far as to stridently downplay the group's interest in workers' inquiry in this traditional sense. He speculates that Socialisme ou Barbarie's aversion to workers' inquiry in the strict sense had its roots either in practical limitations stemming from the small size of the group or in the (no doubt disavowed) belief that the group should serve as the fount of knowledge for the proletariat and not the other way around.[66] Whatever the case with regard to the reasons for this aversion, what is clear is that Lefort forcefully objected to questionnaires in favor of recourse to individual narratives. In soliciting these narratives from workers, Socialisme ou Barbarie participated in a broadly construed tradition of workers' inquiry going at least as far back as Romano's text. It sought to get workers to write about their own experiences at the point of production for the sake of fostering their own activity as a deeply creative class.

In pursuing this objective, Socialisme ou Barbarie drew explicit inspiration from Romano and Stone's *The American Worker*. Philippe Guillaume had translated and introduced the pamphlet for the journal *Socialisme ou Barbarie*.[67] Lefort also took inspiration from *The American Worker* in his elaboration of the rationale for the solicitation of worker narratives in his 1952 article "Proletarian Experience."[68] In this article, he cites Romano's text as a document that stimulates all kinds of questions about the relations between workers and their work, workers and other workers, workers and life beyond the factory, and, finally, workers and proletarian history.[69] However, rather than use these questions to formulate a questionnaire, Lefort goes on to harshly criticize the form of the questionnaire itself. He submits that a questionnaire emanating from outside the proletarian experience lends itself to an inauthentic response. In his words, "a question imposed from the outside might be an irritant for the subject being questioned, shaping an artificial response or, in any case, imprinting upon it a character that it would not otherwise have had."[70] In the previous chapter, we saw something of this irritation in the exasperation of a factory worker over Lenin's steady stream of questions about factory life. Lefort insists that even a "vast statistically-based investigation" involving workers posing questions to other workers would still only result in "numerical correlations" among responses from "anonymous respondents."[71] It would not, in other words, allow for the meaning of these actions to emerge for the workers and their interpreters. But in limiting his critique to questionnaires *outside* the proletarian experience, on the one hand, and *statistical ones inside* the proletarian experience, on the other hand, Lefort engages in a stunning elision of other basic possibilities, such as qualitative questionnaires inside the proletarian experience. More generally, his insistence on a stark inside and outside the proletarian experience forecloses more hybrid forms of engagement involving the formulation of questionnaires by intellectuals *and* workers. We will encounter a movement toward such forms of engagement later in this chapter.

Lefort implies that the open-ended format of individual narratives allows for a more authentic account of proletarian experience, even as he recognizes that narratives necessarily introduce a rupture with action that reconfigures its meaning. In so doing, he bluntly acknowledges the validity of the criticism that individual narratives are limited in value because they are too particular to serve as the basis for a generalization about proletarian life. Lefort nonetheless goes on to defend the general import of individual narratives. He submits that these narratives capture more than the specificity of the individual lives of workers. They capture, in his reasoning, a common and recognizable proletarian frame of experience defined by production, exploitation, and alienation. Lefort also suggests that individual narratives register more than mere opinions. They convey attitudes in the sense of consistent modes of reacting to situations defined by the proletarian frame. Finally, Lefort contends that individual narratives allow for comparisons with other narratives that facilitate "the isolation of meaning and invoke systems of living and thinking that can be interpreted."[72]

Socialisme ou Barbarie saw an opportunity for the practical enactment of worker narratives in the clandestine newspaper *Tribune Ouvrière*, which was founded by a group of workers from the Renault factory at Billancourt in May 1954 and lasted until 1956.[73] Among these workers was a Socialisme ou Barbarie member with the pen name of Daniel Mothé and the real name of Jacques Gautrat.[74] Socialisme ou Barbarie endorsed *Tribune Ouvrière* as an embodiment of a worker newspaper, and Mothé wrote extensively for it. Yet, as Hastings-King notes, "few workers not part of the [*Tribune Ouvrière*] collective itself ever wrote for the paper or worked on its production."[75] In other words, *Tribune Ouvrière* fell short of acquiring the venerated status of a worker newspaper in the sense of a publication that would transmit the oral culture of the shop floor in writing to a worker-readership.[76] Hastings-King stresses the role of written language and its class underpinnings in this failure. He contends that workers were not inclined to approximate the oral culture of the shop floor in their writings because "to write as they spoke would be self-disempowering" in a context that equated being political with an altogether different style of writing.[77] Hastings-King also goes a bit further in his explanation, suggesting that workers did not write at all because literacy in the deeply hierarchical educational system of

France in the 1950s served to thwart their social mobility. It was not, in other words, *illiteracy* so much as *the social function of literacy* that accounted for the failure of worker writings. As Hastings-King pointedly asks with regard to the workers: "Why would they turn, in order to free themselves, to skills that had functioned explicitly to exclude them from non-working-class possibilities for their whole lives?"[78] In formulating such questions, Hastings-King helps us to understand why another experience of workers' inquiry in the broad sense of the practice foundered by conventional measures.

From Conflict to Antagonism: The Workers' Inquiries of *Quaderni Rossi*

The journal *Quaderni Rossi* served as the intellectual space for the most extensive reactivation of Marx's workers' inquiry in the postwar period. Ranierio Panzieri founded the journal in 1961 to grapple with the implications of developments in advanced or planned capitalism for working-class struggles. As part of this overarching focus, *Quaderni Rossi* initiated workers' inquiries at the FIAT factory in Turin in the early 1960s. These inquiries left an indelible mark on the entire trajectory of Italian workerism by giving birth to its central concept of class composition.[79] This concept designates the behavior of the working class that arises from the insertion of its labor-powers into material processes of production. *Quaderni Rossi* reflected a strident focus on class composition in its manifold inquiries. The inquiries sought to access the behavior of the working class *as such*, *before* any mediation by parties and unions.[80] In other words, the emphasis in *Quaderni Rossi*'s inquiries was on the autonomy of the worker as a subject of production who inhabits the space of the factory.

For our purposes, two features of these inquiries stand out. First of all, *Quaderni Rossi* resurrected workers' inquiries in the traditional form of the questionnaire rather than in the form of the narrative. Second, it went much further than Trotskyist and post-Trotskyist currents in theorizing consciousness-raising as an integral component of workers' inquiries. Contributors to *Quaderni Rossi* identified these inquiries as the means of raising the political consciousness of the working class in order to transform this class into an *antagonistic* class. Overall, then, *Quaderni Rossi* returned to a more traditional form of workers' inquiry and intensified the previously implicit focus on consciousness-raising. I elaborate on these modulations through a discussion of the historical experiences of *Quaderni Rossi*'s inquiries at the FIAT factory in Turin as well as through a critical analysis of its theorizations of workers' inquiry.

To begin, it is helpful to establish the connection between the turn to workers' inquiries among members of the *Quaderni Rossi* collective and the experiences of worker narratives among breakaway Trotskyist organizations. The embrace of workers' inquiry within the *Quaderni Rossi* collective had its roots in the enthusiastic reception of the publications of the Johnson-Forest Tendency through the intermediary of Socialisme ou Barbarie. The political militant Danilo Montaldi had translated *The American Worker* into Italian from its French translation in *Socialisme ou Barbarie*. He had also authored its preface.[81] In the preface, Montaldi wrote that *The American Worker* reminds readers of the long-forgotten point "that the worker is first of all someone who lives at the point of production of the capitalist factory before being the member of a party, a revolutionary militant, or the subject of coming socialist power."[82] This view resonated with Panzieri as well as with other contributors to *Quaderni Rossi*. As Wright highlights, they also had sensed a division between the working class and "those bodies—parties and unions—that claimed to represent it."[83] Yet, as he elaborates, *Quaderni Rossi* took a critical stance toward the use of individual worker narratives. It suggested that these narratives simply register individual opinions. They fall short, in other words, of disclosing more general patterns of working-class behavior. *Quaderni Rossi* turned to the form of the questionnaire to capture these patterns. However, as Wright explains, its contributors were well aware of the risks of "the descent into pure empiricism."[84] They sought to offset this risk by adopting the model of Marx's questionnaire, with its emphasis on generating the political self-activity of the working class.[85]

We therefore see that *Quaderni Rossi* inaugurates a deliberate shift from the narrative as a form of workers' inquiry *back* to the more traditional form of the questionnaire. In keeping with the compartmentalized articulation of the main sources of the investigation in Marxism, the main theorizations of workers' inquiry for *Quaderni Rossi* also do not dwell on Mao or even mention his conception of the investigation. Here, however, Michel J. M. Thiollent draws a helpful distinction for us between the *theorization* of workers' inquiry by Panzieri on behalf of *Quaderni Rossi* and the *activities* of the collective (presumably of going to the FIAT factory in Turin to conduct workers' inquiries there).[86] For Thiollent, *Quaderni Rossi*'s attempt to get its political bearings through inquiries directed at factory workers echoed Mao's concept of the investigation as a method for articulating political directives originating in the masses.[87] Thiollent certainly does not develop this fascinating claim in great depth, but it cautions us against going too far in positing a separation between investigations inspired by Marx's questionnaire and those inspired by Mao's investigation. In other words, *Quaderni Rossi*'s adherence to a form of workers' inquiry rooted explicitly in Marx's questionnaire did not necessarily mean that it was simply cut off from other sources of the investigation in the Marxist tradition.

Beyond the appreciative but critical reaction in *Quaderni Rossi* to worker narratives in oppositional Trotskyist and post-Trotskyist currents, the reactivation of workers' inquiry had roots far more particular to the Italian social context. Indeed, among the chroniclers of this form of inquiry, there is a strong consensus that it emerged, paradoxically enough, from studies of classes in Italy *other* than the working class. Andrea Cavazzini, for instance, suggests that the ethnologist Ernesto De Martino had anticipated workers' inquiry through his research of rural communities in southern Italy during the postwar period. For Cavazzini, De Martino anticipated workers' inquiry by casting ethnology as an encounter with a subaltern other that destabilizes "the knowledge of the investigator."[88] Cavazzini even speculates that the founding editor of *Quaderni Rossi*, Raniero Panzieri, "most likely participated" in the writing of De Martino's "masterpiece" *Il Mondo magico*.[89] He claims that, at any rate, both theorists heralded co-research (*conricerca*) as a "practice of inquiry in which the knowledges about a social situation are produced as much by the 'external' investigator as by the 'investigated.' "[90] For his part, Wright suggests that the reactivation of workers' inquiry had its roots in the studies of rural life in southern Italy during the postwar period.[91] In this regard, he draws attention to the social reformer Danilo Dolci, who had used questionnaires to document the "life stories" of the Southern poor in the mid-1950s.[92] Dolci's 1956 *Report from Palermo* contains the narratives of the unemployed from the province of Palermo.[93] The appendix of the report even reproduces Dolci's questions and a lengthy selection of responses.[94] The point of his research had been to draw up a "composite picture" of the plight of the unemployed for a readership that knew very little about it.[95] In carrying out this task, Dolci distanced himself from more militant conceptions of the investigation by adopting the posture of a strictly impartial observer. He took on this posture to allow the voices of the unemployed to be heard.[96]

There were all kinds of connections between Dolci's research among the unemployed and the workers' inquiries of *Quaderni Rossi*. Wright points out that Dolci's efforts to facilitate "the self-expression of the dispossessed" propelled some of the Northern youth who had worked with him toward *Quaderni Rossi*.[97] Among these youth was a figure no less important for Italian workerism than Antonio Negri.[98] Dolci himself thanks Vittorio Rieser for assistance in undertaking his "statistical-sociological survey."[99] This detail is significant because Rieser would go on to participate in a workers' inquiry for *Quaderni Rossi* at the FIAT factory in Turin.[100] He would also represent a faction in *Quaderni Rossi* that identified sociology as the possible basis for a reinvigoration of the workers' movement.[101]

Members of the *Quaderni Rossi* collective conducted their first inquiries at the FIAT factory in Turin between 1960 and 1961. At the time, FIAT presented itself as a company consisting of a workforce with high wages, skills, and robust opportunities for career advancement.[102] Panzieri encouraged inquiries at the FIAT factory in Turin in particular because its workforce was regarded as pacified rather than combative. FIAT, he reasoned, would therefore provide the ideal space from which to test the political efficacy of the inquiry.[103] Dino de Palma, Rieser, and Edda Salvadori undertook one of these inquiries at FIAT between 1960 and 1961 and later recounted their experience in the pages of *Quaderni Rossi*. Their inquiry focused on whether the technical rationalization of the firm through the introduction of new technologies had succeeded in integrating FIAT workers in the sense of adapting them to the new system of production.[104] De Palma, Rieser, and Salvadori sought to construct their knowledge of this topic by going straight to workers rather than relying on contacts in the unions.[105] But there were two contrasting visions of how exactly to proceed with the inquiry: a more sociological one based on questionnaires and interviews formulated in advance by the researchers and a more militant one based on questions formulated through the *interactions* between researchers *and* workers.[106] The latter vision clearly involved a blurring of the division between intellectuals and workers, but the former won out because the mutual formulation of the questions in the questionnaires was deemed excessively spontaneous.[107] However, as Cavazzini recounts, the initial results of the inquiry ended up vitiating its aspiration to take a more objective path concerned mainly with registering facts.[108] These results showed that FIAT workers had not been integrated precisely because the organization of the FIAT factory was not nearly as rationalized as previously thought. More precisely, workers had plenty of room to engage in self-initiated activities that put them at odds with middle management.[109] This implosion of the notion of a pacified workforce at the FIAT factory itself served to instigate political activities there among the researchers. The more sociological approach to the inquiry was retrospectively criticized on two counts. It was criticized for avoiding the solicitation of value judgments and for limiting itself to particularities rather than facilitating processes of inductive reasoning.[110] In short, as Cavazzini poignantly observes, the sociological approach ran the risk of mirroring, rather than undermining, the subjection of workers by sticking to what he describes as "the immediate surface of 'facts.'"[111]

De Palma, Rieser, and Salvadori were not the only ones in *Quaderni Rossi* to conduct an inquiry at the FIAT factory in Turin. Romano Alquati spearheaded his own inquiry there and published its results in the first issue of *Quaderni Rossi* in 1961.[112] Alquati's inquiry set out to determine the political implications of the emergence of a new FIAT workforce consisting of deskilled old workers and unskilled young workers. He based his inquiry on interviews with workers and union militants.[113] The responses of the interviewees revealed a widespread dissatisfaction with the standardized character of their work and the division of labor in the firm.[114] Yet, as Wright stresses, this dissatisfaction among young workers did not equate with support for traditional unions and parties on the left.[115] For Alquati, what it pointed to, rather, was a desire for self-management and forms of political organization more responsive to the working class.[116]

Some of the most important *theorizations* of workers' inquiry appeared in *Quaderni Rossi* roughly four years after its initial inquiries detected new forms of class composition at the FIAT factory in Turin. There was thus a noteworthy lag between the practices of workers' inquiry and these theorizations, as if the temporal interval was necessary to think through and clarify the stakes of the practice. Perhaps unsurprisingly, the theorizations of workers' inquiry in *Quaderni Rossi* built on many of the insights and themes gleaned from the original inquiries at the FIAT factory in Turin. If these inquiries discerned the presence of a potentially antagonistic working class at FIAT, contributors to *Quaderni Rossi* theorized workers' inquiry as a means of *drawing out* this antagonism. These contributors also contended at length with the ongoing debates in the journal about the uses of sociology.

One of the most elaborate but underappreciated theorizations of workers' inquiry to appear in *Quaderni Rossi* was Dario Lanzardo's "Marx and Workers' Inquiry."[117] Originally published in the fifth issue of the journal in 1965, the essay has yet to be translated into English.[118] Part exegesis of Marx's questionnaire and part effort to draw out the lessons of the questionnaire for workers' struggles in a markedly different context, Lanzardo's essay amounts to a veritable tour de force, one of the most sustained and penetrating expositions of Marx's questionnaire to date. Lanzardo construes the questionnaire as a means of both enabling the working class to obtain a consciousness of its exploitation and stimulating this class to develop its own forms of organization against this exploitation. In other words, he discerns in all of the intricacies of Marx's manifold questions a means of raising the political consciousness of the working class in order to transform it into an antagonistic class. From his perspective, the measure of the success of Marx's questionnaire resides less in the concrete answers it generates than in the more diffuse stimulus it provides workers to organize themselves.

From the outset of his essay, Lanzardo latches onto the emphasis in the introduction to Marx's questionnaire on the unique position of workers to describe and remedy the conditions of their exploitation.[119] As we saw in the previous chapter, Marx wrote of the workers, "they alone can describe with full knowledge the misfortunes from which they suffer." He insisted that that "only they, and not saviors sent by Providence, can energetically apply the healing remedies for the social ills to which they are prey."[120] Lanzardo suggests that in these declarations Marx is not suddenly departing from his theories so much as establishing "the principle of a method of political work which is implicitly found in his *Critique of Political Economy*."[121] This method identifies capitalism with a struggle between capital and wage-labor, but it also stresses a whole mystification of this struggle deriving from a more general mystification of wages and surplus value *as* the respective forms of remuneration for labor and capital.[122] This more general mystification rests on the stripping of wage-labor of its socially and historically determinate qualities in a socially and historically determinate mode of production. For Lanzardo, the ensuing naturalization of wage-labor and capital reduces the struggle between them to negotiations over compensation for their respective contributions to the production process.[123] He emphasizes that what gets lost here for workers is the process of exploitation itself, namely, that "labor-power is sold to capitalists as a commodity which they use to accumulate surplus value."[124] The problem for Lanzardo is therefore one of raising the consciousness of workers about their exploitation. Indeed, *only* a clear "consciousness of exploitation" among workers holds the promise for Lanzardo of exceeding "the limits of pure and simple daily conflict against capital."[125]

Lanzardo's emphasis on consciousness-raising then sets the stage for his detailed discussion of Marx's questionnaire. He casts the questionnaire first and foremost as an instrument for raising the consciousness of workers by posing detailed questions to them (in its first three parts) about the precise character of their exploitation in the factory. For Lanzardo, these questions are intended to elicit "explicit clarifications" and "value judgments" from workers about the "conditions they know well."[126] He singles out numerous questions to illustrate this function, from questions pertaining to the hierarchical structure of surveillance in the factory to questions about the payment of wages on the basis of time rates or piece rates. Lanzardo bluntly acknowledges that workers *may* be ill equipped to accurately answer some questions because of their lack of comprehensive information. In this regard, he singles out the seventy-sixth question, which asks workers to "compare the price of the commodities you manufacture or the services you render with the price of your labor."[127] In his brief commentary on this question, Lanzardo recognizes that "the worker can neither calculate the cost of production nor calculate net profit" but what *is* important is that he or she "notice that a difference really exists, and that this difference turns exclusively to the benefit of he who pockets it, namely, the boss."[128] Lanzardo retains this same interpretive lens as he turns to questions in the fourth part of Marx's questionnaire about the organizational forms of opposition to exploitation among the workers. As he observes of a question that asks workers whether strikes have been supported *across* trades:

> It does not matter so much whether the response is negative or even non-existent. The main thing is to clarify that not only this possibility exists but that it's the most effective, and that the union of all of the proletarians is capable of defeating the capitalists already united and organized by production itself and the political power of the state.[129]

Part of the novelty of Lanzardo's reading of Marx's questionnaire resides in his illuminating judgment of its historical destiny. In the previous chapter, we saw that Marx's questionnaire failed to generate enough responses in spite of its widespread distribution. Lanzardo forthrightly acknowledges this detail but proceeds to diminish its significance. In his striking words:

> The fact that the inquiry did not practically have a conclusion, since the answers received by *La Revue socialiste* amount to about a hundred out of twenty five thousand copies distributed throughout France, has only a relative importance on the whole. The main thing was that in reaching workers the questionnaires gave them new possibilities of knowing the manner in which capitalist exploitation functions.[130]

From this perspective, the real significance of Marx's questionnaire resides in enabling workers to generate their own knowledge about capitalist exploitation. The questions themselves serve the immediate purposes of stimulating reflections among workers and generating communications between them. Whether or not these questions yield a dutifully written response delivered to the address of *La Revue socialiste* in Paris is an entirely secondary matter. The ultimate point of Marx's questionnaire for Lanzardo is not to accumulate data for outsiders so much as to incite forms of self-organization among workers.

Yet, as he turns to his present, Lanzardo insists that demystifying capitalist exploitation by piercing the abode of production and recognizing the production of surplus value there entails *more* difficulties than in Marx's time. From his perspective, new forms of capital accumulation have succeeded in mitigating the effects of material poverty and permanent unemployment. Consequently, as Lanzardo observes, "we can no longer approach exploitation itself so directly."[131] He goes on to assert that workers increasingly accept factory wage-labor as the "natural form of existence" because "social production in its entirety" now "influences the working conditions, salary, total life of workers."[132] In the final paragraphs of his essay, Lanzardo rather sweepingly acknowledges other difficulties, such as challenges to the self-organization of workers and impediments to the mere formulation of critiques of capitalist production.[133]

Do all of these difficulties render the task of workers' inquiry more pressing? The scope and thrust of Lanzardo's argument certainly seem to point in this direction. After all, why engage in a dense exegesis of Marx's questionnaire only to conclude that the peculiarities of the conjuncture impugn, if not condemn, its uses? At the same time, it must be acknowledged that Lanzardo refrains from any explicit affirmation of workers' inquiry at the end of his essay. Instead, he gestures to the need for an exploration of instruments to facilitate a critique of capitalist production *among* workers.[134] Such maneuvers seem to hint at a creeping doubt about the viability of workers' inquiry in his present.

Moreover, for all of his deep insights into Marx's questionnaire, Lanzardo commits some fairly obvious (if largely inconsequential) blunders in the fine details of his argument. He identifies questions from the *third part* of Marx's questionnaire with questions from the *fourth part*.[135] Lanzardo quotes from Marx's speech to the First International Working Men's Association in 1865, but he mistakenly dates the speech from 1895, more than a decade after Marx's death.[136] Lanzardo's copious quotations from Marx at the outset of his essay also seem to function too often as tedious substitutes for his own argument. More substantively, if the overall purpose of Marx's questionnaire is to enable the working class to remake itself as an *antagonistic* class, how are we to understand this seemingly important adjective? While there is no straightforward answer to this question in Lanzardo's article, he implicitly opposes antagonism to conflict. His use of the adjective "antagonistic" suggests a self-initiating intensification of the contradiction between labor and capital. "Antagonistic" thus signals a working-class orientation that disrupts the mystification of the struggle between labor and capital. "Conflict," on the other hand, carries the pejorative connotation of a working-class struggle for greater compensation within the (mystified) parameters of capitalist production. From this perspective, workers' inquiry clearly serves the purpose of transforming conflict *into* antagonism.

In a short article titled "Socialist uses of workers' inquiry,"[137] which also appeared in the fifth issue of *Quaderni Rossi* in 1965,[138] Panzieri frames his entire discussion of the socialist uses of workers' inquiry through an *explicit* distinction between conflict and antagonism. Indeed, he outright characterizes the "conflictual" *as* "capitalist" and the "antagonistic" *as* "anti-capitalist."[139] Panzieri goes on to theorize a dynamic relationship between these working-class orientations. In his words, "Given that conflicts are functional to a system that is advanced by them, they can be turned into antagonisms and no longer be functional to the system."[140] Thiollent, in his illuminating interpretation of Panzieri, identifies such moments of conflict as "strikes and forms of class solidarity."[141] He emphasizes that these moments can transform into moments of antagonism when they begin to grate against "the functionality or reproduction of the system." Panzieri himself suggests that this transformation implies a shift in value systems with a tremendously disruptive potential: values embraced by workers during moments of conflict can suddenly dissipate and give way to other values during moments of antagonism.[142]

But instead of offering an exegesis of Marx's questionnaire, Panzieri revisits the debates within *Quaderni Rossi* about the potential uses of sociological methods for socialism. As indicated above, the uses of the questionnaires at the FIAT factory in Turin occasioned these debates. Panzieri directs his criticism against the distrust of sociological methods among *Quaderni Rossi* members.[143] He acknowledges that a general distrust of sociology in Marxism springs from the "metaphysics" resulting from Friedrich Engels's conflation of the social and physical sciences and the consequent (and invariable) failure to establish a proper "science of social facts."[144] For Panzieri, this "metaphysics" betrays a powerful sociological current in Marx. The latter consists in grappling not only with distinctly social facts but also with "social reality as a whole."[145] This detail is quite important. Panzieri insists that what distinguishes Marx's analysis from classical political economy is the refusal to view labor-power from the unilateral standpoint of capital. Marx, as Panzieri reads him, attends to the social dichotomy at the heart of capitalist society and upholds the working class as *both* conflictual and antagonistic.[146] On this basis, Panzieri construes the socialist appropriation of the sociological method of inquiry as a means of not only gauging the degree of antagonism on the part of the working class but also intensifying it by gauging and raising the consciousness of the working class. Consciousness-raising and the movement from conflict to antagonism are thus intimately bound up together in the act of workers' inquiry. In a passage rich enough to quote at length, Panzieri elaborates:

> The method of inquiry should enable us to defy all kinds of mystical ideas about the workers' movement. It should always warrant a scientific observation of the level of consciousness of the working class, and also provide a way of raising it. Thus there is a definite continuity between the moment of sociological investigation guided by rigorous and serious criteria, and political action: sociological inquiry is a kind of mediation that averts the risks of reaching a vision of the level of workers' antagonism and awareness that—whether pessimistic or optimistic—would be completely gratuitous.[147]

For Panzieri, this task implies a whole spatial and temporal orientation for the investigators. They must conduct their inquiries "in the heat of the moment" and "on the spot" because the working class cannot be reduced to a mere reflection of the movements of capital and, more specifically, because conflict can always turn into antagonism.[148] Panzieri can be seen here as articulating the theoretical reason for his earlier insistence that members of *Quaderni Rossi* conduct their inquiries at the ostensibly pacified FIAT factory in Turin.

Obviously, Panzieri goes much further than Lanzardo in elaborating the distinction between conflict and antagonism and the role of workers' inquiry therein. Yet *both* theorists view the purpose of workers' inquiry in identical terms, namely, *to transform the working class into an antagonistic class by raising its consciousness.* Shifting political conditions in Italy nevertheless undermined the resonance of this view before it even appeared in the pages of *Quaderni Rossi* in 1965. As Cavazzini recounts, other prominent contributors to the journal, such as Mario Tronti and Negri, began to envision the new working class *as already antagonistic*, thereby dispensing with the whole need for a long process of consciousness-raising through workers' inquiries.[149] For Cavazzini, one event in particular, the Piazza Statuto revolt of young workers against the headquarters of the Italian Union of Labor in Turin in 1962, catalyzed this transformation.[150]

Yet the emphasis on consciousness-raising through workers' inquiries did not simply go away after losing its momentum in Italy. Working from the Brazilian context in the 1980s, Thiollent used the analyses of Lanzardo and Panzieri for a creative extrapolation. What, he asked, would the seemingly abstract process of consciousness-raising look like from the standpoint of the worker? To be more precise, Thiollent asked how the worker would even begin to understand his or her own exploitation, given his or her lack of training in the critique of political economy and its cherished concepts of "the value of labor, surplus value, constant capital, and variable capital."[151] Thiollent suggested that the very words used by workers to describe their experiences of exploitation in interviews could reveal varying degrees of approximation to an understanding of capitalist exploitation. As a first approximation, workers could invoke a moral universe of the "'rich'" and "'poor'"; as a second approximation, they could refer to "'exploitation'" with reference to income distribution and phenomena such as augmentations in the cost of living; as final approximation, workers could come to perceive a difference between their wages and the effective value of their labor, albeit through the mediation of an interviewer.[152] Though purely speculative, Thiollent's extrapolation has the virtue of at least confronting the vexing problem of how a worker might come to understand his or her exploitation through the process of an inquiry.

We are finally in a position to fully appreciate the significance of taking into account *Quaderni Rossi*'s strong emphasis on consciousness-raising through questionnaires. One of the recurrent themes in the experience of workers' inquiry among post-Trotskyist currents was the overwhelming failure to get workers outside a militant milieu to write about their own experiences on the shop floor. We saw a similar failure in Marx's original project for a workers' inquiry in the previous chapter. Lanzardo's theorization of this practice does not so much deny this failure as reframe the task as one of providing a stimulus to workers to organize themselves. He thus draws our attention away from *worker writing* as an impetus to and verification of an incipient class-consciousness among workers. Instead, Lanzardo gets us to think about the forms of reflection and communication stimulated by *merely posing* a set of questions to workers. He thus compels us to consider the less obvious ways in which a questionnaire might still generate political effects. In light of his major contribution to the theorization of workers' inquiry, the drawbacks of the narrative form of workers' inquiry leap out at us. Quite apart from its shortcomings in capturing and conveying more general patterns of working-class behavior, the individual narrative form is simply too open-ended to facilitate the kinds of political effects that workers' inquiry seeks to generate among its recipients. The open-endedness of this form grates against the kinds of reflections and communications that could be stimulated and drawn out by precise and carefully crafted questions. What is more, the questionnaire as a whole does not necessarily foreclose more open-ended responses. It can accommodate individual narratives through minimal pleas for more information. We have already seen instances of such pleas, and we will encounter them again in chapter 5. Overall, then, the questionnaire is eminently more suited to the task of workers' inquiry than the narrative form.

4

Badiou, the Maoist Investigation, and the Party Form

Mao Zedong's concept and practice of the investigation (*enquête* in French) acquired a deep resonance in Maoist groups in France in the late 1960s and early 1970s.[1] Indeed, variations of his pithy and provocative injunction "No investigation, no right to speak" circulated like a mantra among these groups.[2] Beginning in 1967, French Maoists launched investigations under the stimulus of the still unfolding Chinese Cultural Revolution.[3] Notably, however, their investigations were conducted without any explicit debt to the tradition of investigations inaugurated by Karl Marx's questionnaire nearly a century beforehand. This disconnect is especially noteworthy because the latter document had its origins in the French national context, and it had not receded into obscurity on the radical left in this context by the late 1960s and early 1970s. Quite the contrary, analyses of Marx's questionnaire had been resuscitated through French translations of the *Quaderni Rossi* collective in April 1968 and the theorizations of the radical periodical *Cahiers de Mai* in July 1970.[4] The experience of the investigation in French Maoism thus testifies once more to the autonomous development of different strands of the investigation in the history of Marxism. In the case of the investigation in French Maoism, this autonomy seems to have derived from the conceptualization of the investigation as a comparatively immersive experience. As we saw in chapter 2, Mao rejected individual interviews as the basis of an investigation and conceived of the method behind the practice as much more than the public solicitation of responses to questionnaires distributed en masse. He cast the investigation as an opportunity to engage others in a collective setting for the broad purpose of formulating revolutionary strategies and tactics. French Maoists picked up on Mao's conceptualization of the investigation as this more immersive experience with others, and they pushed it in whole new directions in the context of a highly industrialized country. They began to construe the investigation in varying degrees of relation to *établissement* as the practice of taking up working positions among peasants and workers for prolonged periods of time to radicalize them. Unsurprisingly, their understanding of this relation also had its roots in Mao's pronouncements.[5] In a March 1957 speech, Mao vividly articulated both the similarity and difference between the investigation and the practice that would come to be known as établissement in France. In his partially metaphorical words:

> We encourage the intellectuals to go among the masses, to go to factories and villages. It is very bad if you never in all your life meet a worker or peasant. Our government workers, writers, artists, teachers and scientific research workers should seize every opportunity to get close to the workers and peasants. Some can go to factories and villages just to look around; this may be called "looking at flowers while on horseback" and is better than nothing at all. Others can stay there for a few months, conducting investigations and making friends; this may be called "dismounting to look at the flowers." Still others can stay and live there for a considerable time, say, two or three years or even longer; this may be called "settling down."[6]

Recently, scholarly interest in the French Maoist appropriation of these practices has been undergoing something of a renaissance as part of a much larger renewal of academic interest in French Maoism.[7] This renewal owes no small part to the rise to prominence of Alain Badiou as a "post-Maoist" philosopher.[8] The French Maoist practice of investigations in particular has elicited varying degrees of attention in recent years. But the form of this attention can lend itself to suspicions about the overall import of these investigations in the first place. Discussions of Maoist investigations tend to occupy an illuminating but often fleeting presence in a literature overwhelmingly driven by much broader historical narratives and exegetical imperatives.[9] This literature certainly acknowledges the political, historical, and theoretical significance of Maoist investigations, but it does not tend to engage their contents in much depth at all. There is even a tendency to discuss these investigations in various locales throughout France, such as the region of Brittany, the suburb of Billancourt, and the town of Meulan, without disclosing many details or even citing the source materials for them, as if the knowledge of the investigations in these locales is somehow pervasive enough to simply warrant omitting these materials.[10] One immediate effect of such treatments of investigations is to leave us with occasionally useful but more often sparse and exceedingly general observations about them. In particular, we are left without an elaborate sense of the specificity of French Maoist investigations in the much larger history of the concept and practice of investigations in radical political struggles. We are also left without any kind of strong sense of the kinds of practical and theoretical difficulties posed by this altogether central practice in the French Maoist experience.

This chapter seeks to redress these limitations in the literature by focusing on the lengthiest and most detailed account of Maoist investigations in the French countryside, *Le livre des paysans pauvres: 5 années de travail maoïste dans une campagne française*, published by Badiou's Group for the Foundation of the Union of Marxist-Leninist Communists of France (UCFML) in May 1976.[11] We should linger over the title of this book for just a moment because it tells us a lot about the orientation and temporal scope of the investigations recounted in its pages. Most obviously, *Le livre des paysans pauvres* announces a *return* to a figure whose political significance Mao revealed through his famous investigation in Hunan: the *poor* peasant.[12] Yet the investigations of the UCFML return to this figure in the radically different context of the French countryside of the early 1970s, and these investigations span years rather than just months.

While the economic writings of the UCFML have elicited the attention of interpreters seeking to elucidate Badiou's aversion to the critique of political economy,[13] there appears to be no elaborate discussion of the rich contents of *Le livre des paysans pauvres* in particular. Bruno Bosteels seems to have the *unique* merit of introducing *Le livre des paysans pauvres* to English readers, but even he does not get into its contents beyond the space of a sentence.[14] This little-known book consisting mainly of narratives by UCFML militants written between 1971 and 1975 nonetheless warrants careful attention because it reveals important modulations in the concept and practice of the investigation. These modulations include the fusion of the investigation with établissement, the manifest use of these practices to search for a new type of party, and, finally, the embrace of the militant narrative as the form of the investigation. Beyond the disclosure of these important modulations, *Le livre des paysans pauvres* conveys altogether sharp limitations in the practice of investigations of the UCFML. These limitations stem not only from the sheer practical difficulties of conducting investigations among poor peasants in the countryside over a prolonged period of time but also from the broader political-theoretical framework in which these investigations take place. UCFML militants exude a strident commitment to the goal of poor-peasant autonomy in the presentation and elaboration of their investigations, but their recourse to stark affirmations of proletarian political leadership *over* poor peasants vitiates this commitment.

The resolution of this antinomy in favor of proletarian political leadership reflects the limitations of Badiou's own political orientation during his self-described "'red years'" from the late 1960s to late 1970s.[15] Throughout these years, Badiou viewed the party as a representational body for the transformation of the working class from an objective historical agent into a subjective force in sites of power.[16] If *Le livre des paysans pauvres* unsurprisingly confirms the depth of his commitment to this view, it also foreshadows his extensively discussed shift toward a *critique* of the representational underpinnings of the party form by revealing the difficulties of representing poor peasants in particular. My argument in the following pages thus goes well beyond the already important task of filling a huge lacuna in the literature on investigations in French Maoism. It ultimately affords a far more critical perspective on a crucial moment in Badiou's overall political trajectory.

UCFML Investigations in Context

As the UCFML was a French Maoist organization that goes unmentioned even in otherwise comprehensive analyses of French Maoist practices,[17] it is helpful to begin by dwelling on some basic details about the organization. Founded by Natacha Michel, Sylvain Lazarus, and Badiou between 1969 and 1970, the UCFML was one of a variety of Maoist organizations that flourished in France under the stimulus of the Chinese Cultural Revolution and the events of May 1968. One of the main reasons for the creation of the UCFML was to offset the influence of two other Maoist organizations: the Marxist-Leninist Communist Party of France

(PCMLF) and the increasingly prominent Proletarian Left (GP) led by Benny Lévy (a.k.a. Pierre Victor). In the eyes of UCFML members, the PCFML deviated to the right in identifying itself as the genuine communist party inspired by the French Communist Party (PCF) of the 1920s and 1930s, whereas the GP deviated to the left in its calls for revolts tending toward spectacular displays of violence without sufficient organizational grounding.[18] Unlike the PCMLF, the UCFML did *not* designate itself as a party in its long-winded name because of its openly acknowledged *lack* of a mass base.[19] Nor did it bear the formal attributes of a party, such as "strict rules of affiliation," "membership cards," and "party secretaries."[20] Yet the UCFML remained committed to organization insofar as it sought to constitute a "party of a new type."[21] It thus cast itself in contradistinction to the insufficiently organized GP. The aspiration to found a "party of a new type" was also framed in manifest opposition to "workerism" as the view attributed to anarcho-syndicalists as well as revisionists in the PCF and General Confederation of Labor (CGT) that the working class is "*immediately* a *political* class" by virtue of its "existence as a *social* class."[22] Against this equation of the social being of the working class with its political being, the UCFML identified the party as an organization necessary for the working class to *surpass* its "elementary being of social class to become a political class, a leading class."[23] More elaborately, the UCFML cast the party as "that by which" the working class "substitutes, on the limited horizon of its own class immediacy, the space, no longer only of its own defended interests, but also the political and social interests of the whole of the people."[24]

The activities in the countryside so meticulously recounted in the pages of *Le livre des paysans pauvres* were undertaken to realize this broad vision of the party. On its own account, the UCFML commenced these activities to *test* whether its militants, as the self-styled avant-garde of the proletariat, would *possess* the capacity to lead the whole of the people, not just the proletariat. In its words, "The revolutionary work in the peasantry is—for those who claim to adhere to militant Marxism—the testing ground for the avant-garde of the proletariat to become the leading nucleus of the whole people."[25] This test of whether UCFML militants were ready to lead the people by rallying the peasantry presupposed not only going to the countryside but also taking up positions among the peasants for an extended period of time (établissement) to learn about them. As the opening paragraph of the first chapter of *Le livre des paysans pauvres* explains, the work of these militants in the countryside originated in "simple ideas," namely, that "peasants have a place in the revolution, that they must be rallied to the camp of the people, which demands binding oneself to them in a prolonged manner to acquire an internal knowledge of this social strata."[26] If établissement served as a precondition for acquiring this "internal knowledge," it was intimately connected to two other practices, investigations and the assessment of the experience (*bilan d'éxperience*), in a kind of spiraling movement. Investigations served as a means of generating knowledge about poor peasants and organizing them *in the process*. In a remarkably lucid formulation, the UCFML explained:

> When we speak of an organizing investigation, it refers to the Marxist-Leninist conception (condensed by Mao in the formula: to investigate a problem is to resolve it) which considers that an investigation *already* participates in a process of organization, which contradicts the conception of the investigation as an accumulation of documents, a prelude to all action.[27]

Here we have a straightforward rejection of a teleological understanding of the investigation as a stage of information gathering succeeded by a stage of political action. The investigation for the UCFML was far more dynamic, organizing political action *as* it gathered information in situ. The results of the investigation were then assessed and new investigations launched in light of the lessons learned.

The activities of the UCFML in the countryside began in June 1971 and lasted until at least August 1975.[28] The UCFML conducted its investigations in southwestern France in the area of Millevaches and in the neighboring department of Dordogne as well as in the Var department in southeastern France.[29] The full geographical scope of the investigations nevertheless remains unclear because the UCFML also used fictitious names for villages, presumably to keep its own activities under the police radar and protect the identity of its local supporters.[30] Concerns about police repression would have been well founded. The GP and the PCMLF had already been proscribed and forced underground by the time that the UCFML launched its investigations in the countryside in June 1971.[31]

Owing to the overwhelmingly anonymous character of *Le livre des paysans pauvres*, it is also unclear who exactly in the UCFML composed its contributions, apart from the foreword coauthored by Badiou and

Lazarus. And it is just as unclear who exactly engaged in the investigations. Even so, it seems highly likely that Badiou would have played a fairly prominent role in the production of *Le livre des paysans pauvres*, given his position as coeditor of the Yenan collection to which the book belonged. The language in the book certainly hints at Badiou's editorial hand, echoing precise expressions from his then contemporaneous theorization of contradiction as process of scission between the logic of forces and the logic of places. Such is the case in the aforementioned references of the UCFML to its activities in the countryside as a "testing ground." Badiou had already used this exact expression in his elaboration of the implications of his view of practice as both a *term* in contradiction with theory and an *object* of knowledge as theory. In his concise words, "Without organized application, no testing ground, no verification, no truth."[32]

Bosteels rightly goes so far as to consider the investigation an altogether "fundamental" feature of the UCFML.[33] Yet among French Maoist organizations, the UCFML was hardly alone in practicing investigations in the countryside and elsewhere. Kristin Ross nicely captures the spatial and social breadth of these investigations. She suggests that as early as 1967, French Maoists began undertaking them "with workers and farmers door to door, in market places, in front of metro entrances, and in villages of *la France profonde*."[34] More specifically, Robert Linhart's short-lived Union of Marxist-Leninist Communist Youth (UJCML), the predecessor to the GP, had undertaken investigations among poor peasants and workers in the summer of 1967 to establish contact with the masses for the purpose of ultimately building a genuinely revolutionary communist party. A UJCML leader, Jean-Pierre Le Dantec, suggests that these investigations had their origins in the "will to elaborate a revolutionary political line based on a 'scientific' analysis" inspired in no small measure by Louis Althusser.[35] In his account, UJCML members sought to produce the "equivalent" for the French social formation of the 1960s and 1970s of Lenin's *The Development of Capitalism in Russia* and Mao's "Report on an Investigation of the Peasant Movement in Hunan."[36] The problem was that UJCML members were "students and former students without organic connections with the working class, the poor or middle peasantry and other popular strata of France."[37] They therefore set out to establish these connections through investigations during their summer vacations. However, as Jason E. Smith explains, these investigations were ultimately deemed a mere first and quickly abandoned step toward the more thoroughgoing practice of placing UJCML militants in factories to radicalize workers (établissement) because investigations were seen as facilitating only superficial contact between militants and the masses.[38] Le Dantec corroborates this view. He recounts that investigation groups within the UJCML drew the conclusion from their experiences that "to remain at factory gates to gather together figures and testimonies was a dead end, a position that could lead only to isolated, short-lived contacts."[39] It was necessary, in other words, to engage the masses in a more thoroughgoing manner through établissement. This shift toward établissement as a practice distinct from and superior to the investigation can also be detected in Linhart's famous and deeply moving account of his experiences of attempting to radicalize and organize workers through his employment at the Citroën factory in Porte de Choisy from September 1968 to July 1969.[40] Linhart does not cast these experiences, which took place shortly after the dissolution of the UJCML, in the guise of an investigation. He frames them *exclusively* through the lens of établissement, as if the practice of investigation had already been entirely surpassed or eclipsed.

This practice nevertheless persisted among other Maoist organizations in France. Born from the dissolution of the UJCML, the most famous of these organizations, the GP, also engaged in its own investigations in suburban factories and the countryside. A. Belden Fields notes that the reliance of the GP on investigations was "heavy" and served the broad purpose of "coming to know what people in specific contexts were thinking."[41] One former GP militant, Danielle Rancière, affirms the latter part of this view in her account of her investigations at the Géo factory in the Kremlin-Bicêtre suburb of Paris. She recounts that GP investigations performed a kind of refracting function. They involved gathering information from workers on the basis of interviews, recording this information in notebooks, and then mirroring this information back to workers in the form of pamphlets in order to "liberate" their "speech."[42] Rancière doubts that this practice was at all efficacious, but she claims to have learned a lot from it and used it as a "model" for the activities of the Prisons Information Group (GIP), as we shall see in the subsequent chapter.[43]

However, as indicated above, there is a tendency to discuss Maoist investigations in various locales throughout France without disclosing a lot of details about them or even citing the source materials for them. This tendency manifests itself in discussions of GP investigations.[44] Richard Wolin, for instance, offers nothing more than a passing mention of the investigations undertaken by the GP at the famous Renault factory in Billancourt and in the town of Meulan. In a 2009 interview with Andrea Cavazzini, Yves Duroux provides an astounding and seemingly implausible explanation for such a lack of specificity. He repeatedly insists that the GP *never* practiced the investigation in the first place.[45] In his delicately phrased but altogether jarring words, "I would like to say just a word about this question of the investigation. It was very important and, finally, it was not practiced at the time of the Proletarian Left."[46] From his perspective, the investigation remained more of an important theoretical reference point than a practice. Obviously, Duroux's judgment is extremely difficult to reconcile with the insistence that the GP practiced investigations in the accounts of its interpreters and former militants. Yet, in the sheer audacity of his observation, Duroux may be onto something. We know very little about the contents of the questions or responses in GP investigations. We also know very little about their results and overall political effects. Perhaps the GP investigations were not as widespread as some interpreters of French Maoism have claimed.

Whatever the case, it is also worth noting that not all French Maoist investigations were concerned with the eminently classical figures (in the revolutionary repertoire) of peasants and workers. The more libertarian-leaning Maoist group, Long Live the Revolution (VLR), stands out in this regard.[47] The semi-monthly newspaper of the VLR, *Tout!*, published the responses of two former psychiatric hospital patients to a series of questions about their treatment, the circumstances leading to their hospitalization, and their general views on the distinction between normality and abnormality. These questions and answers were printed in an article aptly titled "Investigation . . ." in the April 1971 issue of *Tout!*[48] There is no indication of whether these questions and answers were based on questionnaires or interviews, but the rationale behind them leaps out at readers in an accompanying declaration from the same page. This untitled declaration highlights the violent silencing of the voices of psychiatric hospital patients in favor of the voices of doctors. In its words, "Only doctors have the right to speak, and the patients are there so that doctors speak of them."[49] From this perspective, the most elementary purpose of the investigation described in the adjacent article was to give patients a voice. Or, more elaborately, the purpose of the investigation was to draw out the voices of the patients to facilitate a contestation of the social system that silences them. The contents of the responses of the former psychiatric hospital patients lent themselves to this goal by disturbing the terms of the distinction between normality and abnormality. As one former patient remarked, "Someone normal is abnormal, which is to say, without any faults."[50] When asked to describe normal people, the other former patient mused skeptically, "Normal people, it's hard to say. Maybe there are some but we have to look for them."[51]

Against the backdrop of all of these remarkably heterogeneous experiences, what made the investigations of the UCFML unique? Let us parse out the response to this question by first addressing what made the UCFML investigations different in the more microcosmic *French Maoist* experience before turning to what made them different in the much larger history of the concept and practice of the investigation in radical political struggles. As we have already seen, the overall emphasis of the UCFML investigations was on *testing* the preparedness of UCFML militants to lead the people rather than on simply establishing an initial point of contact with the masses or facilitating their speech, as in the cases of the UJCML and GP, respectively.[52] In this sense, the overall objective of the investigations was as much self-oriented as externally oriented. For this reason, the investigations of the UCFML were comparatively immersive experiences that relied heavily on two distinct methods: questioning individuals in person and holding collective fact-finding meetings. With regard to the former method, we may note that the UCFML showed its independence from the letter of Mao's prescriptions, which, once again, discouraged investigations based on individual interviews. The immersive character of the UCFML investigations blurred the lines between these investigations and établissement by feeding the latter practice into the former. In other words, investigations were *not* a *prelude* to the realization of a more thoroughgoing and distinct practice of établissement, as in the case of the UJCML. They were, on the contrary, a *product* of this practice. To put the point rather concretely, it was through assisting poor peasants in the collection of hay one summer after another that UCFML militants were able to conduct their investigations. Finally, the temporality of the UCFML investigations set them apart from other investigations within the French Maoist experience. These investigations were conducted in a discontinuous manner over a *prolonged* period of time, half a decade,[53] culminating in a dense document that was meant to stir the political imagination. As Badiou and Lazarus observed in their foreword to *Le livre des paysans pauvres*, "Through this type of contribution, a new debate should be able to start on the revolutionary organization of the people of the countryside and the tasks that result from it for the political organization of the proletariat."[54] Yet, by the time the UCFML concluded its investigations in the countryside, one of its major rivals, the GP, had ceased to exist even in a clandestine manner, and the " 'red years' " were nearly over.

These investigations also stand out against the larger backdrop of the concept and practice of the investigation in the history of radical political struggles. As we saw in chapter 2, investigations in early Marxism were intimately bound up with an impetus toward organization. The questions in these investigations even carried a kind of implicit incitement to organize. However, as indicated in the previous chapter, oppositional strands of Marxism used the investigation in the postwar period in Europe and the United States to question more traditional forms of organization on the radical left. To be more precise, these investigations were used to voice suspicions about the ability of radical parties and unions to adequately represent the working class. In so doing, the investigations rediscovered the worker as a subject of production beyond such forms of association, as if they peeled back these forms to reveal a forgotten substratum. The investigations of the UCFML reversed this trend up to a point. They entailed a more unambiguously affirmative relationship to the party form.[55] The UCFML deemed the latter *the* desired embodiment of collective political subjectivity. The point of its investigations was, once again, to *test* whether its militants would be able to instantiate a "party of a new type" by rallying the peasantry as a crucial segment of the people. Yet, perhaps less expectedly, the very framing of these investigations as a test *also* reflected doubts on the part of the UCFML about whether its militants and, by extension, its desired "party of a new type" *could* adequately represent peasants. The investigations of the UCFML thus sprang from doubts about the representational capacity of the party form *even* as they aspired toward the realization of this form.

These investigations distinguished themselves from other investigations in radical political struggles in another important regard: they intensified the physical displacements and corresponding forms of spatial dislocation that often accompanied the practice of investigations. Physical displacement and spatial dislocation were quite pronounced in Mao's metaphor of the investigation as an act of "dismounting" from a horse "to smell the flowers" and in Raniero Panzieri's appeal to workers' inquiries "on the spot."[56] But they appear to have reached a hiatus in the fusion of UCFML investigations with the practice of établissement in the French countryside. Suddenly, investigations were no longer simply a matter of soliciting information through acts of publicity in newspapers, pamphlets, and posters or even of interviewing workers at the gates of factories. They involved *crossing* the geographical or institutional threshold that traditionally separated investigators and investigated. Militants were to go live with and work alongside poor peasants in particular for extended periods of time. They were, in short, to acquire an *enduring* physical presence in another geographical space to produce knowledge for political purposes. The enduring physical presence of the UCFML militants in this *other* space inflected their investigations with a greater element of unpredictability to the extent that it heightened the possibility of all kinds of unexpected encounters with others.

Finally, another major way in which the investigations of the UCFML differed from other investigations in the larger history of the investigation in radical political struggles concerns their form. In the previous chapter, we addressed the narrative as the preferred form of the investigation in oppositional Trotskyist and post-Trotskyist currents. The UCFML also preferred this form, at least in *Le livre des paysans pauvres*. However, the overwhelming majority of the contributions to this book consist of narratives by militants rather than peasants. What we see, then, is a shift to the militant as the principal narrator of the investigation. And this shift drastically diminishes the burden of having to solicit peasant writings. In other words, the UCFML was not concerned (in the main) with trying to successfully solicit these writings because it was the militant who would narrate the investigation for a militant audience. It was, after all, the subjectivity of the militant that was at stake in the investigation. However, as we shall see in the next section, the UCFML *still* wanted peasants to *speak up* about their conditions and struggles, and it encountered immense difficulties in getting them to carry out this seemingly elementary task. In contrast to the failure of worker writing discussed in chapter 3, we can discern a phenomenon that can be more appropriately described as the failure of *peasant speaking* in the context of UCFML investigations in the French countryside.

Practical Challenges

As we have seen, *Le livre des paysans pauvres* offers a nonteleological theorization of the investigation. But it must be acknowledged that the narratives of the militants in the book disclose very few details about the precise methods employed in their investigations, perhaps because it was widely assumed that these methods simply derived from Mao's theorizations. What is clear is that the UCFML investigations relied heavily on the questioning of individuals as well as on collective meetings and the distribution of texts on particular issues. It is also clear that the spatial and thematic scope of the investigations was quite expansive. The UCFML conducted investigations in various villages and working-class neighborhoods in cities. These investigations addressed a remarkably wide range of topics, such as the relocation of a village cemetery, the need for a milk market among workers in a town and poor peasants in a village, and the use of revenues from logging.

But the UCFML militants encountered all kinds of practical difficulties in their investigations, especially at the outset of their presence in the countryside. Based on the lessons learned from another political experience among peasants in a neighboring department in 1970, the UCFML militants started from the assumption that the practice of establishing one militant per peasant would allow for only for a "unilateral investigation" rather than one on a more collective scale.[57] However, to even begin to conduct their investigations, these militants found that they had no choice as outsiders but to rely on a peasant accordion player, Marcel, who *distrusted* the poor and aged peasants in his own village of Beaumont in southeastern France.[58] To compound this initial problem, the UCFML also discovered that peasants were reluctant to speak at initial meetings designed to determine how militants might assist them.[59] The UCFML militants only began to establish independent contact with poor peasants after immersing themselves in the admittedly "hard" work of collecting hay in July 1971.[60] This work was seen as a way of binding oneself to poor peasants, thereby laying the groundwork for an "investigation of the class situation in Beaumont."[61]

In this context, UCFML militants conducted investigations that led them to plenty of self-acknowledged mistakes. In June and July 1972, militants conducted investigations with residents of a public housing apartment in a working-class neighborhood of a city dubbed simply "V" and with poor peasants from the neighboring village of Beaumont.[62] These residents had been the recipients of the direct sale of milk from the poor peasants over the course of the preceding year. The sale of milk, which took place in a bicycle garage in a basement of the public housing apartment, was seen as a way of circumventing costly intermediaries and, more importantly, establishing contact between peasants and workers for the purpose of an eventual alliance between them. However, as the sale of milk did not precipitate this alliance quickly enough for UCFML militants, these militants decided to conduct individual investigations on the efficacy of the milk market among the residents of the public housing apartment and the poor peasants. These investigations revealed that, from the perspectives of both the residents and peasants, there were simply too few persons around over the summer to make the sale of milk a worthwhile endeavor.[63] In light of these results, the UCFML militants decided to abruptly halt the sale of milk without attempting to convene a meeting between residents and peasants to let *them* decide on the matter. Retrospectively, in the form of an assessment of the experience, the militants criticized themselves for suddenly making this decision. These militants deemed this decision a very serious mistake because it deprived the participants in the milk market of an opportunity to self-organize.[64]

In another instance of the practical challenges involved in investigations, UCFML militants launched an investigation in the summer of 1972 to determine the views of poor peasants toward the use of taxes for the maintenance of paths in the village of Beaumont. These investigations were conducted on an individual basis. They culminated in the production of a poster that displayed three points of view among the peasants, namely, the self-maintenance of paths and corresponding refusal to pay taxes for them, the use of money from the lumber harvest to maintain paths, and, finally, municipal accountability for the maintenance of the paths. The UCFML militants displayed the poster in a public location to solicit the views of others, but it failed to generate any kind of discussion.[65] In their assessment of this experience, the militants concluded that their preceding discussions with peasants had been exhaustive enough to undermine any further reason for a discussion. Perhaps sensing that their own presence may have actually dissuaded others from expressing themselves, UCFML militants also articulated a desire to place the investigation of the population of Beaumont under the direction of poor peasants.[66]

By the summer of 1973, the UCFML even went so far as to claim that its investigations during the preceding summer were conceptually misguided. It maintained that these investigations were seen as ways of identifying stakes and *then* struggling, with organization following on the footsteps of struggle. This approach yielded "investigations without principles" that ultimately left militants in a position of power *rather* than organizing poor peasants.[67] Indeed, the UCFML pointed to the decision to halt the sale of milk in "V" as an example of this outcome.[68] It sought to rectify this error by appealing to a reframing of the practice of investigation in terms of organization. In its emphatic words, "*The investigation will be organizational,* not around organizational proposals, but under the general idea of a program of demands, a program of non-dispersed or punctual stakes."[69]

Proletarian Political Leadership Over Poor Peasants

While all of the problems above certainly convey the immense practical difficulties of carrying out investigations among poor peasants over a prolonged period of time, the core limitation to these investigations resided in the intermediate steps in the realization of their broad purpose. If this overarching purpose was to test the preparedness of the UCFML to found a party by testing the capacity of its militants to lead the people as a whole, how was this leadership to be exercised? The UCFML suggested that it was to be exercised *through* the organization of poor-peasant autonomy. Why did the UCFML retain the emphasis on the need for the constitution of this autonomy, which may so easily arouse suspicions among readers versed in more recent contributions to the literature on peasant mobilizations?[70] For the UCMFL, only autonomous organization would enable poor peasants to handle their own problems as well as larger contradictions among the people. Solutions to these problems or the resolution of these contradictions could not be superimposed from the outside. For this reason, UCFML militants repeatedly insisted that they not only do *not* want to make decisions on behalf of the peasants but also that they *want* to place *their* own concrete activities in the countryside, such as clearing paths of bramble branches and nettles in the village of Beaumont, under the direct supervision of peasants.[71] As the UCFML declared, "The principal question in our eyes is to *place this work under the collective supervision of poor peasants.*"[72] UCFML militants considered the goal of poor-peasant autonomy so important that they criticized *themselves* for *failing* to engender it on a number of occasions, as in the aftermath of investigations leading to their decision to abruptly end the sale of milk in the public housing apartment in "V." By the summer of 1973, the UCFML militants even proposed to cease collecting hay if their presence impeded poor peasants from resolving their own problems.[73]

On the other hand, UCFML militants were quite unequivocal about proletarian political leadership *over* poor peasants. They justified this leadership on grounds that workers possess a more collective outlook on problems. The UCFML suggested that this more collective outlook is rooted in different material situations: workers own only their labor-power, whereas even poor peasants own the instruments of labor and land.[74] The inevitable conclusion for the UCFML was that poor peasants tend to be more individualistic than workers and, therefore, less inclined toward the task of political leadership.[75] The rationale behind this conclusion was, to put things rather mildly, remarkably odd for an organization that rejected the derivation of political being from social being. In according a political privilege to workers over peasants on the basis of their respective material positions, the UCFML slipped into a position akin to the workerism it so fiercely criticized.

One statement of the rationale for going to the countryside concisely captures the twin goals of poor-peasant autonomy and proletarian political leadership, as if no tension exists between them. It declares: "We are going there to support the process of autonomous organization of poor peasants and the idea in the long term of the proletarian direction of this process."[76]

What, however, is the basis for thinking that a genuinely autonomous organization of poor peasants would subject itself to proletarian political leadership? Alternatively, what is the basis for thinking that proletarian political leadership would respect this autonomy? What, in short, is the basis for the conjunction in the quote above?

The appeals of the UCFML to the common interests of the peasantry and proletariat certainly give us an answer about the *basis* of an *alliance* between these classes, but they leave the tension between the goals of proletarian political leadership and poor-peasant autonomy intact. Perhaps the temporal gap—the "long term"—provides one way to make sense of the conjunction. In this interpretive scenario, poor-peasant autonomy would amount to a short-term goal trumped by working-class political leadership in an unspecified "long term." Alternatively, the very of notion of autonomy might be understood in a more qualified and formal sense. There is some basis for this understanding of autonomy in *Le livre des paysans pauvres*. UCFML militants claimed that the role of the communist organization is emphatically *not* to decide on collective matters for the peasants so much as to "lead" and "control" discussions of these matters so that individuals do not take advantage of them.[77]

The sticking point for them was, once again, the threat of individualism from peasants, which was perceived to necessitate a militant body to protect their collective interests. However, among other complications, it is unclear how exactly one can so neatly separate the direction of the discussions about issues from the decisions about them.

Le livre des paysans pauvres seems to take us to a point where *either* working-class political leadership trumps poor-peasant autonomy at some undesignated point in the future *or* where it simply deprives this autonomy of any substance. All of the unforeseen encounters and learning opportunities opened up by the physical displacements of UCFML militants to the countryside to conduct investigations for prolonged periods of time seem to have been swept away in the emphatic defense of proletarian political leadership.

Postscript: Politics Without Party

Of course, the UCFML was not reducible to Badiou, but his name is intimately associated with the organization as well as with the much larger experience of French Maoism. Even today Badiou himself facilitates this identification by easily recalling his years of militancy in the UCFML. However, as is well known, Badiou's politics underwent profound changes after the conclusion in 1975 of the experiences of the investigations meticulously recounted in the militant narratives of *Le livre des paysans pauvres*. Indeed, it would be grossly misleading to finish a discussion of the limitations posed by the search for a "party of a new type" in these investigations without acknowledging that Badiou eventually abandoned the very notion of the party as a form of representation of social forces. In 1983 he cofounded a new organization, the Political Organization (OP), with the other founding members of the UCFML, Michel and Lazarus.[78] Through his activities in the OP, which revolved around support for the struggles of nonstatus migrants in France,[79] Badiou gravitated toward a politics that no longer aspires toward the goal of representing workers and peasants in the party.[80] In a recent interview with Thomas Nail, Badiou succinctly summarized this transformation:

> The *Organisation politique* followed the more openly Maoist organization, created in 1970, called the "UCFml" [*Union des communistes de France marxiste-léniniste*], Marxist-Leninist

> Union of Communists of France. The general inspiration that required the change of name was that the reference to Maoism and Marxism-Leninism was undoubtedly too classical on the one hand, too shared with dogmatic groups—and on the other, it did not place enough emphasis on our own properly political novelty, in particular the fact that our aim was no longer to quickly build a Party to "represent" the working class. But as far as I am concerned, I have always considered there to be a continuity of political practice between the two, and believe that the change of name was not essential.[81]

What, then, was the name of the politics that Badiou adopted through this transformation? It was quite simply a "politics without party." In Badiou's words from a November 1997 interview with Peter Hallward:

> Up to the end of the 1970s, my friends and I defended the idea that an emancipatory politics presumed some kind of political party. Today we are developing a completely different idea, which we call "politics without party." This doesn't mean "unorganized politics." All politics is collective, and so organized one way or another. "Politics without party" means that politics does not spring from or originate in the party. It does not stem from that synthesis of theory and practice that represented for Lenin, the Party. Politics springs from real situations, from what we can say and do in these situations.[82]

This transformation did not take place overnight. Alberto Toscano suggests that the crisis of Marxism for Badiou derived from a crisis of the party specifically as *the* political subject rather than from the "metaphysical tenets" or "sociological shortcomings of Marxism as a science of capitalism."[83] Toscano submits that from roughly 1982 to 1988, the crisis of Marxism propelled Badiou somewhere *between* the search for a "party of a new type" and a "politics without party."[84] Similarly, Hallward notes that the "gradual" character of Badiou's move toward a "politics without party" renders any endeavor to locate it in one source futile,[85] even as he suggests that Badiou anticipated his renunciation of the party form through an appreciation of Jean Paul-Sartre's emphasis on the minimal institutional stability in the group suspension of serial inertia.[86] But Badiou certainly formulated his reasons for abandoning the party form, *without* jettisoning political organization tout court, as early as his 1985 *Peut-on penser la politique?*[87] In this book, Badiou articulates the distinction between "politics" (*la politique*) and "the political" (*le politique*). Whereas "the political" denotes "the communitarian bond, and its representation in an authority,"[88] Badiou insists that "politics" reveals representation as a "fiction" through the event.[89] The event discloses presentation pure and simple,[90] a "there is" ("*il y a*") irreducible to forms of representation.[91] From this standpoint, the core problem with the party is that it remains bound par excellence to "the political," and thus suppresses the evental dimension intrinsic to "politics." Marxist and liberal parties represent classes and opinions, respectively, through their programs at the level of the state. However, far from turning the state into an instrument of their programmatic aspirations, these parties find themselves subjected to it. The state separates to impose the maintenance of a communitarian bond, "if need be by terror."[92] Badiou summarizes the consequences of this process: "Modern parties, whether they are single or multiple, receive their real qualification only from the State."[93]

Much more recently, Badiou has articulated his critique of an emancipatory politics based on the party with reference to the experience of the 1871 Paris Commune. Though formulated in somewhat different terms, this critique also locates the problem of the party in its relationship with the state. Badiou submits that the party bears an ambiguity between an *anti*-state thematic of revolution, on the one hand, and the thematic of a *new* state, on the other hand.[94] He traces this ambiguity back to Marx's famous critique of the shortcomings of the Paris Commune, such as its lack of more vigorous military initiatives at crucial junctures.[95] For Badiou, Marx's critique of these shortcomings *presupposed* the Commune acting *as* an entity endowed with state-like capacities. Owing to this ambiguous position vis-à-vis the state, the party engendered a figure of the *party-state* that historically blocked a politics of emancipation,[96] as in the notable case of the Cultural Revolution in China.[97] For this reason, Badiou dismisses the party as a vehicle for this politics.

How can we locate and make sense of *Le livre des paysans pauvres* within this larger transformation? It serves, first of all, as a lively reminder both of the problems associated with the practices springing from Badiou's earlier position and of the distance he traveled in adopting a "politics without party," even if it is all too easy to exaggerate this distance.[98] While the publication of *Le livre des paysans pauvres* predates Badiou's critique of the party form by nearly a whole decade, it highlights the difficulties of linking the constitution of a "party of a new type" to social representation. As indicated above, the UCFML explicitly framed its activities in *Le livre des paysans pauvres* as a test of whether the avant-garde of the proletariat would be capable of representing the people through this "party of a new type." But the details of its activities reveal the difficulties of enacting this representation through working-class political leadership *and* poor-peasant autonomy. Indeed, the presumption of a facile coherence, if not unity, between the latter aspirations turns out to be problematic. In other words, the whole matter of how exactly to *represent* poor peasants in particular through a "party of a new type" raises a lot of unanswered questions. In eschewing the very notion of the party as a locus of social representation, Badiou ultimately manages to veer his politics away from such questions.

Beyond this transformation, *Le livre des paysans pauvres* attunes us even more to the presence of the investigation in the later Badiou. He locates the investigation at the intersection of two core concepts in his thought: the situation understood as the status quo and the event understood as a rupture with the status quo. Badiou understands ethics in terms of a fidelity to the possibilities opened by the event. He even describes this fidelity as a "sustained *investigation* of the situation, under the imperative of the event itself."[99] Hallward helpfully renders the investigation in the later Badiou as a militant activity intended to establish a positive or negative connection to the event among the elements of the situation. In his strikingly lucid formulation, "Investigation is a militant rather than scholarly process. It is an attempt to win over each element to the event; it is a matter of 'enthusiasm' and 'commitment' rather than of knowledge or interpretation."[100] Few words, we should hasten to note, so nicely capture the specificity of the investigation in radical political struggles. The later Badiou therefore retains from his years in the UCFML an emphasis on the investigation as a militant activity rather than as a simple means of accumulating knowledge.

Finally, the investigations in *Le livre des paysans pauvres* cast Badiou's well-known and long-lasting concern with political novelty in something of a different light. This concern was certainly contemporaneous with the investigations of the UCFML in the French countryside. As militants were conducting these investigations, Badiou insisted that "the true question is always: what happens that is new?"[101] The UCFML tried to take a step toward answering this question by exploring the possibility of enacting something politically new, a "party of a new type," in the

French countryside. Yet the narratives of its militants in *Le livre des paysans pauvres* remind us that the construction of the new amounts to an altogether arduous enterprise susceptible to all kinds of errors, entanglements, and limitations.

5

In the Shadow of Oedipus

Enquêtes in Foucault's Theory and Practice

At the same time that Alain Badiou's Group for the Foundation of the Union of Marxist-Leninist Communists of France (UCFML) launched its investigations of poor peasants in the French countryside, another set of investigations were well under way in France. These investigations targeted an institution: the prison. This institution only *began* to capture the serious attention of the radical left in France two years *after* the tumultuous events of May 1968, as a growing political repression of the extraparliamentary left resulted in the imprisonment of many of its members. Hundreds of Proletarian Left (GP) militants had been arrested and imprisoned after the governmental proscription of their organization in May 1970. This political repression set the stage for the investigations of the Prisons Information Group (GIP), founded by Michel Foucault, Daniel Defert, and others in February 1971. The GIP undertook its own independent investigations of prisons to heighten public intolerance of the prison system through the voices of prisoners themselves. Foucault was very heavily involved in these investigations. During the same period, he was also turning his scholarly attention to the broader history of the investigation in his lectures at the Collège de France.

To fully appreciate Foucault's contributions to the history of the concept and practice of the investigation in radical political struggles, it helps to step back and recall the broad contours of the historical movement charted in the preceding chapters. We addressed the theory and practice of the investigation in the Marxist tradition, from its founding figures in the nineteenth century all the way up to its oppositional currents in the late twentieth century. We saw that the theory and practice of the investigation in Marxism broke along divergent and seemingly noncommunicative tracks: a track inspired by Karl Marx's "A Workers' Inquiry" and a track inspired by Mao Zedong's investigation. Foucault stands out in part for having participated in investigations (under the auspices of the GIP) that *fused together* these divergent tracks, perhaps even for the first time. He thus inhabited and channeled the Marxist practice of investigations in a unique way. But Foucault *also* destabilized the historical parameters of the Marxist tradition of investigations. He gestured to a *pre*-Marxist tradition of workers' inquiries, and he even traced the *official* inquiry itself all the back to Greek antiquity. Foucault thus historicized the investigation in stunningly novel ways in the lecture halls of the Collège *as* he practiced it in equally novel ways in the streets of Paris. Indeed, we can go a bold step further in demarcating the singularity of Foucault's position in the history of the concept and practice of the investigation: he is the *only* major theorist to have *simultaneously* historicized and practiced the investigation, as if it consumed his academic and political being for a short but intense period of time.

However, to even begin to appreciate Foucault's singular standing in the history of investigations, we must engage in a brief detour into some already familiar matters of French-English translation. Notably, Foucault used the same French word, *enquête*, for what has been correctly translated in English as both "inquiry" and "investigation." However, "inquiry" tends to be the predominant translation of enquête in his genealogical analyses whereas "investigation" tends be the predominant translation of enquête in the context of his references to a militant political practice going all the way back to working-class struggles in nineteenth-century France.[1] There is thus an identity in his original terminology that can get easily lost in English translation, to the point that the English reader can be forgiven for thinking that Foucault is discussing two unrelated terms or concepts. If we keep this identity in mind, we can readily see that his interest in the enquête was not just scholarly or purely militant. Throughout the bulk of the *same* period from 1971 to 1973 in which Foucault probed the enquête as a procedure for establishing the truth as fact going all the way back to the classical period of ancient Greece, he *also* conducted enquêtes into prison conditions on behalf of the GIP. Yet, as various interpreters point out, these enquêtes derived from an immediately Maoist political context.[2] As indicated in the previous chapter, Maoist groups of various stripes in France in the late 1960s and early 1970s abided by Mao Zedong's injunction to investigate social conditions in order to know them, learn from them, and eventually change them. And the GIP drew many of its members from the most famous of these groups, the GP. There were therefore direct and palpable connections between the embrace of investigations in the GIP and the more general Maoist deployment of investigations.

Foucault's simultaneous engagement with enquêtes on different registers has not gone unnoticed, but it has not drawn sustained attention either,[3] and it raises the following questions: What exactly was the relationship between the "inquiries" Foucault theorized at such length and the "investigations" he undertook with such tireless commitment during the *same* period? And what point should *we* take away from his simultaneous engagements with these enquêtes? These questions have yet to be formulated, much less tackled, even though there is a lively literature on the implications of Foucault's participation in the investigations of the GIP.[4]

My contention is that a stark but bridgeable gap separates Foucault's analyses of enquêtes from his practical deployment of enquêtes. In his lectures, Foucault disclosed the origins of the enquête in various forms of political power, first in tyranny in Greek antiquity and then in the administrative and judicial practices of the nascent medieval state. Strikingly, however, he barely touched on enquêtes as weapons of resistance to the exercise of power. By contrast, in his activities on behalf of the GIP, Foucault sought to harness enquêtes as precisely such weapons without even hinting at their broader political origins. What we have then are two markedly different presentations of the enquête as we traverse the difficult terrain from Foucault's theory to his practice.

We can certainly find ways of minimizing the gap between these different presentations. The investigations that Foucault undertook for the GIP retained a question and answer format central to the inquiry, and his strident emphasis on the latter as a "form" rather than "content" of knowledge accommodated polyvalent uses.[5] In his lectures, Foucault also gestured to an alternative deployment of investigations among early nineteenth-century workers, and elsewhere he identified this deployment as a source of inspiration for the investigations of the GIP. In the following pages, I elaborate on this important connection through little-known sources that Foucault may have used. But I have no intention of simply closing the gap between his enquêtes in theory and practice. What I want to do, rather, is dwell on the gap itself to tease out its necessarily implicit lesson, namely, that the very practice of the enquête is open, dynamic, and reversible rather than closed and static. In elaborating this point, I also reflect critically on Foucault's oblique concerns about the enquête in his lectures to distinguish between the *knowledge contents* produced through an investigation and the *effects* of *the process* of producing these contents for collective political subjectivity. This distinction is altogether crucial if we are to get away from a facile problematic of failure and evaluate the historical experience of investigations in radical political struggles in a more comprehensive manner.

Foucault's Genealogy of the Enquête

Foucault in his lectures at the Collège de France and elsewhere from March 1971 to May 1973 brought his scholarly acumen to bear on the inquiry as a form of power-knowledge centered on extracting and accumulating knowledge to establish the truth as fact. He depicted the inquiry as a procedure that extracts this knowledge by posing a whole series of questions starting with some variant of the question "Who did what?"[6] In the main, his genealogy of this procedure entailed two somewhat disjointed moves: one that traced the inquiry as far back as the classical period of ancient Greece and another that traced its reappearance and subsequent flourishing back to the administrative and judicial practices of the nascent medieval state. Foucault's genealogy of the inquiry was also inextricably bound up with his genealogies of measure, the test, and the examination as the other major power-knowledge mechanisms in Western societies. He tended to draw out the specificity of the inquiry by way of comparisons with these other power-knowledge mechanisms. His discussion of inquiry thus belonged to a much larger historical and theoretical backdrop.

In this larger context, Foucault stressed the birth of the inquiry in one text in particular, namely, Sophocles's play *Oedipus the King*.[7] Crucially, he cast Oedipus as a figure of a tyrannical form of power-knowledge, rather than as a bearer of ignorance, and he insisted that this form of power-knowledge is intimately related to the inquiry as both a condition and effect. Foucault suggested that Oedipus exemplifies the figure of the tyrant not only because he conquers power and exercises it so as to steer the city of Thebes away from dangers but also because he bases his conquest of power on a particular type of knowledge.[8] This knowledge involves finding answers to the riddle of the Sphinx *all on his own.*[9] More generally, it entails learning on one's own about "what happened and is happening" through witnesses and even witnesses to witnesses.[10] For Foucault, it is this form of power-knowledge that leads Oedipus to opt for the inquiry *over* oracular consultation to figure out who defiled Thebes by murdering King Laius. Oedipus's inquiry starts by questioning persons to determine eyewitnesses to the murder and culminates in questioning these eyewitnesses to obtain testimonies from them in the form of recollections, if need be under the threat of torture.[11] The inquiry at its point of emergence for Foucault thus encompassed a whole series of questions directed toward others to establish the fact of a crime against a deeply coercive backdrop. Foucault elaborated on the contents of these questions: "Who killed? When and in what circumstances was the murder carried out? Who witnessed it? Where is he now? Did you see what you know, or did you hear about it, and from whom? Is the man I am confronting you with, the man you see here, really the man you saw previously?"[12] If all of these questions produce the "tyrant's knowledge,"[13] Foucault claimed that the inquiry as a whole has the paradoxical function in Sophocles of ultimately *discrediting* the tyrannical form of power-knowledge. The inquiry reveals this form as unnecessary by matching the human and the divine, or, more precisely, knowledge of the slave who witnessed the murder of King Laius with the prophecies of the seer Teiresias who identified Oedipus as the murderer.[14] "Inquiry," as Foucault explained, "leads to what was foreseen by divination" and unintentionally discloses the necessity of human laws based on divine decrees.[15] He added that "between knowledge conveyed by oracles and knowledge reported by regular inquiry, there is no longer any place for 'royal' knowledge, for a *gnōmē* that can solve riddles and save cities without calling on anyone."[16] In demonstrating that the king who set out to know only produced a superfluous knowledge, Sophocles, in Foucault's reading, inaugurated the progressive dissolution of the bond of power and knowledge. He thus laid the groundwork for the propagation of the "myth" of "an antinomy between knowledge and power" in Western societies.[17]

In a curious twist to his argument, Foucault maintained that "the history of the birth of the inquiry" nevertheless "remained forgotten and was lost" for centuries after antiquity, being rediscovered only in the late

Middle Ages.[18] He did not offer an elaborate explanation for this loss, observing only that "the Greek method of inquiry had remained stationary, had not achieved the founding of a rational knowledge capable of infinite development."[19] What existed for him in lieu of the inquiry was the test as a judicial practice derived from ancient Germanic law. The test settled disputes between two individuals not by establishing the truth but by determining who was right on the basis of his strength.[20] Foucault insisted that the disappearance of the test and the reappearance of the inquiry only took place through the appropriation and reconfiguration of judicial practices by the nascent medieval state in the twelfth and thirteenth centuries.[21] However, even these transformations did not take place ex nihilo, according to Foucault. The "second birth of the inquiry," as he called it, was rooted in administrative practices of the emergent state during and after the Carolingian Empire, on the one hand, and in the ecclesiastical and administrative practices of the church in the early Middle Ages, on the other hand.[22] In the former, the inquiry involved a meeting between notables convened by the representative of political power to voluntarily decide on how to resolve a problem through sworn testimonies;[23] in the latter, the inquiry took the form of a visit by a bishop to his dioceses and parishes to question those in the know "about what had happened in his absence" and,[24] in particular, "whether there had been a crime, what crime it was, and who had committed it."[25] Still, Foucault maintained that authorities only gravitated definitively toward the inquiry as emergent monarchical states sought to control judicial disputes to preserve their accumulation of wealth and arms in the middle to latter half of the twelfth century.[26] These states introduced sweeping changes into judicial procedures, including the transformation of the sovereign into a victim of an infraction understood as an offense against the laws of the state and the appearance of the prosecutor as his representative.[27] And these innovations undermined the test. As Foucault explained, the king and his prosecutor could not run the risk of failing the test and, consequently, "losing their own lives or their own possessions every time a crime was committed."[28] The inquiry offered a viable alternative to authorities by allowing the prosecutor to facilitate a judgment about the guilt or innocence of a person *without* incurring losses, owing precisely to a consolidation of power relations in favor of the prosecution.[29] The inquiry had the additional advantage of enabling the prosecutor to actualize a crime caught in the act or a "flagrant offense," as it was called, by obtaining testimonies from persons in the know about exactly what had happened.[30]

Apart from explaining how the inquiry reemerged in Western societies after a long lull, Foucault conveyed a more general view of this procedure based on an elaboration of its functional attributes. He emphasized that the inquiry had as its overall goal the restoration of public order in response to a disorder. "The inquiry," Foucault told his auditors, "is the operator of a restoration of order from something that can be an injury but can also be something else: an irregularity."[31] The prosecutor undertook an inquiry by asking a defendant questions to which the latter was *obliged* to respond. The defendant either knew or did not know the answers to the questions.[32] If he ultimately did not know these answers, the prosecutor directed his questions to others. If the defendant confessed, on the other hand, the inquiry came to an end, as it was deemed an overriding success.[33] What emerged from this procedure in the penal system was the "discovery of a truth" based on testimonies from witnesses,[34] and the subsequent transmission of this truth in writing to a judge bearing the responsibility for a decision.[35]

Overall, Foucault depicted the inquiry as a technique to establish the truth as fact through the extraction and accumulation of knowledge. As this technique both sprang from and facilitated the exercise of power, it was "a form of power-knowledge."[36] Indeed, Foucault stressed that because the inquiry consisted of a "form" rather than "content" of knowledge in particular,[37] it was pliable enough to be taken up in other domains of knowledge from the thirteenth to eighteenth centuries. Some of these domains, such as economics and statistics, were manifestly related to political power, while others, such as the natural sciences, were less obviously related to political power.[38] The inquiry thus circulated well beyond its origins for centuries after its second birth. Lest there be any doubt, Foucault also insisted that the inquiry had not gone away in his own present. To the contrary, he claimed that it remained "an integral part of Western justice (even up to our own day)," in spite of his much larger emphasis on the examination as the form of knowledge correlative to the generalization of the exercise of disciplinary power since the eighteenth century.[39]

However, with one exception, which is discussed at great length in the following section, Foucault stopped short of suggesting that the inquiry circulated as a form of resistance in popular struggles, even as he concerned himself to no small degree with these struggles in the past and present.[40] Quite the contrary, what stands out in his genealogy is the origin of the inquiry first in tyranny and then in the medieval state. Foucault himself implored his readers not to "forget" the "political origin" of the enquête and "its link with the birth of states and of monarchical sovereignty."[41]

But we might pause to ask: Why the urgency behind this plea? In other words, *who exactly* ran the risk of forgetting the origins of the inquiry in the birth of states? Moreover, what analytical and political differences arise from the disclosure of these origins? While Foucault directed his plea above to a broad audience consisting of those in the history of science and elsewhere who deem the inquiry a purely disinterested procedure with no history of relations to techniques of power in general and political power in particular, it would have had a different kind of critical resonance among former GIP members and Maoists. After all, *they* had embraced the enquête as an oppositional, if not liberating, practice. It therefore would have come as a deeply unsettling surprise for them to learn that their cherished practice of enquête had its origins in an "authoritarian search for truth" going back to the birth of states.[42] Yet it would be too hasty of us to conclude that Foucault was simply condemning this practice by disclosing its sullied origins. He was up to something else that begins to appear clearly if we expand the scope of our analysis to take into account his political practices.

Foucault's Practice of the Enquête

Foucault participated in enquêtes on behalf of the GIP shortly before he began exploring them in his lectures. His first mention of the enquêtes in his lectures dates from March 17, 1971, whereas his involvement in the enquêtes of the GIP dates from at least as early as its public founding on February 8, 1971.[43] To understand the specificity of these enquêtes, it helps to draw out the historical context leading to the formation of the GIP. The GIP channeled a mobilization around prisons that took place in response to the arrest and imprisonment of hundreds of GP militants after the governmental proscription of their organization in May 1970.[44] This proscription belonged to a larger strategy on the part of the French state of repressing extra-parliamentary leftist organizations that had flourished in the aftermath of May 1968. Yet this effort backfired to the extent that it suddenly transformed the prison system into a prominent site of political struggle for a radical left that had not viewed it as such a site. It is in this context of mobilizations around the prison system by and on behalf of the imprisoned Maoists that the idea of investigating the prisons gained traction. A cell of the GP created after its governmental proscription, the Organization of Political Prisoners (OPP), first promulgated this idea as part of its larger effort to enable imprisoned GP militants to obtain the exercise of rights inherent in the status of political prisoners.[45] The OPP produced a report on the conditions in the prison system.[46] It highlighted the need for an investigation of prison labor in particular at the very end of the report,[47] which appears to have dated from September 1970.[48] A newly re-created radical organization, Red Aid (SR), had plans to launch an investigation of the prisons in January 1971 as part of its much larger effort to defend imprisoned GP militants.[49] But it was the OPP that laid the groundwork for the investigations of the still nonexistent GIP. From the beginning of December 1970, the OPP sought to mobilize intellectuals to publicly support a hunger strike among imprisoned GP militants scheduled to begin in mid-January 1971. In keeping with this goal, one OPP member, Daniel Defert, proposed that the OPP form a commission of inquiry into prisons headed by his partner, Foucault. The OPP enthusiastically embraced this proposal with a view to drawing well-known intellectuals into publicity-generating confrontations with the police at the gates of prisons. Two other militants, Jacques-Alain Miller and Judith Miller, approached Foucault on behalf of the GP about setting up a commission of inquiry into prisons modeled on senatorial commissions into prisons in the United States. The proposal appealed to Foucault because it cohered with his focus on the voices of the excluded in his preceding work on madness and confinement. A group of around twenty persons composed mainly of doctors, lawyers, and intellectuals then gathered to discuss the idea of a commission of inquiry at Foucault's residence at the end of December 1970.[50] Yet this idea did not survive the meeting, which Foucault proceeded to steer in a completely different direction. He rejected the idea of a commission of inquiry and proposed instead a Prisons Information Group (GIP) based on unofficial investigations conducted in the prisons to facilitate the voices of prisoners themselves.[51] What appears to have concerned Foucault about the notion of a commission of inquiry was that it would have operated within traditional political parameters. In the words of Defert, such a commission would necessarily have had "state power" as its "only interlocutor" and "only target."[52] What nonetheless survived of the original plan for a commission of inquiry was a questionnaire for prisoners that had been prepared with the help of prisoners by the lawyer

Christine Martineau and the philosopher Danielle Rancière.[53] While the majority of the participants in the meeting at Foucault's residence expressed doubts about the ability to circulate the questionnaire among prisoners and authenticate the responses, they agreed on the overall need for a questionnaire. Among other advantages, the uniformity of the questions in the questionnaire was seen as facilitating a comparative perspective on conditions across different prisons.[54] It was through such deliberations that the nascent GIP settled on the questionnaire as the basis of its investigations. However, given the general lack of agreement during the first meeting at Foucault's residence, there was never any kind of follow-up meeting, and the GIP ended up shifting the recruitment of its members to "an entirely different social base: students, militants of the GP, of Red Aid or other political groups."[55]

The investigations of the GIP were contemporaneous with the Maoist investigations of the UCFML explored in the previous chapter. Yet they differed radically in their objectives and methods. The investigations of the GIP were undertaken to heighten public intolerance of the prison system through the voices of prisoners themselves rather than to explore the prospects for the foundation of a new party through militant self-testing in the countryside. The GIP specified this objective in the announcement of its first investigation on March 15, 1971.[56] In its words, "Our investigation is not made to accumulate knowledge but to *increase our intolerance and turn it into an active intolerance*."[57] As this declaration was oriented to the public, the second "our" here was a reference not only to GIP militants and prisoners but also to the public at large. Compared with the investigations of the UCFML, the investigations of the GIP aimed to instantiate a *different* kind of collective political subjectivity, one more diffuse and completely unencumbered by the party form. What is more, the GIP distinguished its investigations not only from the concern with amassing knowledge in sociological investigations but also from the weighty task of consciousness-raising so central to the Marxist tradition of investigations. For the GIP, prisoners simply had no need to "'*become conscious*'" because their "consciousness of oppression" was "perfectly clear."[58] The problem was not so much a *lack* of consciousness among prisoners as that "the current system" denied them "the means of expression and organization."[59] The GIP therefore gave itself the task of facilitating the self-expression and organization of the prisoners rather than the marxisant task of raising their consciousness.

The questionnaires used for the first investigation of the GIP dealt with a wide range of aspects of prison life, including visits to the prison, censorship of mail, prison rules and prisoners' rights, material and hygienic conditions in the cells, duration of walks and the space for them, quantity and quality of the food, availability and cost of canteen items, extent and use of leisure time, compensation for work, quality of medical care, and severity of discipline.[60] The final item in the questionnaire even solicited reflections from prisoners about the investigation and questionnaire themselves.[61] In February 1971, Foucault also penned a separate statement introducing the questionnaire to prisoners and their family members.[62] In the statement, which accompanied the distribution of the questionnaires, Foucault insisted that a public opinion campaign to produce durable changes regarding the prisons depends on information from prisoners and their family members. He asked them to send their completed questionnaires to the address of the GIP, which also happened to be his personal address at 285 rue de Vaugirard in Paris.[63]

However, circulating the questionnaires involved very serious challenges, as skeptics at the founding meeting of the GIP had anticipated. Members of the GIP could not simply go to prisons à la Mao to convene fact-finding meetings with prisoners because prisons were not open to the public, and there were all kinds of limitations on the flow of information between prisons and the outside world, including the rampant censorship of mail and the restriction of visitation rights mainly to lawyers and family members. In some cases, the prison administration even employed highly restrictive definitions of the family. For instance, visitation rights were granted to parents but not siblings.[64] The GIP got around these severe limitations by distributing questionnaires to former prisoners, penitentiary personnel, and the families of prisoners.[65] GIP militants distributed questionnaires to the family members of prisoners as they lined up for visits at the entries to prisons during visiting hours. In the absence of these lines, GIP militants engaged the family members of prisoners in other spaces, such as cafés and buses.[66] The geographical scope of the distribution of questionnaires grew with the publicity for the questionnaires. GIP militants initially distributed the questionnaires at the entries to prisons in the Paris region before the appearance of a completed questionnaire in a publication with a national scope, *Esprit*, facilitated its distribution in the provinces.[67] Foucault himself distributed these questionnaires to family members lining up for visits at the entry to La Santé prison in Paris.[68]

But even the act of distributing the questionnaires outside the prisons entailed its own difficulties. Defert recounts an episode in which a family member was initially reluctant to engage GIP militants, no doubt because these militants appeared initially as complete outsiders with unclear agendas.[69] GIP militants set out to allay such concerns among family members by stressing that their investigation was an "*intolerance-investigation*" rather than a "sociological investigation" or "curiosity-investigation."[70] The investigation was, in other words, a way of demonstrating solidarity with the prisoners (and their family members) rather than simply treating them as objects of knowledge. GIP militants also ran the risk of police monitoring and intimidation as they distributed questionnaires to the families.[71] The families in turn had to overcome certain difficulties in merely accepting the questionnaires. In a document written on behalf of the GIP, Defert nicely sums up these difficulties:

> It's not an easy act for the families of prisoners to accept the questionnaire, to speak in a loud voice about the prison before or after the visit, to participate in meetings. It's to accept a grouping with people who do not have loved ones in prison. It's to accept it in spite of the police checkpoint and threats. It's to accept it on a political basis. It's a political act.[72]

Family members experienced other difficulties as they took on the task of transmitting the questions to loved ones in prison. They were not allowed to hand the questionnaires to their loved ones or even speak about the questionnaires during visiting hours. Family members therefore had to transmit the contents of the questionnaires in a more illicit manner. Defert recalls an episode in which a mother copied the questions on scraps of paper and read them quickly to her son while a guard turned his back on them. The guard eventually caught them in the act of communicating questions and answers, and the son was reported and punished with time in solitary. Yet, even after his punishment, the son wanted to continue answering the questionnaire, which he completed with the help of his mother in two months.[73]

The completed questionnaires were sent to the address of the GIP listed at the very top of the questionnaire. Members of the GIP met there with former prisoners and prisoners' family members to select answers from the completed questionnaires for publication.[74] GIP members were especially concerned about verifying the responses they received for the obvious reason that false information could lead to a loss of their credibility.[75] However, as Defert acknowledges, the GIP did not possess a lot of means of either verifying these responses or identifying its informants.[76]

The GIP resolved this vexing problem by (successfully) gambling on the believability of the responses that aroused its own suspicions. In this regard, Defert recalls that the GIP was initially reluctant to publish the response of a prisoner from Toul. The prisoner claimed that another prisoner had been attached in solitary confinement to a sheet metal bed with a hole for urinating and defecating for a period of more than a week. GIP members simply found the account too outrageous to believe. Yet Defert claims that, at Foucault's prompting, they went ahead and published it on the grounds that they had believed and published other responses by prisoners.[77] The GIP ultimately felt vindicated in this decision. The revolt at the Toul prison in 1971 brought to light precisely the practices described by the prisoner.[78]

All of the selected answers to the questionnaire were eventually published in a report titled *Investigation in 20 Prisons* in May 1971.[79] The GIP also conducted other investigations and published the results of these investigations in various reports belonging to a numbered "Intolerable" series over the succeeding months and years.[80] However, as Foucault appears to have been most heavily involved in the investigation culminating in *Investigation in 20 Prisons*, we will focus our attention on this report in particular.

Before proceeding to the contents of *Investigation in 20 Prisons*, let us dwell on its form because this form stands out in the history of investigations in radical political struggles even as it draws implicitly from other contributions to this history. *Investigation in 20 Prisons* opens with a preface anonymously authored by Foucault under the collective name of the GIP. In this regard, Foucault followed a convention practiced by Marx in his questionnaire. However, there was one noteworthy difference between them: Marx anonymously introduced a *published questionnaire* that *never* yielded *published* results whereas Foucault anonymously introduced a *published report* based on completed questionnaires. In their anonymous declarations, Marx and Foucault nonetheless revealed a point of affinity: they appealed to the *self-activity* of the investigated against exploitation and oppression, respectively. Just as Marx stressed that "only" workers "can energetically apply the healing remedies for the social ills to which they are a prey,"[81] Foucault insisted that "it is up to" the newly expanding strata of the oppressed to "*take charge of the struggle that will put an end to oppression being exercised.*"[82] It was, in short, the *investigated themselves* who would act politically on the knowledge *they* generated to change *their* conditions.

The singularity of the form of *Investigation in 20 Prisons* begins to appear more readily in the substantive sections of the report consisting of responses from prisoners. What is striking from the first of these sections is that the GIP blurred the distinction between the preparatory materials of its investigation and the more synthetic presentation of the results of these materials. It reproduced two completed questionnaires *in* the report to elucidate its method of investigation. One of these questionnaires is from a prisoner at La Santé and the other is from a prisoner at Province.[83] The GIP nonetheless left its decision to publish these completed questionnaires over others entirely unclear. It may be that the responses in them were more consistent and robust than the responses in other questionnaires. Whatever the rationale for the reproduction of the completed questionnaires in *Investigation in 20 Prisons*, their inclusion broke with the tendency in many other investigations in the history of the practice to efface preparatory materials from the published presentation of the final results. The second major blurring in *Investigation in 20 Prisons* concerns a theme that figured prominently in previous chapters, namely, the distinction between the narrative and the questionnaire. The GIP blurred this distinction by including two narratives that address the themes from the questionnaire in its report. One of the narratives is from a prisoner at La Santé and the other is from a prisoner at Nevers.[84] The GIP claimed that these narratives follow the order of questions in the questionnaire, but it takes only one look at them to realize that they deviate to varying degrees from that order. The GIP also blurred the distinction between narratives and questionnaires in another way. It published responses to the questionnaire that assumed narrative qualities rather than the more punctual qualities of succinct responses to precise questions.[85]

Measured purely in terms of accumulating and publishing responses, the first investigation of the GIP was a resounding success. Prisoners completed enough questionnaires for the answers to them to be selected and published in a dense report. This success stands in marked contrast to the stark failure of some investigations in the Marxist tradition to merely elicit the writings of workers, much less publish them. We must therefore ask why the investigation of the GIP succeeded where some Marxist investigations failed, especially because the GIP did not enjoy the benefit of any kind of direct access to then current prisoners. This question is very difficult to answer because these investigations did not necessarily occupy the same time and space. Part of the answer to the question may reside in the relative simplicity of the questions in the GIP questionnaires. These questions were not abstract or excessively demanding, no doubt owing to the involvement of former prisoners in their formulation. Indeed, they were straightforward enough to elicit a simple "yes" or "no" in a tremendous number of cases. The different temporalities of prison life and factory life may also explain the success of the GIP and failure of some Marxist investigations. Both factories and prisons belong to a disciplinary matrix of institutions that captures and uses the time of individuals, as Foucault never tired of repeating in the early 1970s.[86] Yet, to put the matter bluntly, prisoners *had* time to fill out the questionnaires. Or, more precisely, they had an excess of their captured and regimented time to fill out the questionnaires even under highly restrictive conditions. Workers, on the other hand, filled in their so-called free time after the end of the working day with the pursuit of other activities.[87] Paradoxically, then, prisoners may have been better positioned to fill out the questionnaires than factory workers. Finally, organization may have accounted for the success of the GIP investigations and failure of some Marxist investigations. The circulation and completion of the GIP questionnaires were premised on ramified networks of confidants, including loved ones. These networks simply did not exist in the case of some Marxist investigations.

The actual contents of the hundreds of anonymous responses in *Investigation in 20 Prisons* vary considerably. Apart from responses consisting of a simple "yes" or "no," there are responses that involve varying degrees of elaboration about the fine details of prison life. These details range from the use of chamber pots in the cells due to the lack of plumbing,[88] to descriptions of prisoners in solitary tied to pipes and physically attacked by guards,[89] to an account of prisoners groped by guards while standing nude in the hallway for searches.[90] Taken together, however, the responses in the report vividly document not only the harsh material conditions in the prisons but also the extreme violence and petty humiliations inflicted on prisoners, not to mention the desperation and grim absurdity of life in the prisons. To briefly illustrate the magnitude of the latter phenomena, we can defer to the response of one prisoner from Fresnes. This prisoner recalled that prisoners at Fresnes had ingested "nails, razor blades, glass, metal buttons" to commit suicide.[91] The prisoner went on to recount that doctors at the Fresnes hospital had extracted these objects and collected them in jars with the intention of displaying them at a medical conference but that the warden had circulated a memo declaring that all objects found in the bellies of prisoners are the property of the prison administration, as if the problem merely resided in an embarrassing infringement of the property rights of the prison administration.[92]

Such revelations from the enquêtes of the GIP certainly contrasted with the core presentation of the enquête in Foucault's lectures. He introduced the former as weapons of resistance in political struggles over intolerable conditions in the prison without even hinting at their origins in the birth of states, no doubt because the latter move would have been unnecessary. As Foucault declared in his anonymous preface to *Investigation in 20 Prisons*, "These investigations are not intended to improve, soften or render more bearable an oppressive power. They are intended to attack it where it is exercised under a different name—that of justice, technique, knowledge, objectivity."[93] What is more, the GIP undertook its investigations without any state sanction. Indeed, the investigations were outright illegal. Based on the synopsis above, we can also see that differences burst through the otherwise similar forms taken by Foucault's practical deployment of enquêtes and the enquête in judicial procedures that he analyzed at such length. If both types of enquêtes extracted knowledge by directing questions toward others to obtain answers from them, the contents of these questions and answers differed sharply owing to markedly different, if not opposed, objectives. The GIP relied for its investigations on written questionnaires rather than on initially verbalized questions and answers. These questionnaires were used to heighten intolerance of a state institution, the prison, rather than to incriminate a person suspected of a crime. Accordingly, the questionnaires revolved around the solicitation of the fine details of what makes the prison intolerable rather than who committed a crime. The questions were also framed through the collective anonymity of the GIP, rather than through a prosecutor, and the answers were presented in a similarly anonymous fashion to protect the identity of prisoners. Finally, the knowledge extracted through the questionnaires consisted mainly of facts from prisoners in writing, but these facts were selectively publicized rather than transmitted to a judge responsible for a decision about the guilt or innocence of a person. In other words, the GIP investigations yielded a knowledge for the mobilization of popular resistance to the prison rather than a knowledge for the state administration of justice.

Stepping back a bit in Foucault's genealogy of the enquête, we can also ask about the broader implications of his reading of Oedipus for his understanding of the enquêtes of the GIP. It is altogether striking that not long after Foucault began participating in these enquêtes, he turned his attention to the enquête launched by Oedipus, as if his activities in the streets of Paris were surreptitiously animating his research agenda in the lecture halls of the Collège and elsewhere. It stands to reason that Foucault sought to critically explore a popular practice among radical organizations that he had fully embraced. If the lesson of Oedipus's enquête was that knowledge could turn out to be politically superfluous, then it seems that Foucault may well have been raising implicit questions about the political effects of the knowledge that the GIP sought to constitute through its enquêtes. He certainly rationalized these enquêtes on grounds that the public did *not* know a great deal about what was happening in the prison system *from the perspective of prisoners* because of the paucity of published information about this system from their perspective.[94] And, like Oedipus, Foucault and other members of the GIP set out to figure out what was happening. But would their collective quest for knowledge about the prison system turn out to be a politically superfluous endeavor? What, in other words, would be the political effects of this knowledge?

Foucault was not alone in raising such questions. In chapter 2, we saw that V. I. Lenin arrived at the harsh and sobering conclusion that the knowledge constituted through his own workers' inquiries *was* superfluous because official sources of knowledge afford a more comprehensive view of working conditions in factories. Foucault himself could not have had definitive answers to questions about the superfluity of the investigations of the GIP at the time of his lectures on Oedipus from 1971 to 1972 because these investigations were still ongoing. However, Foucault's reading of Oedipus hints at a way of critically assessing these investigations as well as other militant investigations.

It behooves us to hasten to stress that this way of assessing these investigations is problematic. While the question of the political effects of the knowledge constituted through investigations is no doubt important, the focus on the already constituted character of this knowledge implicit in suspicions about its superfluity can too easily take our attention away from the political effects generated through its *process of production*. In other words, what were the political effects of merely posing questions to subalterns about their conditions and struggles, regardless of whether they even answered these questions? How did the questions themselves impact the way these subalterns envisioned themselves and their world? Beyond the whole matter of the political effects of knowledge constituted through investigations, there is the matter of the political effects of the *process* of *producing* this knowledge. The formulation and communication of questions figure centrally in this process, and questions have lives of their own, regardless of whether they yield written and verbalized answers from their recipients. Of course, discerning the political effects of questions is no straightforward matter because questions are neither inherently liberating nor inherently constraining. Questions may be experienced as burdensome, annoying, absurd, invasive, painful, and even terrifying.[95] They may be ignored, tolerated, ridiculed, or rejected by their intended recipients. Questions may also be forgotten with the passing of time. But they may also linger in the minds of their recipients and others to induce doubts and disquiet with political ramifications. Carefully framed questions may, in short, incite the political imagination in certain contexts. It is this less tangible possibility that gets effaced as soon as we focus exclusively on the knowledge already constituted through investigations as *the* measure of their success or failure.

Crossing the Gap: Workers' Inquiries

Beyond general questions about the enquêtes of the GIP raised by Foucault's reading of Oedipus, there is a very concrete point of articulation between his enquêtes in theory and practice. It resides in his repeated gestures to *another* history of investigations, namely, the history of nineteenth-century workers' inquiries. We can ascertain a sense of the novelty and import of these gestures if we refer to how other prominent members of the GIP construed the sources of inspiration for the practice of investigation in the group. To make this move, it helps to recall the broader historical and political context of radical political organizations in France in the late 1960s and early 1970s. Throughout a period of roughly three and a half years *prior* to the creation of the GIP, various Marxist organizations had undertaken investigations in France by drawing explicitly from Marx's questionnaire and Mao's investigation. We addressed the reactivation of Mao's investigation in France in some detail in the previous chapter. As we saw there, this reactivation tended to concentrate in factories and the countryside, but it also spilled out into less conventional institutional spaces (for a classical revolutionary orientation), such as the psychiatric hospital. Obviously, the GIP participated in this extension of the investigation to such spaces by concentrating on the prison.

Even before the creation of the GIP, however, Maoists were not the only ones engaged in investigations in France. The radical periodical *Cahiers de Mai*, which sprang up in the immediate aftermath of May 1968 and lasted into the early 1970s,[96] offered a fairly elaborate theorization of workers' inquiry in an anonymous article titled "The Political Role of the Inquiry" in its July 1970 issue.[97] Opening with an epigraph from the introduction to Marx's 1880 questionnaire for French workers that had also appeared in the opening to Dario Lanzardo's dense analysis of the questionnaire,[98] the article sought to clarify the overall political approach of *Cahiers de Mai* by elucidating the practice of workers' inquiry in particular. It did so by stridently opposing its conception of this practice to the more commonplace sociological version of workers' inquiry prominent at universities: the latter placed the investigator in a position *exterior* to objects of study, whereas the former revolved around "the active participation, from beginning to end, of workers with which it is done" *and* resulted in an "article" produced "under their collective control and under their effective direction."[99] Workers' inquiry, as construed here by *Cahiers de Mai*, thus entailed the *dissolution* of hierarchies in the production of knowledge.[100] Beyond this general characteristic, *Cahiers de Mai* spelled out four theoretical "functions" of workers' inquiry: first, "giving speech to revolutionary workers in firms" rather than relying on information "ultra-manipulated as much by the bourgeoisie as by the traditional organizations of the working class"; second, "grouping together militant workers around the inquiry" so that they *self*-organize on the basis of the experience of producing an article together; third, using the article "as an instrument of propaganda and agitation" within the firm and between firms from different industries; and, finally, "diminishing the segregation between militants outside of firms and militant workers" by enabling the former to respond to the demands of the latter.[101] The article went on to stress that the realization of these functions depends in its turn on militant practices formed in struggle rather than on practices superimposed from without. In its cautionary words: "There is no royal road to conducting an inquiry, but a certain practice to acquire."[102] Ultimately, *Cahiers de Mai* formulated workers' inquiry as a means of "consciousness-raising and organization" through workers themselves rather than through militants outside firms.[103]

Cahiers de Mai conveys a strong sense of the extent to which the Marxist investigation circulated as a practice that elicited careful reflections among its practitioners. In a testimony of the sheer extent to which it circulated among radical organizations in France in the late 1960s and early 1970s, two founding members of the GIP, who were tasked with the composition of the questionnaires for its first investigation, insist in no uncertain terms that the group drew from different variants of the Marxist investigation for its practice of investigation. One GP militant and founding member of the GIP, Rancière, maintains that the GIP inherited its model of investigations from the Maoism of the GP, and she even credits herself with having quietly introduced this model into the group at its founding meeting.[104] For Rancière, this model performed a kind of refracting function, as we saw in the previous chapter. It basically consisted of interviewing workers at the gates of factories to gather information from them, recording this information in notebooks, and then reflecting this information back to the workers through pamphlets in order to "liberate" their "speech."[105] Another GP militant and founding member of the GIP, Defert, suggests that the whole focus of the questionnaires of the GIP derived from Marx's lengthy questionnaire for French workers about their working conditions. Defert maintains that the GIP drew inspiration for its questionnaires from the meticulous attention to material conditions in Marx's questionnaire even as he expresses reservations about the relative significance of the focus on material conditions for the prisoners themselves.[106] In his concise and revealing words, "Our model was Marx's workers' inquiry."[107] For Defert, the focus on the materiality of the prisons inspired by Marx amounted to one way for the GIP to express its seriousness to prisoners.[108]

Of course, Defert and Rancière were not the only GIP members tasked with the composition of the questionnaire for its first investigation. The sociologist Jacques Donzelot and Martineau were also given this task.[109] The sociologist Jean-Claude Passeron even reviewed the first GIP questionnaire after Rancière and Martineau had composed a draft of it.[110] Former prisoners were also involved in the composition of the questions in the questionnaire.[111] There were thus many sources for the formulation of the questionnaire, and there was even a kind of co-research in its formulation akin to the co-research debated among members of the *Quaderni Rossi* collective. However, the statements of Defert and Rancière attest to the general weight of Marxism in the formulation of the practice of the investigation in the GIP. Taken together, they suggest that the GIP not only drew the investigation from a broadly Marxist political milieu but also fused together different sources of the investigation in the Marxist tradition to facilitate the speech of prisoners about the materiality of the prison.

Foucault certainly did not deny that these sources served as the immediate backdrop to the practice of investigations in the GIP. To do so would have been strangely out of sync with his marxisant orientation at the time.[112] But Foucault's pronouncements peeled back a historical layer, so to speak, suggesting that investigations were *already* practiced in nineteenth-century proletarian struggles. He gestured to this history in various documents from 1971 to 1972. Foucault alluded to it as early as his preface to *Investigation in 20 Prisons*. In the preface, he identified workers' inquiries into their own conditions in the nineteenth century as a source of inspiration for the GIP in its struggle against a far-reaching political oppression in the aftermath of May 1968.[113] In an interview with high school students from November of the same year, Foucault referred to nineteenth-century workers' inquiries to suggest that they yielded a knowledge *excluded* by "official knowledge."[114] He returned to these same inquiries in his Collège course from 1971 to 1972, *Théories et institutions pénales*. In the final lecture of this course, delivered on March 8, 1972, Foucault went so far as to *oppose* workers' inquiries to administrative inquiries. Turning to possible avenues of research into "struggles over inquiries, for or against the constitution of a surplus knowledge," Foucault mentioned "the struggles of workers to assure themselves their own inquiries, to speak in their own name, *against* administrative inquiries."[115] His reference to surplus knowledge was clearly a play on Marx's surplus value, suggesting that the stakes in political struggles are as much about the production and appropriation of this knowledge as of the production and appropriation of surplus value.

In their deeply informative commentary, Philippe Artières, Laurent Quéro, and Michelle Zancarini-Fournel also identify nineteenth-century workers' inquiries as a source of inspiration for the investigations of the GIP. But they go on in the very same sentence to reduce this "tradition" of nineteenth-century workers' inquiries *to* Marx's "A Workers' Inquiry," as if the latter exhausts the former.[116] Whatever else might be said, Foucault himself did not make this equation in any of his remarks above. He did not even refer explicitly to Marx's questionnaire. His disparate remarks above thus open up the way for a consideration of workers' inquiries in the nineteenth century *beyond* Marx's questionnaire. Unfortunately, however, Foucault's discussions of these nineteenth-century workers' inquiries not only remain fragmentary and underdeveloped, but they also do not point explicitly to sources that offer a more robust account of the history of these inquiries. This lack of detail may explain the conflation of nineteenth-century workers' inquiries with Marx's questionnaire in Artières, Quéro, and Zancarini-Fournel. Fortunately, the editorial team of the recently published *Théories et institutions pénales* cites a source that *does* offer a more substantive account of these inquiries. That source is Hilde Rigaudias-Weiss's *Les enquêtes ouvrières en France entre 1830 et 1848*, first published in 1936.[117] We are already familiar with this source from previous chapters. It is not surprising that the editorial team of Foucault's newly published course defers to the authority of Rigaudias-Weiss. She is a major figure in the history of workers' inquiries in her own right. Quite apart from publishing a whole book on workers' inquiries in early nineteenth-century France, Rigaudias-Weiss translated Marx's questionnaire into German and undertook a nonmilitant, psychosociological inquiry of German workers during the Weimar Republic on behalf of Erich Fromm at the Frankfurt Institute for Social Research.[118]

The reference to Rigaudias-Weiss's book appears in an endnote to Foucault's quote from *Théories et institutions pénales* on the opposition between workers' inquiries and administrative inquiries.[119] It is not entirely clear from the endnote whether Foucault had actually read Rigaudias-Weiss's little-known book. However, thanks to the meticulous research of Stuart Elden at the Bibliothèque nationale de France, it is now possible to establish that Foucault at least knew about Rigaudias-Weiss's book and intended to consult it because he referred to it in a handwritten bibliography.[120] More importantly for our purposes, the details of her book lend much greater substance to Foucault's point about workers' inquiries into their own conditions. They also speak to the larger literature on workers' inquiries. Rigaudias-Weiss's rich narrative complicates the view in this literature that governments and representatives of the dominant class were mainly responsible for undertaking inquiries into the working class in the first half of the nineteenth century, and that workers only got around to seriously undertaking inquiries into their own conditions in the second half of the nineteenth century under the aegis of socialism.[121] Thiollent explicitly formulates this view, and Artières, Quéro, and Zancarini-Fournel offer a similar perspective, as we have seen.

Though Rigaudias-Weiss somewhat ambiguously traces the first attempt at workers' inquiries in France as far back as 1830,[122] she claims that the momentum for them really took off as the effects of industrial transformations intensified demands from workers for social reforms in the early 1840s. Rigaudias-Weiss recounts that inquiries were undertaken by workers through worker-run newspapers to realize these reforms. As she explains, worker-journalists in charge of the inquiries believed that a detailed description of the social conditions of workers *by* workers would vividly demonstrate the need for social reforms.[123] In her narrative, workers from two newspapers in particular, the Catholic, democratic, and worker-run *L'Atelier* and Étienne Cabet's *Le Populaire*, conducted inquiries by soliciting and then publishing the responses of workers to pleas for information on a wide range of topics, including wages, hygiene, the length of the working day, and the employment of women and children.[124] The inquiries of *L'Atelier* and *Le Populaire* lasted from 1840 to 1843 and from 1841 to 1845, respectively.[125] Rigaudias-Weiss shows that *L'Atelier* in particular was altogether emphatic about launching its inquiries to facilitate the speech of workers in the defense of their interests. She quotes the following excerpt from an October 1840 issue of the newspaper: "'Henceforth, they (the workers) will speak themselves; what is said will be less well said, but it will be true, and we will believe workers speaking in the name of all workers.'"[126] In accordance with this aspiration, the same newspaper criticized the inquiries of economists for seeking information from bosses and foremen rather than from workers.[127]

Rigaudias-Weiss suggests that while the pleas for information in workers' inquiries were straightforward enough to generate precise responses,[128] the inquiries were eventually discontinued for failing to elicit *enough* responses.[129] In a perfectly marxisant fashion, she chalks this failure up to the absence of "preliminary" conditions requisite for workers to obtain a "consciousness of their social situation."[130] Yet her explanation is far too sweeping to be convincing, and it suspends her otherwise scrupulous attention to the detailed reasons why other inquiries failed to elicit the interest of workers. Rigaudias-Weiss's account of the failure of the *official* inquiry of 1848 illustrates this scrupulous attention. Her reasons for this failure range from the prevalence of illiteracy among workers to their fear of reprisals from bosses, and the disbelief among workers that the inquiry would serve their interests.[131] Beyond these reasons, Rigaudias-Weiss emphasizes that the official inquiry relied on questions in questionnaires that were simply too "abstract and general" to be comprehensible to workers.[132] The questions functioned, in other words, to exclude workers.[133] To make this point, Rigaudias-Weiss draws attention to the following exceedingly general and abstract question: "What would be the means of augmenting production and assuring the progressive development of consumption?"[134] Of course, workers' inquiries were exempt from this kind of question for Rigaudias-Weiss because their pleas for information were straightforward. She therefore cannot be faulted for failing to bring her criticism of questions in other investigations to bear on the questions in workers' inquiries. Where Rigaudias-Weiss falls short is in simply not as vigorously exploring the other more detailed reasons for the failure of nineteenth-century workers' inquiries to generate enough responses. She nevertheless succeeds in distilling a dynamic interaction between workers' inquiries and official inquiries. Rigaudias-Weiss acknowledges that workers' inquiries transformed public opinion to the point of precipitating eventually successful calls after the 1848 revolution for an official inquiry into the conditions of the working class.[135] As mentioned in chapter 2, Rigaudias-Weiss even claims that conservative politicians undertook this official inquiry to appease the workers' movement and counter socialist doctrines in particular.[136] Her emphasis on the fluidity and reversibility of inquiries *may* have rubbed off on Foucault even as he had other routes to it.

Apart from Rigaudias-Weiss's contribution, there is a more direct way in which Foucault could have familiarized himself with workers' inquiries in the nineteenth century. In the fourth section of *Discipline and Punish,* he relied heavily on excerpts from *L'Atelier* to demonstrate the basis of opposition to penal labor in workers' newspaper in France in the 1840s. Foucault used these excerpts to show that this opposition was rooted in the view that penal labor would reduce wages and generate unemployment for workers.[137] To make this point, he even drew from an article titled "Inquiry: The Condition of Women" in a December 1842 issue of *L'Atelier.*[138] Foucault highlighted the claim in the article that competition from penal labor deprives women of employment with the effect of forcing them into prostitution and consequently the prison, where they also end up competing with women outside the prison.[139] It is not at all clear when exactly he came across this article in his research, but it provides proof that he was at least familiar with the workers' inquiries carried out by *L'Atelier.* It is therefore possible that Foucault learned about these inquiries while consulting *L'Atelier* for his research on what would become *Discipline and Punish,* if he did not already know about these inquiries from other sources.

Regardless of how exactly Foucault familiarized himself with nineteenth-century workers' inquiries, it should be obvious that the history of these inquiries abounds with implications. This history demonstrates not only that workers' inquiries were used as weapons of resistance in political struggles *prior* to Marxism but also that the whole emphasis on undertaking such inquiries to facilitate the *speech* of the investigated was hardly novel to radical political organizations in the late twentieth century. This emphasis had a whole history that goes at least as far back as *L'Atelier*'s stated aspiration in 1840 to enable workers to speak for themselves in defense of their own interests.[140] Most importantly for our purposes, Foucault's frustratingly brief invocation of nineteenth-century workers' inquiries in *Théories et institutions pénales* goes a distance in minimizing the otherwise stark gap between his enquêtes in theory and practice because it finally gestures to a usage of these inquiries as weapons of resistance in the context of his larger genealogy of the official inquiry. Indeed, as Foucault invoked workers' inquiries in both his political statements on behalf of the GIP and in his lectures, these inquiries stand out as the *only* concrete point of convergence between the enquêtes in his theory and practice.

Learning from the Gap

We thus can minimize the gap between these enquêtes, but there is also a lesson to be learned from simply dwelling on it. Indeed, the gap itself speaks volumes about Foucault's overall method. It may be tempting to think that the takeaway from it consists in a kind of cautionary tale according to which the ostensibly oppositional or liberating practice of investigations turns out to have been tainted or compromised by its roots in what Foucault called an "authoritarian search for truth" going back to Greek tyranny and the birth of states.[141] This tale in its turn might even feed into a kind of paranoia about practicing the investigation in the first place. Notably, however, Foucault did not exhibit any signs of this paranoia. Quite the contrary, he wielded the investigation to the utmost of his capacities in a short period of time without any apparent qualms. The editors of Foucault's *Théories et institutions pénales* claim that he was "above all" worried that "the 'investigation' form that he himself retained for the GIP" would enable intellectuals to extract, confiscate, and ultimately nullify popular knowledge, but they base this rather strong claim on his more general concerns about the privileging of intellectuals in political struggles rather than on anything that he actually said or wrote about the investigation.[142] Indeed, they do not muster a shred of documentary evidence to suggest that Foucault was somehow exceptionally worried about the investigation. In fact, it is possible to draw the opposite conclusion. We can surmise that what made the investigation different in Foucault's judgment from other political practices that ran the risk of privileging intellectuals, such as the popular tribunals in vogue among GP Maoists, was the *absence* of what he described as a space for a "position of neutrality."[143] He and others in the GIP embraced a form of the investigation that did not allow for any such position for intellectuals to occupy precisely because it was animated through and through by the manifestly partisan goal of heightening intolerance of the prison system.[144] Foucault bluntly affirmed this lack of neutrality by describing GIP investigations as "*intolerance-investigations*."[145]

If there was a more specific reason to be cautious about such investigations, it had to do with the prospect of the *reinsertion* of the contents of knowledge unleashed through them in an ensemble of hierarchical practices. Obviously, this problem was quite different from the problem of the *exclusion* of knowledge contents *by* official knowledge. Foucault had cast his passing remarks about early nineteenth-century workers' inquiries in terms of the latter problem. In his words from an interview with high school students in November 1971:

> The workers, at the beginning of the nineteenth century, carried out detailed investigations into their material conditions. This work served Marx for the bulk of his documentation; it led, in large part, to the political and trade-union practices of the proletariat throughout the nineteenth century; it maintains and develops itself through continuing struggles. Yet this knowledge has never been allowed to function within official knowledge. *It is not specific processes that have been excluded from knowledge, but a certain kind of knowledge. And if we become aware of it today, it is in a secondary sense: through the study of Marx and those elements in his text that are most easily assimilated into official knowledge.*[146]

Roughly half a decade later, however, Foucault struck a much more cautionary note. He warned his Collège auditors about the threat of the *resubjugation* of recently "desubjugated knowledges."[147] These "desubjugated knowledges" referred not only to historical knowledges unmasked through scholarly erudition but also to popular knowledges "disqualified" by the hierarchy of knowledges as inadequately conceptual or scientific.[148] And it was precisely such popular knowledges in the form of the knowledge of prisoners in particular that Foucault had mobilized through enquêtes on the behalf of the GIP.

If, however, he put his finger on the vexing problem of the reabsorption of these knowledges within an ensemble of hierarchical practices long after the dust of battle had settled, Foucault did not offer any kind of resolution to this problem. Admittedly, it is tremendously difficult to see what kind of a resolution he could have offered, because nothing can resolutely guarantee that knowledge contents will not be absorbed within hierarchical practices. We can nevertheless use his problem as a springboard to move forward. Rather than seeking to insulate knowledge contents from a potential reinsertion into hierarchical practices *or* simply giving up on the forms for producing these contents, it might be far more useful to concentrate on the *very task* of producing popular knowledges because the *mere* execution of this task can lend itself under certain conditions to the constitution of alternative forms of collective political subjectivity, *regardless* of the destiny of the knowledges themselves. The intricate (and seemingly self-generating) interplay of questions and answers in an investigation can yield political effects well beyond their formal knowledge contents. In other words, the value of this task resides less in *what* it produces than *whom* it produces. For its part, the GIP construed this whom as a public less tolerant of intolerable conditions in the prisons.[149]

Returning to our initial question, what then is the lesson of the gap between the enquêtes in Foucault's theory and practice? It is quite simply that the enquête is not static. It can be reinhabited and practiced otherwise. More precisely, the enquête can be used for purposes entirely at odds with the purpose for which it was originally intended because it is a generic enough form to circulate from one political position to another, especially during moments of social and political upheaval. Just as early nineteenth-century workers took over the inquiry during a period of industrialization in France and harnessed it for purposes *other* than economic administration, Foucault and other members of the GIP took over the investigation in a climate of intensive political repression after May 1968 and refashioned it for their own unique purposes. Foucault's *practices* demonstrated that the enquête amounts to an even more fluid, open, and reversible practice than what can be gleaned from his rich genealogy. Foucault's political practices in this instance thus perform the useful service of telling us something that we cannot ascertain to the same degree from his analyses.

However, lest there be any misunderstanding about the scope of the malleability and reversibility of enquêtes illuminated through these practices, it would be helpful to sound two cautionary notes. The first is relatively basic: radical movements, organizations, and publications do not hold a monopoly on the practice of the investigation. Jamie Woodcock formulates this point in his own deeply innovative and compelling consideration of the American television show *Undercover Boss*, which features executives who go undercover among the workers in their companies. In the typical plot of the show, the disguised executives come face to face with both the hardships of the workers and problems in the production process before finally revealing their identities to selected workers. The executives then discuss ways of overcoming problems of inefficiency with the workers and offer rewards to deserving workers. Woodcook writes, "*Undercover Boss* shows that the method of workers' inquiry is not the sole preserve of those seeking to understand exploitation and resistance on the part of workers. There are instances in which management will use somewhat similar techniques to gain a better understanding of the production process."[150] We can make this point with regard to the results of a militant investigation. Radical organizations and publications do not even hold a monopoly on the knowledge contents of their own previously undertaken investigations because changing historical and political conditions may alter the fate of these contents. One altogether noteworthy use of knowledge contents from a militant investigation for alternative, if not opposed, ends took place through the posthumous publication of Mao's previously discussed *Report from Xunwu* in China in 1982. The use of these contents is striking because it involved an *alternative* deployment of the *same* knowledge contents in an investigation undertaken by a founding figure in the history of investigations in radical political struggles. As Roger R. Thompson explains, the posthumous publication of "the *Report from Xunwu* was part of a campaign associated with Deng Xiaoping that stressed the importance of 'seeking truth from facts.'"[151] Thompson nicely (and bluntly) spells out the upshot of the publication of the report in the changing China of the early 1980s: "if facts required China to move away from Mao's final vision for the Peoples' Republic of China, then so be it."[152]

Ben Golder helps us formulate another cautionary note, one about the risks of exaggerating the fluidity and reversibility of the investigation. In his probing analysis of Foucault's engagement with rights, Golder echoes Susan Marks's warnings against "'false contingency'" as the conviction that practices can be *easily remade* simply because they are *not necessary*.[153] There are, in other words, "operative and material dynamics" that inhibit the remaking of certain practices.[154] A consideration of the practices of the GIP teaches us that its remaking of the investigation was full of challenges, especially at the outset. More generally, the preceding chapters demonstrate that radical organizations and publications encountered immense difficulties in their efforts to reappropriate the investigation for their own political purposes. By conventional measures, they failed in these efforts more often than not. Then again, it is precisely these conventional measures that the discussion in the preceding chapters has sought to question so as to open up other ways of appraising investigations in radical political struggles and theories.

6

Conclusion

The preceding chapters of this book have revisited (and in some cases more simply visited) the dense, obscure, overlooked, and often forgotten details of the history of the investigation in radical political struggles. There were many reasons to explore these details. One was to simply establish a more comprehensive or at least less fragmentary account of the militant investigation than what is available in the existing literature. This more comprehensive rendering of the militant investigation in turn enabled us to gauge the sheer diversity of the practice in terms of methods, contexts, subjects, objectives, and results. It also equipped us to begin to chip away at the pervasive problematic of failure in the history of militant investigations by highlighting instances of success in this history and providing us with more theoretical insights to challenge this problematic. As I have already restated a huge portion of the larger historical argument in the opening to the previous chapter, I do not engage in the labor of rehashing its details here. Suffice it to fill in the remaining gap by emphasizing that Michel Foucault *takes us back* in two fundamental ways: he takes us back to the birth of the *official* inquiry, and he takes us back to the birth of the *militant* investigation. Yet, in keeping with Foucault's genealogical method, his examination of these interrelated but distinct births is an engagement with a prominent political practice from his own present. It renders what was an all-too-familiar practice of knowledge production (to Foucault and his militant fellow travelers) strange by historicizing this practice and locating its emergence in the more general birth of political power in the West. However, these moves do not underhandedly condemn the militant investigation (by revealing its authoritarian origins) so much as affirm alternative and oppositional ways of inhabiting what first appeared as an eminently *official* practice of knowledge production.

If Foucault takes us as far *back* as antiquity, the core historical argument in the preceding chapters has gone *no further forward* than the early 1970s. The reason for this self-limitation is that militant investigations flourished from the early 1960s to the early 1970s, only to then go into precipitous decline as the movements practicing them experienced enormous setbacks with the general rise of more conservative political forces. As we saw in the introduction, Andrea Cavazzini locates the decline of workers' inquiry in Italy in particular in the hollowing out of the working class as *the* subject of social emancipation (and its corresponding reduction to a merely empirical referent warranting humanitarian pity at certain junctures).[1] If the working class was no longer understood as *the* class harboring the potential for its own emancipation as well as the emancipation of society as a whole, what was the point in undertaking a practice centered on drawing out this potential? The very fount of the practice of the investigation in radical political struggles had been undermined. While illuminating, one problem with this strand of argument is that it tends to implicitly diminish the forms of the political self-activity of the working class that fall short of the grandiose goal of social emancipation. What about workers' inquiries that might still facilitate these forms? What about the role of these inquiries in generating everyday resistances among workers?

In purely historical terms, the breakdown in the very powerful notion of the working class as a subject of social emancipation did not mean that the militant investigation simply disappeared after reaching a kind of hiatus in the early 1970s. In the last two decades, there have been deeply innovative attempts to revisit the militant investigation in theory and practice, especially in its iteration as a workers' inquiry. To offer a still more comprehensive sense of the investigation in radical political struggles and theories, it is helpful to briefly take stock of these attempts. It is also helpful to engage them for two other reasons. One is that some of the more critical insights from the recent experiences in militant investigations allow us to further finesse the theoretical point in the preceding pages about the importance of the political afterlives of questions. To be precise, these insights caution us against any tendency to think that questions are somehow intrinsically oppositional or liberating. The other related reason for engaging recent experiences in militant investigations is something of the inverse of the previous one. The elaboration of the history of militant investigations in the preceding chapters allows us to draw out the *limitations* in the critical insights of some of the recent experiences in these investigations. Some of these insights simply go too far in divesting questions of any oppositional or liberating potential. I suggest that context and the relationship between the investigator and investigated offer ways of delineating the potential promises and problems in the questions at the core of militant investigations.

Rebirths of the Militant Investigation

One very important point of reference and source of inspiration for recent experiences in militant investigations comes from the Argentine group Colectivo Situaciones. This group was formed against the backdrop of the social and political crises in Argentina at the end of the 1990s and the beginning of the 2000s. Colectivo Situaciones is significant for articulating a conception of research militancy or militant research (*militancia de investigación* in Spanish) that stresses the *immanence* of the militant researcher to the situation understood as a space of affective bonds for nurturing alternative, noncapitalist forms of sociability.[2] From this perspective, the researcher is not a subject who relates to objects from a transcendental position. Colectivo Situaciones picks out two figures to illustrate this negative point. It emphatically opposes its conception of research militancy or militant research to the relationship to political action embodied in the figure of traditional political militant, on the one hand, and to the relationship to knowledge production embodied in the figure of the academic, on the other hand.[3] For Colectivo Situaciones, *both* of these figures share a commitment to "predefined schemes" that reduce others to objects.[4] In the case of the traditional militant, that scheme is the " 'party line,' " and in the case of the academic, that scheme is the pursuit of "preexisting theses."[5] In contradistinction to these figures, Colectivo Situaciones insists that subjects of knowledge and political action appear *as a consequence* of "encounters" *within* the situation.[6] For the group, such encounters take the form of engaging a wide range of social movements through workshops and publications.[7]

Notably, Colectivo Situaciones elucidates its conception of militant research or research militancy in direct response to the queries of another group that embraces variations of the militant investigation. That group is the Spanish-based Precarias a la Deriva. Precarias first appeared in the context of a general strike against the European Union in Spain in June 2002. The initiative for the creation of the group came from women in the squatting community of Eskalera Karakola in Madrid. Frustrated by the calls for a strike that privileged established and unionized workers, the women wanted to find forms of political engagement and opposition that spoke to their specific conditions and struggles as precarious and gendered laborers. They settled on a picket-survey that involved the mobilization of small groups of women around Madrid on the day of the strike.[8] These groups used "cameras, recorders, notebooks, and pens" to pose questions to laborers in "the invisible, non-regulated, temporary, undocumented, house-based sectors of the market."[9] The question "What is your strike?" figured centrally in their survey.[10] The encounters generated through the survey served as a basis for further research into the theme of the diverse experiences of "feminine precarity."[11] This research relies on an adoption and feminist adaptation of the Situationist method of drifting. Precarias drifted rather deliberately through everyday spaces to draw out connections among women engaged in precarious labor in these spaces.[12]

Precarias and Colectivo Situaciones have served as sources of inspiration for other more recent experiments in militant investigations. In response to the cancellation of the Labor Day holiday for large segments of the workforce at the University of North Carolina at Chapel Hill, a group of students and instructors launched their own militant investigations in 2005. These investigations concerned the nature of work on the campus. The group of students and instructors, which eventually acquired the name 3Cups Counter-Cartographies Collective, engaged in what has been described as a "stationary drift."[13] From a busy corner on the campus, it engaged in the well-established techniques (in the history of militant investigations) of conducting interviews, holding collective discussions, and distributing questionnaires. The interviews started with the rather open-ended question "What's your labor like, today and everyday?"[14] The group also had recourse to less traditional techniques, such as video recordings and the production of participatory maps. The purely quantitative results of its investigation appear to have been impressive. Maribel Casas-Cortés and Sebastian Cobarrubias describe them as follows: "The ad-hoc group generated four audio-taped interviews, three audio-taped collective conversations, fifty surveys and questionnaires, four color-coded maps, one page of conclusions on butcher paper, thirty digital photos, twenty minutes of videotape, a three-page research log, as well as signs, flyers, and some graffiti."[15] Like Precarias, from which it now draws explicit inspiration, the nascent 3Cups Counter-Cartographic Collective used its initial experience to eventually establish a more ongoing militant research project.[16] This project would set out to probe labor at the university through the use of drifts and mapping.

Apart from these forms of militant research, there have been even more recent attempts to resuscitate and critically enact Marx's version of workers' inquiry in particular. What makes these attempts different from the attempts discussed in the previous chapters is that they are focused intensely on the role of affective labor in the context of the bourgeoning service sectors of various economies. For instance, Jamie Woodcock recently undertook a workers' inquiry at a call center responsible for selling insurance to trade union members in the United Kingdom. He engaged in the inquiry to "explore the possibilities for resistance and organization" among the call center workers.[17] In a manner that easily recalls the practices of French Maoists, Woodcock even took up a working position at the call center for a period of five months to pursue this exploration. He based his inquiry on his own experiences as a worker as well as on his own conversations with fellow workers inside and outside the workplace. Woodcock found that call center workers are caught up in a contradiction between quantitative and qualitative pressures. They are required to meet sales targets through the rigid use of scripts and computer surveillance, yet they are also required to verbally communicate enthusiasm toward customers and provide them with an overall positive experience, even through recourse to jokes. These twin demands of meeting sales targets and performing an emotional labor for customers take their toll, resulting in feelings of stress and guilt among workers. For Woodcock, these feelings help explain the quick turnover among call center workers. To provide some measure of this turnover based simply on his own experiences, Woodcock recalls being one of the "longest lasting workers" in his "training cohort" after *only* five months of employment. Such turnover, he concludes, poses serious problems for organizing resistance among call center workers.[18]

Woodcock has not been alone in attempting to reactivate Marx's version of workers' inquiry in the context of the growing service industries. In the spring of 2012, Jennifer M. Murray undertook a workers' inquiry of female servers at an upscale cocktail lounge in the lobby of a Manhattan hotel.[19] The lounge creates a falsely intimate environment where servers perform an affective labor for generally well-to-do customers in return for potentially large tips.[20] Murray based her inquiry on recorded interviews with twelve of the fourteen servers at the lounge. As Murray herself had previously worked at the lounge, her familiarity with the servers facilitated incredibly fluid conversations in the interviews.[21] Murray found through these interviews that her former coworkers experience various kinds of *shame* about their work: shame as a stigma about working in an occupation with a negative status; shame as an internalized *and* projected revulsion at being subject to harassment and humiliation; and shame at being the object of deeply invasive inquiries from customers.[22] Murray imparts the scope of these inquiries: "It is not uncommon for customers to ask a server her age, her birthplace, about her family, about her dating or marital status, where she lives, what she does for fun, what her habits are, or what her goals are for her life."[23] For Murray, the shame generated through such relentless and deeply intrusive questions complicates the traditional notion of a workers' inquiry as borrowed from Marx because it turns questions into possible sources for reliving shame among the investigated with potentially damaging effects for their emotional well-being. In light of this complication, Murray writes, "we sometimes must resist inquiring at all, socially or sociologically."[24] She appeals to "stories of resistance and agency rather than inquiry per se."[25] For Murray, these stories allow workers to recognize their shame and harness it critically to facilitate their own autonomy. The steps in her critical deployment of a workers' inquiry thus reenact the shift from the questionnaire to individual narratives in the larger history of militant investigations, albeit in one experience of affective labor in a service industry setting.

In a short narrative about his working experiences as a bartender in Berlin, Jacob Blumenfeld goes one provocative step further.[26] He insists that knowledge about working conditions and struggles brings *no* empowerment, and that the notion that it would appears as a cruel but tantalizing illusion in retrospect. Blumenfeld writes, "A self-inquiry into the actual conditions of work seems ideal. But the more I think about work, the more alienated I feel. Knowledge brings no power here, only shame."[27] He does not attempt to harness this shame through the endorsement of a more narrative form. Blumenfeld simply dismisses the very idea of a workers' inquiry and appeals instead to an *anti*-workers' inquiry in the sense of a practice that explores the "negative relation" that workers have "to themselves as both dependent on, and external to, their own class belonging."[28]

Back in 2009, Yves Duroux declared in an interview that the disappearance of the militant investigation had resulted in ignorance about labor. In his blunt and definitive words, which I quote in the opening paragraph of this study, "Today we know nothing about the world of labor. There is no longer the investigation."[29] It is not clear whether the "we" in this declaration refers to academics, militants, or the public at large. Whatever the case, the overview above of recent experiences in the militant investigation reveals a less definitive historical trend with less dire consequences. Far from simply disappearing after a period of popularity among radicals in the late 1960s and early 1970s, the militant investigation has undergone something of a rebirth in the last two decades in response to profound changes in labor. It is now deployed to grapple with the conditions and struggles of workers who do not tend to fit the mold of the traditional full-time, permanent, unionized, and predominantly male factory workers of yesteryear. These workers may be part-time, self-employed, or even unemployed. They may perform affective labor in the service economy, and they may occupy more precarious positions on the margins of formal economies. Yet, as we have seen from the preceding chapters, the adaptability of the militant investigation to markedly different conditions is nothing new. It has a very long history. There has also been a noteworthy shift in the points of reference in recent practices of the investigation. To the extent that a source of inspiration from early Marxism remains intact, that source is Marx's project for a workers' inquiry *rather* than Mao's investigation. The latter has been left aside with the disrepute and precipitous decline of Maoism even on the radical left after the mid-1970s. Yet, as can be seen through Murray's analysis of her own workers' inquiry, Marx's version of workers' inquiry has also remained subject to severe criticism in recent experiences. Overall, the rebirth of the militant investigation renders a more comprehensive examination of its history all the more germane to the extent that this history speaks back to us, offering insights into the difficulties and possibilities opened up by this practice in markedly different conditions.

The critiques of Murray and Blumenfeld also provide a nice point of transition into a clarification of the more theoretical thread of argument in the preceding chapters. As indicated back in the introduction, failure figures as a central leitmotif in the literature on investigations. This leitmotif is based in large part on the view that the investigations failed to generate verbal, written, and published responses from workers in particular. This type of failure can be seen in Marx's project for a workers' inquiry. And, to be resolutely clear once again, I have not rejected the leitmotif of failure so much as aspired to complicate *how* we measure failure (and success) in the history of militant investigations. This task seems especially important because the militant investigation is not like other investigations. It is not based on generating empirical contents that serve as the basis for the elaboration of social-scientific theories. The militant investigation is based explicitly on generating political effects and outcomes. We therefore need a measure of success and failure that is more appropriate to attending to those effects and outcomes. With this imperative in view, I have built on Dario Lanzardo's insights to draw attention to the far less tangible ways in which questions might generate political effects and outcomes without necessarily yielding written and verbalized responses, much less published ones. Here the questionnaire and the interview have a unique advantage over the narrative form of workers' inquiry. This advantage does not consist simply in disclosing general patterns of behavior through the accumulation of comparable responses. It also consists in serving as a *focused* stimulus for reflections and communications among workers. As the narrative form poses no questions to workers, it does not possess this possibility. It only possesses the possibility of stimulating reflections and communications among workers once it is in circulation in draft form at least, as in case of Paul Romano's essay. Yet even this possibility presupposes that workers will actually read the narratives. By contrast, investigations based on verbalized questions in particular retain the possibility of stimulating political effects among workers from the very outset without waiting for the publication and dissemination of their responses within a worker readership. To recap, I have stressed that, once expressed, questions have lives of their own that cannot be reduced to the written and verbalized responses to them. They may resonate among workers in unforeseen and informal ways long after their communication through interviews and questionnaires. They may spur conversations and reflections that yield political effects long after the formal completion of an investigation. If that is the case, then questions (without answers) may dovetail into the production of collective political subjectivity at the heart of the militant investigation. We should pause, then, before hastily concluding that the absence of responses equates with the outright failure of an investigation. Such a pause matters because it ultimately affords a more robust understanding of political efficacy itself.

Here, however, it is also worth keeping in mind that there is nothing inherently liberating or oppositional about questions. Far from spurring forms of collective resistance to exploitation and oppression, questions may simply turn away their intended recipients. They may be experienced as incomprehensible, boring, and annoying. V. I. Lenin and Claude Lefort point to the latter possibility. Questions may also have more far more pernicious effects on their recipients. Blumenfeld and Murray remind us that questions may be sources of shame for workers. Blumenfeld, however, takes his argument a bit too far. He is outright dismissive of *any* oppositional or liberating potential in workers' inquiry, as vividly illustrated by his use of the word "shit" to describe the assumption that knowledge generated from this inquiry would suddenly reveal the exploitation of workers, which would then just as suddenly unify them and mobilize them to dismantle capitalism.[30] What goes missing in Blumenfeld's gross caricature of workers' inquiry is any sense of the rather complicated, arduous, untidy, and precarious *process* of merely producing knowledge with political outcomes. We know from the preceding pages that many of the principal theorists of workers' inquiry, such as Lanzardo and Raniero Panzieri, understood the practice in terms of a *drawn-out* process of political consciousness-raising. Moreover, to the extent that organizers of workers' inquiries subscribed to the naive assumption that political knowledge would lead swiftly to revolution, they tended to be quickly disabused of this assumption in their own experiences. Put differently, shame may indeed result from an inquiry, but it need not be the *only* result. In this regard, the example of Murray's inquiry is far more instructive. Her former coworkers experienced questions as intrusive and invasive when they emanated from customers at the workplace, but they did not experience *Murray's* questions in quite this manner. In fact, she succeeded in eliciting rich narratives from her former coworkers. What are we to conclude from this distinction? Perhaps simply that everything depends on context. Murray's status as a kind of insider by virtue of her former employment at the cocktail lounge enabled her to pose questions to her former coworkers without eliciting their shame. This fact alone grates against her ultimate dismissal of questions in favor of narratives and highlights the practical importance for organizers of an inquiry of establishing deeper bonds with the investigated. One of Murray's former coworkers and interviewees even emphasizes the invasive *and* oppositional possibilities in questions, albeit in the context of social interactions. In her words:

> Sometimes I'll go back to a table, and they'll say to me, "What's your deal? Where are you from? What do you do

> outside this bar? What neighborhood do you live in? How old are you? Where did you go to school?" All these personal questions. So I've started saying, in response, "And how old are you? Where are you from? What do you do?" It keeps things in balance. What makes people think they can ask us things like that? I mean, you shouldn't know so much stuff about me, when I don't know anything about you.[31]

These defiant words, uttered by an anonymous server from an anonymous cocktail lounge in Manhattan, provide an eminently appropriate conclusion to our exploration of militant investigations. They stand, first and foremost, as a testimony to the continuing ability of workers' inquiry to attempt to elicit the voices of workers after nearly two centuries of the practice. Obviously, however, the substance of these words concerns questions uttered in the context of everyday social interactions at a workplace rather than in the context of a workers' inquiry. The server clearly directs her anger toward questions from a customer rather than questions from a militant investigator. Her remarks nonetheless serve as a vivid reminder of some of the basic points elaborated in the preceding pages: questions have lives of their own above and beyond the intentions of those who utter them, and they are reversible in direction and purpose. Even deeply intrusive and demeaning questions can be reoccupied, turned around, and foisted against those who enjoy the privilege of uttering them. The history of militant investigations is nothing less than the history of the practice of formulating, inhabiting, and channeling questions in new social directions to produce new forms of collective political subjectivity.

Notes

Chapter 1

1. Louis Althusser, *The Future Lasts Forever: A Memoir*, ed. Olivier Corpet and Yann Moulier Boutang, trans. Richard Veasey (New York: The New Press, 1993), 209. I thank Diogo Sardinha for referring me to the passage containing Althusser's praise of Duroux.

2. Yves Duroux, "Sur la question du savoir dans le maoïsme," in *Le sujet et l'étude: idéologie et savoir dans le discours maoïste suivi de dialogue avec Yves Duroux*, by Andrea Cavazzini (Reims: Le Clou dans le Fer, 2011), 107.

3. Ibid.

4. Ibid.

5. For an exploration of the uses of investigations among workers, philanthropists, and the state in early nineteenth-century France, see Hilde Rigaudias-Weiss, *Les enquêtes ouvrières en France entre 1830 et 1848* (1936; repr., New York: Arno Press, 1975). For an examination of the relationship between workers' inquiries and Frankfurt School theories in Italy in the 1960s, see Andrea Cavazzini, *Enquête ouvrière et théorie critique: Enjeux et figures de la centralité ouvrière dans l'Italie des années 1960* (Liège: Presses Universitaires de Liège, 2013). It is difficult to overstate the importance of these books for any study of the history of militant investigations, but as they restrict themselves to the uses of these investigations in distinct national contexts separated by more than a century, they leave a huge gap in our understanding of these practices. For an analysis that traces the reactivation of Marx's project for a workers' inquiry from oppositional Trotskyist and post-Trotskyist tendencies in the United States and France in the 1940s and 1950s to Italian workerism in the 1960s, see Asad Haider and Salar Mohandesi, "Workers' Inquiry: A Genealogy," *Viewpoint Magazine*, September 27, 2013, https://viewpointmag.com/2013/09/27/workers-inquiry-a-genealogy/. Haider and Mohandesi cover a lot of historical ground in great detail, yet in leaping from the Marx of 1880 to postwar Trotskyism, they skip over nearly three-quarters of

a century of experiences in militant investigations. For a tremendously fecund but excessively brief comparison between investigations in the French Maoist experience and workers' inquiries in the Italian workerist experience, see Duroux, "Sur la question du savoir dans le maoïsme," 102–10. The compartmentalized articulation of the investigation in the founding figures of Marxism seems at least partially responsible for the fragmented state of research about militant investigations. As we shall see in the next chapter, Marx, Lenin, and Mao *each* formulated the militant investigation *as if* starting from scratch, without any apparent knowledge of preceding efforts to employ this practice in radical political struggles. For this very reason, an obscure Portuguese pamphlet that simply brings together Marx and Mao's writings on the militant investigation does much more than stand out as an excellent collection of primary materials. It grates against the fragmented state of research on militant investigations by inviting readers to compare the writings of Marx and Mao on the topic. For this pamphlet, see Karl Marx and Mao Tsetung, *Cadernos da prática 1: Inquérito operário e luta política*, trans. and ed. Amadeu Lopes Sabino and Sebastião Lima Rego (Lisbon: printed by the authors, 1971).

6. Michel J. M. Thiollent, *Crítica metodológica, investigação social e enquete operária*, 4th ed. (São Paulo: Polis, 1985) 101–26.

7. Panel on Responsible Conduct of Research (Government of Canada), "RCR Framework Interpretations," January 2015, http://www.rcr.ethics.gc.ca/eng/policy-politique/interpretations/inquiry-enquetes/.

8. Erich Fromm, *The Working Class in Weimar Germany: A Psychological and Sociological Study*, trans. Barbara Weinberger, ed. Wolfgang Bonss (Cambridge, MA: Harvard University Press, 1984), 41. I thank Karsten Piep for provoking me to find this important study.

9. Ibid., 42; Wolfgang Bonss, "Critical Theory and Empirical Social Research: Some Observations," in *Working Class in Weimar Germany*, 1.

10. Fromm, *Working Class in Weimar Germany*, 51.

11. Ibid., 49.

12. Bonss, "Critical Theory and Empirical Social Research," 2.

13. Fromm, *Working Class in Weimar Germany*, 43.

14. Ibid.

15. Bonss, "Critical Theory and Empirical Social Research," 23–26.

16. Fromm, *Working Class in Weimar Germany*, 41, brackets in the original.

17. Ibid., 49, italics mine.

18. Ibid., 50–51.

19. Peter Hallward, *Badiou: A Subject to Truth* (Minneapolis: University of Minnesota Press, 2003), 126.

20. Thiollent, *Crítica metodológica*, 124.

21. I thank Philippe Artières for (rather forcefully) reminding me of this point at the Time Served: *Discipline and Punish* 40 Years On conference at Galleries of Justice in Nottingham, England, on September 11, 2015.

22. Stevphen Shukaitis and David Graeber, eds., *Constituent Imagination: Militant Investigations // Collective Theorization*, with the assistance of Erika Biddle (Oakland: AK Press, 2007), 316, brackets added. There are plenty of deeply incisive contributions in this volume, but only a handful of them deal directly with investigations in the sense employed here.

23. Sebastian Touza and Nate Holdren, Translator's introduction to "Something More on Research Militancy: Footnotes on Procedures and (In)Decisions," by Colectivo Situaciones, in *Constituent Imagination*, 74, italics mine.

24. Shukaitis, Graeber, and Biddle, *Constituent Imagination*, 316.

25. Of course, I borrow the terms of this distinction from Michel Foucault's famous reformulation of genealogy in *"Society Must Be Defended": Lectures at the Collège de France, 1975–76*, ed. Mauro Bertani and Alessandro Fontana, trans. David Macey (New York: Picador, 2003), 8.

26. Duroux, "Sur la question du savoir dans le maoïsme," 109.

27. Cavazzini, *Enquête ouvrière et théorie critique*, 143–44. I thank Richard A. Lynch for his assistance in the translation of this passage.

28. Hilde Weiss, "Karl Marx's 'Enquête Ouvrière,'" in *Interpretations of Marx*, ed. Tom Bottomore (New York: Basil Blackwell, 1988), 262. Incidentally, before ever learning about Weiss, much less her important interpretation of Marx's questionnaire, I also described the "failure" of Marx's questionnaire to generate results. See Marcelo Hoffman, "Investigations from Marx to Foucault," in *Active Intolerance: Michel Foucault, the Prisons Information Group, and the Future of Abolition*, ed. Perry Zurn and Andrew Dilts (New York: Palgrave Macmillan, 2016), 173. My thoughts on this matter have evolved, as the succeeding discussion should make clear.

29. Duroux, "Sur la question du savoir dans le maoïsme," 102.

30. Stephen Hastings-King, *Looking for the Proletariat: Socialisme ou Barbarie and the Problem of Worker Writing* (Chicago: Haymarket Books, 2015), 166, 203.

31. Ibid., 224.

32. Dario Lanzardo, "Marx et l'enquête ouvrière," in *Luttes ouvrières et capitalisme d'aujourd'hui*, by Quaderni Rossi, trans. Nicole Rouzet (Paris: François Maspero, 1968), 127–29.

33. Colectivo Situaciones, "Something More on Research Militancy: Footnotes on Procedures and (In)Decisions," trans. Sebastian Touza and Nate Holdren, in *Constituent Imagination*, 81.

34. Duroux, "Sur la question du savoir dans le maoïsme," 107.

35. Jodi Dean, *The Communist Horizon* (New York: Verso, 2012), 207–50; Jodi Dean, *Crowds and Party* (New York: Verso, 2016). For my own highly critical reflections on these contributions, see Marcelo Hoffman, "Sources of Anxiety About the Party in Radical Political Theory," *Theoria: A Journal of Social and Political Theory* 63, no. 149 (December 2016): 18–36.

36. Claire Duchen, *Feminism in France: From May '68 to Mitterand* (Boston: Routledge & Kegan Paul, 1986), 9–10.

37. "Communique de presse," *L'idiot liberte: Le torchon brûle!*, n.d., 20, http://archivesautonomies.org/IMG/pdf/feminisme/torchonbrule/letorchonbrule-n000.pdf.

38. Ibid.

39. Duchen, *Feminism in France*, 9–10.

40. Ibid., 10.

Chapter 2

1. English translations of "A Workers' Inquiry" abound, but they vary considerably in form and content. These translations appear in pamphlets, journals, anthologies, collected volumes, and online. For a translation from the Communist Party of Great Britain that includes the introduction as well as all 101 questions in consecutive order, see Karl Marx, *A Workers' Enquiry* (London: Utopia Press, 1933). For the first translation in the United States that contains the introduction as well as all 101 questions in consecutive order, see Karl Marx, "A Workers' Inquiry," *New International: A Monthly Organ of Revolutionary Marxism* 12, no. 4 (1938): 379–81. For a translation that omits the introduction to the questionnaire but includes all 101 questions in consecutive order, see Karl Marx, "Marx's *Enquête Ouvrière*," in *Karl Marx: Selected Writings in Sociology & Social Philosophy*, trans. T. B. Bottomore, ed. Bottomore and Maximilien Rubel (New York: McGraw-Hill, 1964), 204–12. For a more recent translation that includes the introduction as well as all 101 questions in consecutive order, see Karl Marx, *A Workers' Inquiry* (Tougaloo, MS: Freedom Information Service; Detroit: Bewick, 1973). For an apparent translation from German that retains the introduction as well as the consecutive ordering of all 101 questions, see Hilde Weiss, "Karl Marx's 'Enquête Ouvrière,'" in *Interpretations of Marx*, ed. Tom Bottomore (New York: Basil Blackwell, 1988), 263–68. For a translation that leaves out the introduction as well as the final item in the questionnaire and organizes the questions consecutively only in *each* of the four sections, see Karl Marx, "Workers' Questionnaire," in *Collected Works*, vol. 24, *Marx and Engels: 1874–83* (New York: International Publishers, 1989), 328–34. For an online transcription that includes the introduction and the first hundred questions in consecutive order, see Karl Marx, "A Workers' Inquiry," Works of Karl Marx 1880, 1997, https://www.marxists.org/archive/marx/works/1880/04/20.htm. The glaring differences between the translation in the *Collected Works* and the other translations derive from the use of different source materials. The translation in the *Collected Works* is based on Marx's original manuscript, whereas the other translations derive from the published version of the questionnaire in *La Revue socialiste*. On the derivation of the translation in the *Collected Works* from Marx's original manuscript, see the editorial commentary in Marx, "Workers' Questionnaire," 24:636–37n377. I stick to the translation in *A Workers' Inquiry*

for a number of reasons: first and foremost, it is faithful to the presentation of the original questionnaire in *La Revue socialiste* in terms of the contents, ordering, and range of the questions; second, it is based on American rather than British English; third, it does not derive from a translation based on a language other than the original French; fourth, it is much more recent than the first American translation; and, finally, it is free of the errors and omissions in the online version.

2. [Karl Marx], "Enquête ouvrière," *La Revue socialiste*, April 20, 1880, http://gallica.bnf.fr/ark:/12148/bpt6k5817422b.item.r=Revue+Socialiste+1880.

3. *L'Égalité*, April 28, 1880, http://gallica.bnf.fr/ark:/12148/bpt6k68307182/f3.item.r=l'egalite+journal;jsessionid=8EFF1ADF444E3A9C275C1E7AE689A61C; *L'Égalité*, May 5, 1880, http://gallica.bnf.fr/ark:/12148/bpt6k6830719g/f1.item.r=l'egalite+journal;jsessionid=8EFF1ADF444E3A9C275C1E7AE689A61C. Unfortunately, the insert of the questionnaire does not appear in the holdings of *L'Égalité* in the Gallica digital library of the Bibliothèque nationale de France.

4. Michel J. M. Thiollent, *Crítica metodológica, investigação social e enquete operária*, 4th ed. (São Paulo: Polis, 1985), 103.

5. Karl Marx, *Capital: A Critique of Political Economy*, vol. 1, trans. Ben Fowkes (New York: Vintage Books, 1977), 91.

6. David Harvey, *A Companion to Marx's Capital* (New York: Verso, 2010), 151.

7. Marx, *Capital*, 349–50, 398–99.

8. Marx, *Workers' Inquiry*, 4.

9. Andrew R. Aisenberg, *Contagion: Disease, Government, and the "Social Question" in Nineteenth-Century France* (Stanford: Stanford University Press, 1999), 26–27.

10. Ibid., 26–34.

11. Ibid., 35–40.

12. Ibid., 40.

13. Hilde Rigaudias-Weiss, *Les enquêtes ouvrières en France entre 1830 et 1848* (1936; repr., New York: Arno Press, 1975), 184–233.

14. Ibid., 192–94.

15. Ibid.,

16. Ibid., 210–18.

17. Ibid., 228–30.

18. Ibid., 227.

19. Marx, *Workers' Inquiry*, 4.

20. Ibid.

21. Ibid.

22. Ken Lawrence, introduction to *Workers' Inquiry*, 3.

23. Weiss, "Karl Marx's 'Enquête Ouvrière,'" 261.

24. Marx, *Workers' Inquiry*, 4, italics in the original.

25. Ibid., 5.

26. Ibid.

27. Ibid.

28. Andrew Rothstein, foreword to *Workers' Enquiry*, 5, italics in the original.

29. Marx, *Workers' Inquiry*, 5–6.

30. Ibid., 6, italics in the original.

31. Ibid., 7.

32. Ibid., 8.

33. Ibid.

34. Ibid., 8–9.

35. Ibid., 10–12.

36. Ibid., 11.

37. Ibid., 12.

38. Ibid., 5.

39. Lawrence, introduction to *Workers' Inquiry*, 3; Weiss, "Karl Marx's 'Enquête Ouvrière,'" 262.

40. Marx, *Workers' Inquiry*, 5.

41. Rothstein, foreword to *Workers' Enquiry*, 5.

42. James Burnham, Max Shachtman, and Maurice Spector, Introduction to Karl Marx's "A Workers' Inquiry," *New International: A Monthly Organ of Revolutionary Marxism* 12, no. 4 (1938): 379.

43. Marx, *Workers' Inquiry*, 5.

44. Ibid.

45. Asad Haider and Salar Mohandesi, "Workers' Inquiry: A Genealogy," *Viewpoint Magazine*, September 27, 2013, https://viewpointmag.com/2013/09/27/workers-inquiry-a-genealogy/.

46. Marx, *Workers' Inquiry*, 12.

47. Ibid.

48. Dario Lanzardo, "Marx et l'enquête ouvrière," in *Luttes ouvrières et capitalisme d'aujourd'hui*, by Quaderni Rossi (Paris: François Maspero, 1968), 129.

49. Haider and Mohandesi, "Workers' Inquiry."

50. "Enquête ouvrière," *La Revue socialiste*, July 5, 1880, http://gallica.bnf.fr/ark:/12148/bpt6k58174319/f32.item.r=Revue+Socialiste+1880.

51. Weiss, "Karl Marx's 'Enquête Ouvrière,'" 258.

52. "Enquête ouvrière."

53. T. B. Bottomore and Maximilien Rubel, Introductory note to Marx's *Enquête Ouvrière*," in *Karl Marx*, 204n.

54. Rigaudias-Weiss, *Enquêtes ouvrières en France*, 221–22.

55. Weiss, "Karl Marx's 'Enquête Ouvrière,'" 262n11.

56. Ibid., 262–63.

57. *L'Égalité*, May 5, 1880, http://gallica.bnf.fr/ark:/12148/bpt6k6830719g/f1.item.r=l'egalite+journal;jsessionid=8EFF1ADF444E3A9C275C1E7AE689A61C.

58. In this regard, see Lanzardo, "Marx et l'enquête ouvrière," 129.

59. Thiollent, *Crítica metodológica*, 106.

60. Marx, *Workers' Enquiry*.

61. Thiollent, *Crítica metodológica*, 115–16, 124–25.

62. Ibid., 116.

63. Ibid., 124–25.

64. V. I. Lenin, *What Is to Be Done? Burning Questions of Our Movement* (New York: International Publishers, 1969), 54–57.

65. V. I. Lenin, "Questionnaire on the Situation of Workers in Enterprises," in *Marxism in Russia: Key Documents, 1879–1906*, ed. Neil Harding, trans. Richard Taylor (New York: Cambridge University Press, 1983), 138–39; Lars T. Lih, *Lenin* (London: Reaktion Books, 2011), 55.

66. Lih, *Lenin Rediscovered: "What Is to Be Done?" in Context* (Chicago: Haymarket Books, 2008), 602.

67. Lenin, "Questionnaire on the Situation of Workers in Enterprises," 138–39.

68. Ibid.

69. Lih, *Lenin Rediscovered*, 111–58.

70. Lenin, "Questionnaire on the Situation of Workers in Enterprises," 139, brackets in the original.

71. Lenin, *What Is to Be Done?*, 148n.

72. Ibid.

73. Ibid.

74. Ibid.

75. Ibid.

76. V. I. Lenin, *Collected Works*, vol. 3, *The Development of Capitalism in Russia* (Moscow: Progress Publishers, 1972).

77. Ibid., 643–44n40.

78. Ibid., 43–44.

79. Ibid., 42, 68, 166, 181.

80. Ibid., 103.

81. Ibid., 103, 105.

82. Ibid., 180.

83. Ibid., 454–84.

84. Ibid., 484.

85. Ibid., 468.

86. Ibid., italics in the original.

87. Jean-Pierre Le Dantec, "D'où vient l'établissement?," *Les Temps Modernes*, nos. 684–85 (July–October 2015): 17.

88. Roger R. Thompson, introduction to *Report from Xunwu*, by Mao Zedong, trans. Roger R. Thompson (Stanford: Stanford University Press, 1990), 24.

89. Mao Tsetung, "Report on an Investigation of the Peasant Movement in Hunan," in *Selected Readings from the Works of Mao Tsetung* (Peking: Foreign Languages Press, 1971), 23–39.

90. Rebecca E. Karl, *Mao Zedong and China in the Twentieth-Century World: A Concise History* (Durham: Duke University Press, 2010), 30–31.

91. Mao, "Report," 23.

92. Karl, *Mao Zedong and China in the Twentieth-Century World*, 31.

93. Mao, "Report," 35.

94. Ibid., 23.

95. Mao, *Report from Xunwu*, 45.

96. Mao, "Report," 23.

97. I owe a debt of gratitude to Rebecca E. Karl for pointing out Mao's investigation in Xunwu.

98. Thompson, introduction to *Report from Xunwu*, 11.

99. Ibid., 25.

100. Mao, *Report from Xunwu*, 45.

101. Ibid., 47.

102. Ibid., 46–47.

103. Thompson, introduction to *Report from Xunwu*, 18.

104. Mao, *Report from Xunwu*, 85.

105. Mao Tsetung, "Oppose Book Worship," in *Selected Readings*, 40–50.

106. Ibid., 44–45.

107. Ibid., 47, brackets added.

108. Ibid., 48.

109. Mao, *Report from Xunwu*, 64–65.

110. Mao, "Oppose Book Worship," 48.

111. Thompson, introduction to *Report from Xunwu*, 31.

112. Mao, "Oppose Book Worship," 48.

113. Ibid., 48–49.

114. Ibid., 49.

115. Ibid.

116. Mao, *Report from Xunwu*, 64.

117. Mao, "Oppose Book Worship," 40.

118. For these reflections, see Mao Tsetung, "On Contradiction," in *Selected Readings from the Works of Mao Tsetung*, 85–133.

119. Mao Tsetung, "Preface to *Rural Surveys*," in *Selected Readings*, 196.

Chapter 3

1. Asad Haider and Salar Mohandesi, "Workers' Inquiry: A Genealogy," *Viewpoint Magazine*, September 27, 2013, https://viewpointmag.com/2013/09/27/workers-inquiry-a-genealogy/; Jamie Woodcock, "The Workers' Inquiry from Trotskyism to Operaismo: A Political Methodology for Investigating the Work-

place," *ephemera: theory & politics in organization* 14, no. 3 (2014): 493–513, http://www.ephemerajournal.org/sites/default/files/pdfs/contribution/14-3woodcock.pdf.

2. Haider and Mohandesi, "Workers' Inquiry." Haider and Mohandesi instructively draw out the goal of consciousness-raising in the inquiries of the Johnson-Forest Tendency, Correspondence, and Socialisme ou Barbarie, yet they stop short of discerning this *same* objective in the workers' inquiries of *Quaderni Rossi*, as if it had been surpassed or eclipsed in the affirmation of an *already* antagonistic class. In so doing, they miss some of the most elaborate theorizations of workers' inquiry in the history of the practice.

3. Karl Marx, "A Workers' Inquiry," *New International: A Monthly Organ of Revolutionary Marxism* 12, no. 4 (1938): 379–81.

4. Haider and Mohandesi, "Workers' Inquiry."

5. C. L. R. James, *State Capitalism and World Revolution*, in collaboration with Raya Dunayevskaya and Grace Lee (Chicago: Charles H. Kerr, 1986), 13. For a helpful synopsis of Leon Trotsky's view of bureaucracy as a mere outgrowth of Joseph Stalin's illegitimacy, see Stephen Hastings-King, *Looking for the Proletariat: Socialisme ou Barbarie and the Problem of Worker Writing* (Chicago: Haymarket Books, 2015), 38–39.

6. James, *State Capitalism and World Revolution*, 30, 32, 39–44, 49.

7. Ibid., 40.

8. Haider and Mohandesi, "Workers' Inquiry."

9. Hastings-King, *Looking for the Proletariat*, 183.

10. Haider and Mohandesi, "Workers' Inquiry," italics mine; Paul Romano and Ria Stone, *The American Worker* (Detroit: Bewicked, 1972).

11. Haider and Mohandesi, "Workers' Inquiry." I stick to these pseudonyms in this discussion mainly for the sake of remaining consistent with the references to them in quotes from *The American Worker*.

12. Christian Høgsbjerg, "A 'Bohemian Freelancer'? C.L.R. James, His Early Relationship to Anarchism and the Intellectual Origins of Autonomism," in *Libertarian Socialism: Politics in Black and Red*, ed. Alex Prichard et al. (New York: Palgrave Macmillan, 2012), 154.

13. Paul Romano, "Life in the Factory," in *American Worker*, 1–41.

14. Martin Glaberman, introduction to *American Worker*, v.

15. Stone, "The Reconstruction of Society," in *American Worker*, 42–70.

16. Høgsbjerg, "A 'Bohemian Freelancer'?," 154.

17. Woodcock, "Workers' Inquiry from Trotskyism to Operaismo," 498–500.

18. Ibid., 493, 509.

19. See Haider and Mohandesi, "Workers' Inquiry"; Woodcock, "Workers' Inquiry," 500; Hastings-King, *Looking for the Proletariat*, 124–34.

20. Romano, "Life in the Factory," 1.

21. Ibid.

22. Ibid., 41.

23. Ibid., 1.
24. Ibid., 12.
25. Ibid.
26. Ibid., 14.
27. Ibid., 36–37.
28. Ibid., 37.
29. Stone, "Reconstruction of Society," 42.
30. Ibid., 46.
31. Ibid., 46–47.
32. Ibid., 49.
33. Ibid., 53.
34. Ibid., 70.
35. Ibid., 59.
36. Ibid., 59n.
37. Marx, "Workers' Inquiry," 379–81.
38. Haider and Mohandesi, "Workers' Inquiry."
39. Ibid.
40. Haider and Mohandesi, "Workers' Inquiry."
41. Karl Marx, *A Workers' Inquiry* (Tougaloo, MS: Freedom Information Service; Detroit: Bewick, 1973), 12.
42. Glaberman, introduction to *American Worker*, vi.
43. Stone, "Reconstruction of Society," 58.
44. Glaberman, introduction to *American Worker*, vi.
45. Correspondence, *The Correspondence Booklet: Selections from a Paper That Is Written, Edited and Circulated by Its Readers* (Detroit: Correspondence Publishing, 1954), 59.
46. Ibid., 1.
47. Hastings-King, *Looking for the Proletariat*, 17–18, 177.
48. Ibid., 181. Hastings-King identifies Dunayevskaya as the author of this column.
49. Correspondence, *Correspondence Booklet*, 62. Dunayevskaya's declaration that *Correspondence* was the first workers' newspaper in the world was simply misinformed. As we shall see in chapter 5, workers' newspapers date from at least as early as nineteenth-century France. Another contributor to *Correspondence* described the newspaper in more modest terms as a workers' newspaper in the making. In the candid words of this self-described intellectual: "*Correspondence* is not yet a workers' newspaper" (ibid., 57).
50. Hastings-King, *Looking for the Proletariat*, 170.
51. Ibid., 179.
52. Correspondence, *Correspondence Booklet*, 1.
53. Ibid., 25–27, 30, 47–48, 55–56, 61–63.
54. Hastings-King, *Looking for the Proletariat*, 181.

55. Ibid., 183.

56. Ibid., 169.

57. Ibid., 183.

58. Ibid., 36. Hastings-King identifies the precise catalyst for this break as the decision of the Trotskyist International Communist Party to support Josip Broz Tito's Yugoslavia, which the Chaulieu-Montal Tendency considered Stalinist.

59. Ibid., 19–22.

60. Ibid., 14, 41.

61. Ibid., 42.

62. Ibid., 41–43.

63. Ibid., 15.

64. Ibid., 16.

65. Ibid.

66. Henri Simon, "Workers' Inquiry in Socialisme ou Barbarie," trans. Asad Haider and Salar Mohandesi, *Viewpoint Magazine*, September 26, 2013, https://viewpointmag.com/2013/09/26/workers-inquiry-in-socialisme-ou-barbarie/.

67. Hastings-King, *Looking for the Proletariat*, 124–25; Haider and Mohandesi, "Workers' Inquiry: A Genealogy."

68. Claude Lefort, "Proletarian Experience (1952)," trans. Stephen Hastings-King, *Viewpoint Magazine*, September 26, 2013, https://viewpointmag.com/2013/09/26/proletarian-experience/.

69. Ibid.

70. Ibid.

71. Ibid.

72. Ibid.

73. Hastings-King, *Looking for the Proletariat*, 197; 202.

74. Ibid., 7.

75. Ibid., 203, brackets added.

76. Ibid., 166, 217.

77. Ibid., 222.

78. Ibid., 224.

79. Steve Wright, *Storming Heaven: Class Composition and Struggle in Italian Autonomist Marxism* (Sterling, VA: Pluto Press, 2002), 49.

80. Quaderni Rossi, introduction to *Luttes ouvrières et capitalisme d'aujourd'hui*, trans. Nicole Rouzet (Paris: François Maspero, 1968), 10.

81. Haider and Mohandesi, "Workers' Inquiry."

82. Danilo Montaldi, "Introduction to L'Operaio Americano (1954)," trans. Salar Mohandesi, *Viewpoint Magazine*, September 27, 2013, https://viewpointmag.com/2013/09/27/introduction-to-loperaio-americano-1954/.

83. Wright, *Storming Heaven*, 24.

84. Ibid., 25.

85. Ibid.

86. Michel J. M. Thiollent, *Crítica metodológica, investigação social e enquete operária*, 4th ed. (São Paulo: Polis, 1985), 117.

87. Ibid., 116–17.

88. Andrea Cavazzini, *Enquête ouvrière et théorie critique: Enjeux et figures de la centralité ouvrière dans l'Italie des années 1960* (Liège: Presses Universitaires de Liège, 2013), 24.

89. Ibid., 25.

90. Ibid., 25–26.

91. Wright, *Storming Heaven*, 22.

92. Ibid.

93. Danilo Dolci, *Report from Palermo*, trans. P. D. Cummins (New York: Hillman/MacFadden Books, 1961).

94. Ibid., xiii, 211–56.

95. Ibid., xiii.

96. Ibid.

97. Wright, *Storming Heaven*, 23.

98. Antonio Negri, "Marx Is Still Marx: Interview With Rainer Ganahl," http://semiotexte.com/?p=660.

99. Dolci, *Report*, xiv.

100. Cavazzini, *Enquête ouvrière*, 109.

101. Haider and Mohandesi, "Workers' Inquiry."

102. Ibid., 49.

103. Woodcock, "Workers' Inquiry," 504.

104. Cavazzini, *Enquête ouvrière*, 110–11.

105. Ibid., 109.

106. Ibid., 109–10.

107. Ibid., 110.

108. Ibid., 110, 112.

109. Ibid., 112.

110. Ibid.

111. Ibid.

112. Haider and Mohandesi, "Workers' Inquiry."

113. Wright, *Storming Heaven*, 46.

114. Ibid., 48–50.

115. Ibid., 49.

116. Ibid., 50–51.

117. Dario Lanzardo, "Marx et l'enquête ouvrière," in Quaderni Rossi, *Luttes ouvrières*, 117–31.

118. Ibid., 131.

119. Ibid., 117.

120. Marx, *Workers' Inquiry*, 4.

121. Lanzardo, "Marx et l'enquête ouvrière," 117.

122. Ibid.
123. Ibid., 119.
124. Ibid.
125. Ibid., 121.
126. Ibid.
127. Marx, *Workers' Inquiry*, 10.
128. Lanzardo, "Marx et l'enquête ouvrière," 125.
129. Ibid., 127.
130. Ibid., 129.
131. Ibid.
132. Ibid., 130.
133. Ibid., 130–31.
134. Ibid., 131.
135. Ibid., 125.
136. Ibid., 127; Karl Marx, "[Value, Price and Profit]," in *Collected Works*, vol. 20, *Marx and Engels: 1864–68* (Moscow: Progress Publishers, 1985), 101–49.
137. Raniero Panzieri, "Socialist Uses of Workers' Inquiry," trans. Arianna Bove, *Transversal*, http://transform.eipcp.net/transversal/0406/panzieri/en.
138. Raniero Panzieri, "Conception socialiste de l'enquête ouvrière," in Quaderni Rossi, *Luttes ouvrières et capitalisme d'aujourd'hui*, 116.
139. Panzieri, "Socialist Uses of Workers' Inquiry."
140. Ibid.
141. Thiollent, *Crítica metodológica*, 119.
142. Panzieri, "Socialist Uses of Workers' Inquiry."
143. Ibid.
144. Ibid.
145. Ibid.
146. Ibid.
147. Ibid.
148. Ibid.
149. Cavazzini, *Enquête ouvrière*, 106.
150. Ibid. Cavazzini mistakenly dates the revolt from 1963.
151. Thiollent, *Crítica metodológica*, 108.
152. Ibid.

Chapter 4

1. Enquête translates as "investigation," "inquiry," and "survey." I explain my reasons for tilting toward "investigation" in the introduction, and I address the English translation of enquête in a bit more detail in the subsequent chapter.

For the moment, it suffices to add that the rendering of enquête as "investigation" is especially appropriate in this chapter because it tends to be the most common translation of enquête in the literature on French Maoism.

2. Thanasis Lagios, "Foucauldian Genealogy and Maoism," *foucaultblog*, February 6, 2016, doi: 10.13095/uzh.fsw.fb.130. The original injunction comes from a subheading in Mao Tsetung, "Oppose Book Worship," in *Selected Readings from the Works of Mao Tsetung* (Peking: Foreign Languages Press, 1971), 40. Incidentally, other Maoist slogans continued to circulate among non-Maoist groups even after French Maoism went into precipitous decline. Perhaps surprisingly, Daniel Defert recalls that he retained the Maoist slogan "The eye of the peasant sees clearly" in his AIDS activism in *Une vie politique: Entretiens avec Philippe Artières et Eric Favereau avec la collaboration de Joséphine Gross* (Paris: Seuil, 2014), 49. Defert used the slogan rather liberally with reference to AIDS patients.

3. Kristin Ross, *May '68 and Its Afterlives* (Chicago: University of Chicago Press, 2002), 109; Donald Reid, "*Etablissement*: Working in the Factory to Make Revolution in France," *Radical History Review*, no. 88 (Winter 2004): 85. I want to thank Thanasis Lagios for drawing my attention to Reid's article and generously providing me with a copy of it.

4. Dario Lanzardo, "Marx et l'enquête ouvrière," in *Luttes ouvrières et capitalisme d'aujourd'hui*, trans. Nicole Rouzet (François Maspero: Paris, 1968), 117–31; "Le rôle politique de l'enquête," *Cahiers de Mai*, July 1970, 13–16.

5. Reid, "*Etablissement*," 86.

6. Mao Tsetung, "Speech at the Chinese Communist Party's National Conference on Propaganda Work," in *Selected Readings from the Work of Mao Tsetung*, 485.

7. For a rich account of établissement in the French Maoist experience, see Reid, "Etablissement," 83–111. For Maoism as an enduring influence in Badiou, see Bruno Bosteels, "Post-Maoism: Badiou and Politics," special issue, *positions: east asia cultures critique* 13, no. 1 (2005): 575–634. For the claim that French Maoism nurtured a turn to human rights and associative democracy after May 1968, see Richard Wolin, *The Wind From the East: French Intellectuals, the Cultural Revolution and the Legacy of the 1960s* (Princeton: Princeton University Press, 2010). For the role of Maoism in Louis Althusser's critique of humanism, see Camille Robcis, "'China in Our Heads': Althusser, Maoism, and Structuralism," *Social Text 110* 30, no. 1 (2012): 51–69. For an examination of the move to the political right among French Maoists who had practiced établissement, see Jason E. Smith, "From Établissement to Lip: On the Turns Taken by French Maoism," *Viewpoint Magazine*, September 25, 2013, https://viewpointmag.com/2013/09/25/from-etablissement-to-lip-on-the-turns-taken-by-french-maoism/. For the effervescence of French Maoism through prominent readings of Mao's theory of contradiction, see Julian Bourg, "Principally Contradiction: The Flourishing of French Maoism," in *Mao's Little Red Book: A Global History*, ed. Alexander C.

Cook (New York: Cambridge University Press, 2014): 225–44. For Maoism as an underappreciated source of inspiration for Michel Foucault's reformulation of genealogy in the mid-1970s, see Mads Peter Karlsen and Kaspar Villadsen, "Foucault, Maoism, Genealogy: The Influence of Political Militancy in Michel Foucault's Thought," *New Political Science: A Journal of Politics and Culture* 37, no. 1 (2015): 91–117. For a contrasting take on Maoism as a source of Foucault's genealogical method, see Lagios, "Foucauldian Genealogy and Maoism." It is noteworthy that *all* of these very different contributions touch at least in one way or another on the Maoist practice of investigations, as if discussions of French Maoism *oblige* a reference to this practice.

8. On the characterization of Badiou as a "post-Maoist," see Bosteels, "Post-Maoism," 581.

9. Ross offers a synopsis of crucial aspects of the investigation in her analysis of social amnesia about May 1968 in France in *May '68 and its Afterlives*, 109–113. Bosteels dwells briefly on the investigation in his dialectical interpretation of the later Badiou in "Post-Maoism," 580–81. Wolin devotes a few scattered pages of his lengthy book to the popularity of investigations among organizations concerned with the struggles of prisoners, gays, and women in *Wind from the East*, 18, 131–32, 138, 159, 303, 305–7, 323, 330, 338.

10. In this regard, see Reid, "Etablissement," 85; Wolin, *Wind from the East*, 138. It should go without saying that this elision of source materials does a disservice to researchers of the French Maoist experience.

11. Groupe pour la fondation de l'Union des communistes de France marxiste-léniniste (UCFML), *Le livre des paysans pauvres: 5 années de travail maoïste dans une campagne française* (Paris: François Maspero, 1976).

12. The word *paysans* in the title of the book translates as "small farmers" as well as "peasants." I opt for the latter translation to more clearly stress that the UCFML embraced Mao's affirmation of the revolutionary role of poor peasants in the very different context of late twentieth-century France. Admittedly and perhaps unsurprisingly, however, the UCFML's understanding of poor peasants diverged from Mao's understanding. The UCFML treated poor peasants as a class fraction unable to cultivate *owned* land because of an *insufficiency* of labor-power in ibid., 149. This rendering contrasts with Mao's treatment of poor peasants as a class fraction that gravitates between a *complete dispossession* of the land and instruments of labor, on the one hand, and an *insufficient ownership* of land and money to cover the costs of living, on the other hand. For his rendering of poor peasants, see Mao Tsetung, "Report on an Investigation of the Peasant Movement in Hunan," in *Selected Readings from the Works of Mao Tsetung*, 35.

13. Gavin Walker critically revisits the intricacies of the UCFML's economic writings from the mid-1970s to suggest that Badiou's aversion to the critique of political economy has its roots in critiques of economism in these writings in "On

Marxism's Field of Operation: Badiou and the Critique of Political Economy," *Historical Materialism* 20, no. 3 (2012): 39–74.

14. Bosteels, "Post-Maoism," 680.

15. Alain Badiou, "May '68 Revisited, 40 Years On," in *The Communist Hypothesis*, trans. David Macey and Steve Corcoran (New York: Verso, 2010), 59–60.

16. Ibid., 52–54.

17. As an example, see Reid, "Etablissement," 83–111. Stunningly, Reid makes no mention of the UCFML in his otherwise comprehensive analysis of établissement among French Maoist organizations.

18. Bosteels, "Post-Maoism," 629–30n50.

19. A. Belden Fields, *Trotskyism and Maoism: Theory and Practice in France and the United States* (New York: Praeger, 1988), 98.

20. Bosteels, "Post-Maoism," 585.

21. In invoking a "party of a new type," the UCFML adopted a phrase that has been mistakenly attributed to Lenin. Lars T. Lih suggests that Lenin did not use this phrase because there was nothing new in his core conceptualization of the party. The latter, as Lih explains, drew extensively from an already established Social-Democratic view of the party as a fusion of the working-class movement and socialist doctrine. On the imputation of the phrase "party of a new type" to Lenin, see Lars T. Lih, *Lenin Rediscovered: "What Is to Be Done?" in Context* (Chicago: Haymarket Books, 2008), 31n54.

22. UCFML, *Livre des paysans pauvres*, 15, italics mine.

23. Ibid., 16.

24. Ibid.

25. Ibid.

26. Ibid., 21.

27. Ibid., 92, italics mine.

28. Ibid., 19, 219n1.

29. Ibid., 17.

30. Ibid.

31. On these proscriptions, see Fields, *Trotskyism and Maoism*, 94, 107. We address the consequences of the proscription of the GP in much greater detail in the subsequent chapter.

32. Alain Badiou, *Théorie de la contradiction* (Paris: François Maspero, 1975), 20.

33. Bosteels, "Post-Maoism," 579.

34. Ross, *May '68*, 109.

35. Jean-Pierre Le Dantec, "D'où vient l'établissement?," *Les Temps Modernes*, nos. 684–85 (July–October 2015): 16.

36. Ibid., 17.

37. Ibid.

38. Jason E. Smith, "From Établissement to Lip." On the disappointment of UJCML militants with investigations, see also Reid, "Etablissement," 85. For the recollections of one militant who conducted investigations among peasants in the Vosges region of northeastern France only to then take up a position in a factory, see Michèle Manceaux, *Les maos en France* (Paris: Gallimard, 1972), 54–57.

39. Le Dantec, "D'où vient l'établissement?," 20.

40. Robert Linhart, *The Assembly Line*, trans. Margaret Crosland (Amherst: University of Massachusetts Press, 1981).

41. Fields, *Trotskyism and Maoism*, 122.

42. Danielle Rancière, "Militer ensemble: Entretien avec Danielle Rancière," in *Michel Foucault*, ed. Philippe Artières et al. (Paris: Éditions de l'Herne, 2011), 53–54. Rancière and other GP members were certainly not alone in thinking of the investigation in terms of a kind of mirror function. As we saw in chapter 2, Ken Lawrence and Hilde Weiss construed the investigation precisely in such terms.

43. Ibid., 53.

44. Wolin, *Wind from the East*, 138.

45. Yves Duroux, "Sur la question du savoir dans le maoïsme," in *Le sujet et l'étude: idéologie et savoir dans le discours maoïste*, by Andrea Cavazzini (Reims: Le Clou dans le Fer, 2011), 102, 106.

46. Ibid., 106.

47. For a helpful overview of the VLR, see Fields, *Trotskyism and Maoism*, 100–1.

48. "Enquête . . . ," *Tout!*, April 23, 1971.

49. *Tout!*, April 23, 1971.

50. "Enquête . . ."

51. Ibid.

52. Of course, the focus of the UCFML on testing the preparedness of its militants to lead the people by going to the countryside to work with peasants did not necessarily mean that it was disinterested in facilitating the voices of peasants. Notably, the UCFML published a letter authored by poor peasants in *Livre des paysans pauvres*, 144–48.

53. From a temporal perspective, it appears that there were at least two kinds of UCFML militants who worked in the countryside: those who spent an entire summer there and those who stayed for much shorter periods of two weeks to a little over a month. On the latter, see ibid., 26.

54. Ibid., [8].

55. I want to thank Çigdem Çidam for helping me draw out this point through her comments on an earlier draft of this chapter delivered at the annual meeting of the Association for Political Theory at the University of Colorado in Boulder on October 22, 2015.

56. Mao, "Speech," 485; Raniero Panzieri, "Socialist Uses of Workers' Inquiry," trans. Arianna Bove, *Transversal*, http://transform.eipcp.net/transversal/0406/panzieri/en.

57. UCFML, *Livre des paysans pauvres*, 21. The UCFML described "Beaumont" as a mountain village located close to the village of "Saint-Jean" in the commune of la Verdière. This commune is located in the Var department in southeastern France. On the location of Sant-Jean in the commune of la Verdière and its proximity to Beaumont, see ibid., 52–53.

58. Ibid., 22.

59. Ibid., 24–25.

60. Ibid., 25.

61. Ibid.

62. Ibid., 43.

63. Ibid., 48.

64. Ibid., 45, 48, 59.

65. Ibid., 49.

66. Ibid., 50.

67. Ibid., 97.

68. Ibid.

69. Ibid., 92, italics in the original.

70. For an analysis highly critical of the presumption that peasants *lack* autonomy and therefore necessitate the political leadership of outside social forces, see Ranajit Guha, *Elementary Aspects of Peasant Insurgency in Colonial India* (Durham: Duke University Press, 1999).

71. UCFML, *Livre des paysans pauvres*, 24, 28, 128.

72. Ibid., 24, italics in the original.

73. Ibid., 95–96.

74. Ibid., 204–5, 211.

75. Though the reasoning behind this ascription of individualism to peasants was reductionist, the charge of individualism against peasants was hardly unique to the UCFML. A theorist no less emphatic about the revolutionary potentialities of the peasantry in the decolonizing world than Frantz Fanon still considered individualism an "objectively reactionary" trait of the peasantry in Western industrialized countries in *The Wretched of the Earth*, trans. Richard Philcox (New York: Grove Press, 2004), 66.

76. UCFML, *Livre des paysans pauvres*, 21.

77. Ibid., 267.

78. Thomas Nail, "Alain Badiou and the *Sans-Papiers*," *Angelaki: Journal of the Theoretical Humanities* 20, no. 4 (December 2015): 111.

79. Ibid., 109–30.

80. For an overview of the prescriptions and activities of the OP as well as their implications for Badiou's understanding of politics, see Peter Hallward, *Badiou: A Subject to Truth* (Minneapolis: University of Minnesota Press, 2003), 227–42.

81. Alain Badiou, "The Nomadic Proletariat: An Interview with Alain Badiou," by Thomas Nail, *Philosophy Today* 61 (forthcoming), brackets in the original.

82. Alain Badiou, "Politics and Philosophy: An Interview with Alain Badiou," in *Ethics: An Essay on the Understanding of Evil*, trans. Peter Hallward (New York: Verso, 2001), 95–96.

83. Alberto Toscano, "Marxism Expatriated: Alain Badiou's Turn," in *Critical Companion to Contemporary Marxism*, ed. Jacques Bidet and Stathis Kouvelakis (Boston: Brill, 2008), 535.

84. Ibid.

85. Hallward, *Badiou*, 41.

86. Ibid., 43.

87. Alain Badiou, *Peut-on penser la politique?* (Paris: Seuil, 1985), 85–86.

88. Ibid., 15.

89. Ibid., 12.

90. Ibid., 87.

91. Ibid., 67.

92. Ibid., 108.

93. Ibid., 109.

94. Alain Badiou, "The Paris Commune: Political Declaration on Politics," in *The Communist Hypothesis*, 181–82.

95. Ibid., 179–80. Karl Marx criticized the Communards for failing to attack the government of Adolphe Thiers in Versailles at its moment of greatest vulnerability in "The Civil War in France," in *Marx: Later Political Writings*, ed. and trans. Terrell Carver (New York: Cambridge University Press, 2006), 178. V. I. Lenin echoed a more general variation of this criticism in *State and Revolution* (New York: International Publishers, 1943), 37.

96. Badiou, "The Paris Commune," 182.

97. Ibid., 113–14, 155–56.

98. Bruno Bosteels astutely emphasizes that what *persists* in Badiou's shift toward a politics without party "is the idea that any emancipatory politics must take an organized form" in "Translator's Introduction," in *Theory of the Subject*, by Alain Badiou (New York: Bloomsbury Academic, 2009), xi.

99. Alain Badiou, *Ethics: An Essay on the Understanding of Evil*, trans. Peter Hallward (New York: Verso, 2001), 67, italics mine.

100. Hallward, *Badiou*, 126.

101. Badiou, *Théorie*, 110.

Chapter 5

1. For the one glaring exception to the translation of enquête as "inquiry" in Foucault's analyses, see Michel Foucault, *Discipline and Punish: The Birth of the*

Prison, trans. Alan Sheridan (New York: Vintage Books, 1978), 225–27. Sheridan renders enquête as "investigation." For the original French, see Michel Foucault, *Surveiller et punir: Naissance de la prison* (Paris: Gallimard, 1975), 226–28.

2. Richard Wolin, *The Wind from the East: French Intellectuals, the Cultural Revolution, and the Legacy of the 1960s* (Princeton: Princeton University Press, 2010), 18; Mads P. Karlsen and Kaspar Villadsen, "Foucault, Maoism, Genealogy: The Influence of Political Militancy in Michel Foucault's Thought," *New Political Science: A Journal of Politics and Culture* 37, no. 1 (2015): 91–117; Thanasis Lagios, "Foucauldian Genealogy and Maoism," *foucaultblog*, February 6, 2016, doi: 10.13095/uzh.fsw.fb.130.

3. Lagios briefly highlights the simultaneity of Foucault's focus on enquêtes in his lectures and political activities in "Foucauldian Genealogy and Maoism." See also the editorial commentary in Michel Foucault, *Théories et institutions pénales: Cours au Collège de France (1971–1972)*, ed. Bernard E. Harcourt in collaboration with Elisabetta Basso and Claude-Olivier Doron and with the assistance of Daniel Defert (Paris: Seuil/Gallimard, 2015), 224n38.

4. Cecile Brich, "The Groupe d'information sur les prisons: The Voice of Prisoners? Or Foucault's?," *Foucault Studies*, no. 5 (January 2008): 26–47, http://rauli.cbs.dk/index.php/foucault-studies/article/view/1408; Marcelo Hoffman, "Foucault and the 'Lesson' of the Prisoner Support Movement," *New Political Science: A Journal of Politics and Culture* 34, no. 1 (March 2012): 21–36; Karlsen and Villadsen, "Foucault, Maoism, Genealogy," 91–117.

5. Michel Foucault, "Truth and Juridical Forms," in *Essential Works of Foucault, 1954–1984*, ed. Paul Rabinow, vol. 3, *Power*, ed. James Faubion, trans. Robert Hurley et al. (New York: The New Press, 2000), 51.

6. Michel Foucault, "Penal Theories and Institutions," in *Essential Works of Foucault, 1954–1984*, ed. Paul Rabinow, vol. 1, *Ethics: Subjectivity and Truth*, ed. Paul Rabinow, trans. Robert Hurley et al. (New York: The New Press, 1997), 19.

7. Foucault, "Truth and Juridical Forms," 5.

8. Michel Foucault, *Lectures on the Will to Know: Lectures at the Collège de France, 1970–1971 and Oedipal Knowledge*, ed. Daniel Defert, trans. Graham Burchell (New York: Palgrave Macmillan, 2013), 241–42, 244.

9. Ibid., 245–46.

10. Ibid., 248.

11. Ibid., 249.

12. Ibid., 237.

13. Ibid., 249.

14. Ibid., 254–55.

15. Ibid., 255.

16. Ibid., 256.

17. Foucault, "Truth and Juridical Forms," 32.

18. Ibid., 34.
19. Ibid.
20. Ibid., 34–39.
21. Ibid., 39–40.
22. Ibid., 34.
23. Ibid., 44–45.
24. Ibid., 46.
25. Ibid., 47.
26. Ibid., 42.
27. Ibid., 42–43.
28. Ibid., 44.
29. Foucault, *Théories et institutions pénales*, 200.
30. Foucault, "Truth and Juridical Forms," 47.
31. Foucault, *Théories et institutions pénales*, 202.
32. Ibid.
33. Ibid., 203, 205.
34. Ibid., 206.
35. Ibid., 203.
36. Ibid., 209.
37. Foucault, "Truth and Juridical Forms," 51.
38. Ibid., 49–50.
39. Foucault, *Discipline and Punish*, 225.
40. Noteworthy in this regard is Foucault's lengthy exposition of the repression of the peasant-based, antifiscal revolt of the bare feet in Normandy from 1639 to 1640 in *Théories et institutions pénales*, 3–109. For a helpful review of this course, see Stuart Elden, "Peasant Revolts, Germanic Law and the Medieval Inquiry," review of *Théories et institutions pénales: Cours au Collège de France, 1971–1972*, by Michel Foucault, *Befrois*, June 2, 2015, http://www.berfrois.com/2015/06/foucaults-politics-of-truth-stuart-elden/.
41. Foucault, *Discipline and Punish*, 225.
42. Ibid.
43. Foucault, *Lectures on the Will to Know*, 185; David Macey, *The Lives of Michel Foucault: A Biography* (New York: Pantheon Books, 1993), 257–58.
44. Philippe Artières, Laurent Quéro, and Michelle Zancarini-Fournel, "Genèse du GIP," in *Le Groupe d'Information sur les Prisons: Archives d'une lutte, 1970–1972*, ed. Philippe Artières, Laurent Quéro, and Michelle Zancarini-Fournel (Paris: Éditions de l'IMEC, 2003), 27.
45. Daniel Defert, "L'émergence d'un nouveau front: les prisons," in *Groupe d'Information sur les Prisons*, 316.
46. Organisation des prisonniers politiques (OPP), "Rapport sur les prisons," in *Groupe d'Information sur les Prisons*, 34–36.

47. Ibid., 36.

48. Artières, Quéro, and Zancarini-Fournel, *Groupe d'Information sur les Prisons*, 34.

49. Ibid., 42.

50. Defert, "L'émergence d'un nouveau front," 316–17.

51. Ibid., 318.

52. Ibid., 321.

53. Ibid., 318–19.

54. Ibid., 318.

55. Daniel Defert, *Une vie politique: Entretiens avec Philippe Artières et Eric Favereau avec la collaboration de Joséphine Gross* (Paris: Seuil, 2014), 57.

56. Artières, Quéro, and Zancarini-Fournel, *Groupe d'Information sur les Prisons*, 52.

57. GIP, "Le GIP vient de lancer sa première enquête," in *Groupe d'Information sur les Prisons*, 52, italics in the original.

58. Ibid., italics in the original.

59. Ibid.

60. GIP, "Questionnaire aux détenus," in *Groupe d'Information sur les Prisons*, 55–62.

61. Ibid., 62.

62. Artières, Quéro, and Zancarini-Fournel, *Groupe d'Information sur les Prisons*, 50.

63. Michel Foucault, "La situation dans les prisons est intolérable . . . ," in *Groupe d'Information sur les Prisons*, 50–51.

64. GIP, "Nous venons discuter dans les files d'attente . . . ," in *Groupe d'Information sur les Prisons*, 63.

65. Defert, "L'émergence d'un nouveau front," 319.

66. GIP, "Enquête-intolérance," in *Groupe d'Information sur les Prisons*, 53.

67. Philippe Artières, Laurent Quéro, and Michelle Zancarini-Fournel, " 'Nous voulons savoir,' " in *Groupe d'information sur les Prisons*, 48.

68. Michel Foucault, "La prison partout," in *Groupe d'Information sur les Prisons*, 79.

69. Defert, *Vie politique*, 73.

70. GIP, "Enquête-intolérance," 53, italics in the original.

71. GIP, "Quand l'information est une lutte," 72.

72. Ibid., 72–73.

73. Ibid., 72.

74. Macey, *Lives of Michel Foucault*, 267–68.

75. GIP, "Enquête-intolérance," 54.

76. Defert, "L'émergence d'un nouveau front," 324.

77. Ibid.; Defert, *Vie politique*, 73–74. The account that the GIP actually published differs from what Defert recounts, but it is no less scandalous. In the

report of the first investigation of the GIP, a prisoner from Toul describes another prisoner who was placed in a straitjacket in solitary confinement for ten days. As the straitjacket of the latter prisoner was never detached, his urine and fecal matter accumulated around him during this period. See Information Group on Prisons (GIP), *Investigation in 20 Prisons*, in *Foucault and Power: The Influence of Political Engagement on Theories of Power*, by Marcelo Hoffman (New York: Bloomsbury, 2014), 202.

78. Defert, *Vie politique*, 73–74.

79. GIP, *Investigation in 20 Prisons*, 155–204.

80. Groupe d'Information sur les Prisons (GIP), *Enquête dans une prison-modèle: Fleury-Mérogis* (Paris: Éditions Champ Libre, 1971); Groupe d'Information sur les Prisons (GIP), *L'assassinat de George Jackson* (Paris: Gallimard, 1971); Groupe d'Information sur les Prisons (GIP), *Suicides de prison (1972)* (Paris: Gallimard, 1973). To my knowledge, none of these reports has been fully translated into English. However, an English translation of a section of *L'assassinat de George Jackson* can be found in Michel Foucault, Catharine von Bülow, and Daniel Defert, "The Masked Assassination," in *Warfare in the American Homeland: Policing and Prison in a Penal Democracy*, ed. Joy James (Durham: Duke University Press, 2007), 140–58.

81. Karl Marx, *A Workers' Inquiry* (Tougaloo, MS: Freedom Information Service; Detroit: Bewick, 1973), 4.

82. GIP, *Investigation in 20 Prisons*, 156, italics in the original.

83. Ibid., 158–72.

84. Ibid., 172–80.

85. Ibid., 166–67.

86. See, for instance, Michel Foucault, *La société punitive: Cours au Collège de France (1972–1973)*, ed. Bernard E. Harcourt (Paris: Gallimard/Seuil, 2013), 215–16.

87. For a deeply thoughtful reflection on the colonization of so-called free time by capital, see Nichole Marie Shippen, *Decolonizing Time: Work, Leisure, and Freedom* (New York: Palgrave Macmillan, 2014).

88. GIP, *Investigation in 20 Prisons*, 186.

89. Ibid., 202.

90. Ibid., 198.

91. Ibid., 201.

92. Ibid. Well over four decades after the publication of this shocking revelation, scandalous conditions, including overcrowding and rat infestations, continue to beset the Fresnes prison. See Jean-Baptiste Jacquin, "A la prison de Fresnes, alerte sur le 'traitement inhumain' et 'dégradant' des détenus," *Le Monde*, December 14, 2016, http://www.lemonde.fr/police-justice/article/2016/12/14/la-controleure-des-prisons-alerte-sur-le-traitement-inhumain-des-detenus-a-fresnes_5048494_1653578.html.

93. GIP, *Investigation in 20 Prisons*, 156.

94. Michel Foucault, "Nul de nous n'est sûr d'échapper à la prison . . . ," in *Groupe d'Information sur les Prisons*, 43–44.

95. The Brazilian journalist Paulo Markun offers a vivid reminder of the extent to which filling out a questionnaire can amount to an absurd and terrifying experience in *Meu querido Vlado: A história de Vladimir Herzog e do sonho de uma geração*, 2nd ed. (Rio de Janeiro: Objetiva), 155–57. He recalls the obligation to fill out a questionnaire *after* having been tortured at an army center in São Paulo but *before* being released from a prison at another security center in November 1975. Markun describes his situation through a neologism that ingeniously combines the Portuguese words *pergunta* (question) and *purgatório* (purgatory): "*perguntório*" (ibid., 158, italics in the original).

96. Kristin Ross, *May '68 and Its Afterlives* (Chicago: University of Chicago Press, 2002), 111–12.

97. "Le rôle politique de l'enquête," *Cahiers de Mai*, July 1970, 13–16. Ross offers a rich but somewhat misleading discussion of this article in *May '68 and its Afterlives*, 111–12. She does not distinguish *Cahiers de Mai*'s theorization of workers' inquiry from the Maoist investigation in the larger context of her elaboration of the latter. Ross may have lumped together these different types of enquêtes because *Cahiers de Mai* dabbled with a Maoist language in its theorization of workers' inquiry.

98. "Rôle politique de l'enquête," 13; Dario Lanzardo, "Marx et l'enquête ouvrière," in *Luttes ouvrières et capitalisme d'aujourd'hui*, trans. Nicole Rouzet (François Maspero: Paris, 1968), 117. Still, it should be noted that the epigraph is not a word-for-word reproduction of the quote as it appeared in the original introduction to Marx's questionnaire in *La Revue socialiste*. The precise source for the epigraph is not listed, and I have not been able to track it down.

99. "Rôle politique de l'enquête," 16.

100. Ross makes this point, albeit through an opposition between politics and police borrowed from Jacques Rancière in *May '68 and Its Afterlives*, 211–12.

101. "Rôle politique de l'enquête," 13–14.

102. Ibid., 15. Of course, these cautionary words are a play on Karl Marx's famous warning to his French readers that "there is no royal road to science" in *Capital: A Critique of Political Economy*, vol. 1, trans. Ben Fowkes (New York: Vintage Books, 1977), 104.

103. "Rôle politique de l'enquête," 16. The whole preceding paragraph owes an enormous debt of gratitude to Stuart Elden, who generously sent me a copy of the article about workers' inquiry in *Cahiers de Mai*.

104. Danielle Rancière, "Militer Ensemble: Entretien avec Danielle Rancière," in *Michel Foucault*, ed. Philippe Artières et al. (Paris: Éditions de l'Herne, 2011), 54.

105. Ibid., 53.

106. Defert acknowledges that the "filthy materiality" of the prison *was* important, but he emphasizes that former prisoners spoke more often of the "humiliation" and "debasement" that the "filth" transmitted in *Vie politique*, 54.

107. Defert, "L'émergence d'un nouveau front: les prisons," 318.

108. Ibid.

109. Artières, Quéro, and Zancarini-Fournel, "Genèse du GIP," 30.

110. Artières, Quéro, and Zancarini-Fournel, " 'Nous voulons savoir,' " 47.

111. GIP, "Quand l'information est une lutte," 69.

112. We can be even more precise here: *Maoism* inflected Foucault's conceptual vocabulary at the time. For his mobilization of this vocabulary, see Foucault, *Théories et institutions pénales*. Quite apart from focusing in this course on a peasant-based revolt and honing in on the strategies for breaking up worker-peasant alliances, Foucault embraced a whole dialectical language replete with references not only to "internal" (ibid., 89) and "immanent" (ibid., 92) contradictions but also to the "principal contradiction" (ibid., 92) in particular. He claimed that the repression established by Chancellor Pierre Séguier in the aftermath of the revolt of the bare feet in Normandy generated "the contradiction between popular armament (i.e. warrior) and selective armament (repressive). This contradiction was without a doubt the principal contradiction at the end of the Middle Ages at the level of the exercise of power" (ibid., 92). In making this claim, Foucault employed a *distinctly* Maoist concept. Mao Tsetung had famously articulated the concept of the principal contradiction to accentuate the unevenness of contradictions in "On Contradiction," in *Selected Readings from the Works of Mao Tsetung* (Peking: Foreign Language Press, 1971), 109–17. Louis Althusser had latched onto the concept in his critique of Hegelian dialectics in "On the Materialist Dialectic: On the Unevenness of Origins," in *For Marx*, trans. Ben Brewster (New York: Verso, 2005), 194–95, 205, 210–11.

113. GIP, *Investigation in 20 Prisons*, 156.

114. Michel Foucault, "Revolutionary Action 'Until Now,' " in *Language, Counter-Memory, Practice: Selected Essays and Interviews*, ed. Donald F. Bouchard, trans. Donald F. Bouchard and Sherry Simon (Ithaca, NY: Cornell University Press, 1977), 219.

115. Foucault, *Théories et institutions pénales*, 212, italics mine.

116. Artières, Quéro, and Zancarini-Fournel, " 'Nous voulons savoir,' " 47. Priscila Piazentini Vieira carefully avoids this reduction even as she draws exclusively from Artières, Quéro, and Zancarini-Fournel in her brief discussion of the Marxist sources of inspiration for Foucault's use of questionnaires on behalf of the GIP. See Priscila Piazentini Vieira, *A coragem da verdade e a ética do intelectual em Michel Foucault* (São Paulo: Intermeios, 2015), 157.

117. Hilde Rigaudias-Weiss, *Les enquêtes ouvrières en France entre 1830 et 1848* (1936; repr., New York: Arno Press, 1975).

118. For her translation of Marx's questionnaire, see Hilde Weiss, "Karl Marx's 'Enquête Ouvrière,'" in *Interpretations of Marx*, ed. Tom Bottomore (New York: Basil Blackwell, 1988), 263–68. For the details of her extensive involvement in Fromm's inquiry, see Wolfgang Bonss, "Critical Theory and Empirical Social Research: Some Observations," in *The Working Class in Weimar Germany: A Psychological and Sociological Study*, by Erich Fromm (Cambridge, MA: Harvard University Press, 1984), 1, 24.

119. Foucault, *Théories et institutions pénales*, 224n39.

120. Michel Foucault, handwritten bibliography on Collège de France headed notepaper, BNF NAF28730 (13), Folder 3, Subfolder 3 "Biblio," 57. Fonds Michel Foucault, Bibliothèque nationale de France, Paris. Words cannot capture my deep sense of gratitude to Elden for finding and pointing out this archival document.

121. For this view, see Michel J. M. Thiollent, *Crítica metodológica, investigação social e enquete operária*, 4th ed. (São Paulo: Polis, 1985), 103. Paradoxically, Thiollent cites Rigaudias-Weiss's book in his admittedly brief historical overview of nineteenth-century workers' inquiries (ibid., 102n3).

122. Rigaudias-Weiss, *Enquêtes ouvrières en France entre 1830 et 1848*, 15–16. The ambiguity resides in her account of whether workers were the first to undertake inquiries into the conditions of the working class. On the one hand, Rigaudias-Weiss claims that workers were the first "to put to work an inquiry into their working conditions" (ibid., 235) and that philanthropic and governmental inquiries into these conditions followed suit. On the other hand, she insists that it was not "workers themselves who were the first to conduct inquiries into their social condition" (ibid., 158). However, this point is difficult to reconcile with the fine details of her historical narrative. Rigaudias-Weiss traces workers' inquiries back to 1830, before any other types of inquiries into the conditions of workers.

123. Ibid., 162.

124. Ibid., 160, 166.

125. Ibid., 159, 164, 166.

126. Ibid., 159.

127. Ibid., 160.

128. Ibid., 244.

129. Ibid., 165.

130. Ibid.

131. Ibid., 210–12.

132. Ibid., 216.

133. Ibid.

134. Ibid., 217.

135. Ibid., 171, 235–36.

136. Ibid., 192–94.

137. Foucault, *Discipline and Punish*, 241–42.

138. Ibid., 241. For the original article, see "Enquête: De la condition des femmes," *L'Atelier*, December 30, 1842, http://gallica.bnf.fr/ark:/12148/bpt6k6863q/f230.image.

139. Foucault, *Discipline and Punish*, 241.

140. In this regard, it should perhaps come as little surprise that Socialisme ou Barbarie drew explicit inspiration from the historical example of *L'Atelier* in its support for and participation in the worker newspaper *Tribune Ouvrière*. A Socialisme ou Barbarie study group based at the Renault factory in Billancourt even went so far as to propose the reading of a reprinted issue of *L'Atelier* in 1954. On this detail, see Stephen Hastings-King, *Looking for the Proletariat: Socialisme ou Barbarie and the Problem of Worker Writing* (Chicago: Haymarket Books, 2015), 200n70.

141. Foucault, *Discipline and Punish*, 225.

142. Foucault, *Théories et institutions pénales*, 224n38.

143. Michel Foucault, "On Popular Justice: A Discussion with Maoists," in *Power/Knowledge: Selected Interviews and Other Writings, 1972–1977*, ed. Colin Gordon, trans. Colin Gordon, Leo Marshall, John Mepham, and Kate Soper (New York: Pantheon Books, 1980), 27.

144. Brich turns Foucault's suspicion about the connection between spaces of neutrality and the privileging of intellectuals on its head in "Groupe d'information sur les prisons," 26–47. She maintains that Foucault ended up privileging *his own* political voice in the GIP owing precisely to his *lack* of neutrality vis-à-vis the voices of prisoners. What is problematic in her argument is not the observation that Foucault lacked neutrality so much as the premise he sought to adhere to it. This premise brushes aside Foucault's commitment to the GIP's larger goal of heightening public intolerance of the prison system. As I argue elsewhere, this goal most likely structured the inclusion, exclusion, and ordering of the voices of prisoners in the publications of the GIP, but it did so in ways surprisingly critical of the GIP itself. See Marcelo Hoffman, "Investigations from Marx to Foucault," in *Active Intolerance: Michel Foucault, the Prisons Information Group, and the Future of Abolition*, ed. Perry Zurn and Andrew Dilts (New York: Palgrave Macmillan, 2015), 169–85.

145. GIP, *Investigation in 20 Prisons*, 156, italics in the original.

146. Foucault, "Revolutionary Action 'Until Now,'" 219–20, italics mine.

147. Michel Foucault, *"Society Must Be Defended": Lectures at the Collège de France, 1975–1976*, ed. Mauro Bertani and Alessandro Fontana, trans. David Macey (New York: Picador, 2003), 11.

148. Ibid., 7.

149. I owe Jason Read, Todd May, and Keith Harris a debt of gratitude for raising enough critical questions to enable me to elaborate the point in the preceding paragraph in greater detail. They raised these questions at The

Political Philosophy and Michel Foucault and Gilles Deleuze conference at Purdue University in West Lafayette, Indiana, on November 13, 2015.

150. Jamie Woodcock, "Smile Down the Phone: An Attempt at a Workers' Inquiry in a Call Center," *Viewpoint Magazine*, September 25, 2013, https://viewpointmag.com/2013/09/25/smile-down-the-phone-an-attempt-at-a-workers-inquiry-in-a-call-center/.

151. Roger R. Thompson, introduction to *Report from Xunwu*, by Mao Zedong, trans. Roger R. Thompson (Stanford: Stanford University Press, 1990), 36.

152. Ibid., 32.

153. Ben Golder, *Foucault and the Politics of Rights* (Stanford: Stanford University Press, 2015), 87.

154. Ibid.

Chapter 6

1. Andrea Cavazzini, *Enquête ouvrière et théorie critique: Enjeux et figures de la centralité ouvrière dans l'Italie des années 1960* (Liège: Presses Universitaires de Liège, 2013), 143–44.

2. Colectivo Situaciones, "Something More on Research Militancy: Footnotes on Procedures and (In)Decisions," trans. Sebastian Touza and Nate Holdren, in *Constituent Imagination: Militant Investigations // Collective Theorization*, ed. Stevphen Shukaitis and David Graeber with the assistance of Erika Biddle (Oakland: AK Press, 2007), 84.

3. Ibid., 81–82.

4. Ibid., 84.

5. Ibid., 81–82.

6. Ibid., 82.

7. Ibid., 85.

8. Maribel Casas-Cortés and Sebastián Cobarrubias, "Drifting Through the Knowledge Machine," in *Constituent Imagination*, 116.

9. Ibid.

10. Ibid.

11. Ibid.

12. Ibid., 117.

13. Ibid., 112.

14. Ibid.

15. Ibid., 113.

16. Ibid.

17. Jamie Woodcock, "Smile Down the Phone: An Attempt at a Workers' Inquiry in a Call Center," *Viewpoint Magazine*, September 25, 2013, https://viewpointmag.com/2013/09/25/smile-down-the-phone-an-attempt-at-a-workers-inquiry-in-a-call-center/.

18. Ibid.

19. Jennifer M. Murray, "The Shame of Servers: Inquiry and Agency in a Manhattan Cocktail Lounge," *ephemera: theory & politics in organization* 14, no. 3 (2014): 431–45, http://www.ephemerajournal.org/contribution/shame-servers-inquiry-and-agency-manhattan-cocktail-lounge.

20. Ibid., 431–32.

21. Ibid., 434.

22. Ibid., 435–42.

23. Ibid., 433.

24. Ibid., 444.

25. Ibid.

26. Jacob Blumenfeld, "Anti-workers' Inquiry," *The Brooklyn Rail: Critical Perspectives on Arts, Politics, and Culture*, July 13, 2015, http://brooklynrail.org/2015/07/field-notes/anti-workers-inquiry.

27. Ibid.

28. Ibid.

29. Yves Duroux, "Sur la question du savoir dans le maoïsme," in *Le sujet et l'étude: idéologie et savoir dans le discours maoïste*, by Andrea Cavazzini (Reims: Le Clou dans le Fer, 2011), 107.

30. Blumenfeld, "Anti-workers' Inquiry."

31. Quoted in Murray, "The Shame of Servers," 441.

Bibliography

Aisenberg, Andrew R. *Contagion: Disease, Government, and the "Social Question" in Nineteenth-Century France*. Stanford: Stanford University Press, 1999.

Althusser, Louis. *The Future Lasts Forever: A Memoir*. Edited by Olivier Corpet and Yann Moulier Boutang. Translated by Richard Veasey. New York: The New Press, 1993.

———. "On the Materialist Dialectic: On the Unevenness of Origins." In *For Marx*, translated by Ben Brewster, 161–218. New York: Verso, 2005.

Artières, Philippe, Laurent Quéro, and Michelle Zancarini-Fournel. "Genèse du GIP." In *Le Groupe d'Information sur les Prisons: Archives d'une lutte, 1970–1972*, edited by Artières, Quéro, and Zancarini-Fournel, 27–30. Paris: Éditions de l'IMEC, 2003.

———, eds. *Le Groupe d'Information sur les Prisons: Archives d'une lutte, 1970–1972*. Paris: Éditions de l'IMEC, 2003.

———. "Nous voulons savoir." In *Le Groupe d'Information sur les Prisons: Archives d'une lutte, 1970–1972*, edited by Artières, Quéro, and Zancarini-Fournel, 47–49. Paris: Éditions de l'IMEC, 2003.

L'Atelier. "Enquête: De la condition des femmes." December 30, 1842. http://gallica.bnf.fr/ark:/12148/bpt6k6863q/f230.image.

Badiou, Alain. *Ethics: An Essay on the Understanding of Evil*. Translated by Peter Hallward. New York: Verso, 2001.

———. "May '68 Revisited, 40 Years On." In *The Communist Hypothesis*, translated by David Macey and Steve Corcoran, 43–67. New York: Verso, 2010.

———. "The Nomadic Proletariat: An Interview with Alain Badiou." By Thomas Nail. *Philosophy Today* 61 (forthcoming).

———. "The Paris Commune: Political Declaration on Politics." In *The Communist Hypothesis*, translated by David Macey and Steve Corcoran, 168–228. New York: Verso, 2010.

———. *Peut-on penser la politique?* Paris: Seuil, 1985.

———. "Politics and Philosophy: An Interview with Alain Badiou." In *Ethics: An Essay on the Understanding of Evil*, translated by Peter Hallward, 95–144. New York: Verso, 2001.

———. *Théorie de la contradiction*. Paris: François Maspero, 1975.

Blumenfeld, Jacob. "Anti-workers' Inquiry." *The Brooklyn Rail: Critical Perspectives on Arts, Politics, and Culture*, July 13, 2015. http://brooklynrail.org/2015/07/field-notes/anti-workers-inquiry.

Bonss, Wolfgang. "Critical Theory and Empirical Social Research: Some Observations." In *The Working Class in Weimar Germany: A Psychological and Sociological Study*, by Erich Fromm, translated by Barbara Weinberger, and edited by Wolfgang Bonss, 1–38. Cambridge, MA: Harvard University Press, 1984.

Bosteels, Bruno. "Post-Maoism: Badiou and Politics." Special issue, *positions: east asia cultures critique* 13, no. 1 (2005): 575–634.

———. "Translator's Introduction." In *Theory of the Subject*, by Alain Badiou, vii–xxxvii. New York: Bloomsbury Academic, 2009.

Bottomore, T. B., and Maximilien Rubel. Introductory note to "Marx's *Enquête Ouvrière*." In *Karl Marx: Selected Writings in Sociology & Social Philosophy*, edited by T. B. Bottomore and Maximilien Rubel, 203–4. New York: McGraw-Hill, 1964.

Bourg, Julian. "Principally Contradiction: The Flourishing of French Maoism." In *Mao's Little Red Book: A Global History*, edited by Alexander C. Cook, 225–44. New York: Cambridge University Press, 2014.

Brich, Cecile. "The Groupe d'information sur les prisons: The Voice of Prisoners? Or Foucault's?" *Foucault Studies*, no. 5 (January 2008): 26–47. http://rauli.cbs.dk/index.php/foucault-studies/article/view/1408.

Burnham, James, Max Shachtman, and Maurice Spector. Introduction to Karl Marx's "A Workers' Inquiry." *New International: A Monthly Organ of Revolutionary Marxism* 12, no. 4 (1938): 379.

Cahiers de Mai. "Le rôle politique de l'enquête." July 1970.

Casas-Cortés, Maribel, and Sebastián Cobarrubias. "Drifting Through the Knowledge Machine." In *Constituent Imagination: Militant Investigations // Collective Theorization*, edited by Shukaitis and Graeber with the assistance of Biddle, 112–26. Oakland: AK Press, 2007.

Cavazzini, Andrea. *Enquête ouvrière et théorie critique: Enjeux et figures de la centralité ouvrière dans l'Italie des années 1960*. Liège: Presses Universitaires de Liège, 2013.

Colectivo Situaciones. "Something More on Research Militancy: Footnotes on Procedures and (In)Decisions." In *Constituent Imagination: Militant Investigations // Collective Theorization*, edited by Shukaitis and Graeber with the assistance of Biddle, 79–93. Oakland: AK Press, 2007.

Correspondence. *The Correspondence Booklet: Selections from a Paper That Is Written, Edited and Circulated by Its Readers*. Detroit: Correspondence Publishing, 1954.

Dean, Jodi. *The Communist Horizon*. New York: Verso, 2012.

———. *Crowds and Party*. New York: Verso, 2016.

Defert, Daniel. "L'émergence d'un nouveau front: les prisons." In *Le Groupe d'Information sur les Prisons: Archives d'une lutte, 1970–1972*, edited by Artières, Quéro, and Zancarini-Fournel, 315–26. Paris: Éditions de l'IMEC, 2003.

———. *Une vie politique: Entretiens avec Philippe Artières et Eric Favereau avec la collaboration de Joséphine Gross*. Paris: Seuil, 2014.

Dolci, Danilo. *Report from Palermo*. Translated by P. D. Cummins. New York: Hillman/McFadden Books, 1961.

Duchen, Claire. *Feminism in France: From May '68 to Mitterand*. Boston: Routledge & Kegan Paul, 1986.

Duroux, Yves. "Sur la question du savoir dans le maoïsme." In *Le sujet et l'étude: idéologie et savoir dans le discours maoïste suivi de dialogue avec Yves Duroux*, by Andrea Cavazzini, 93–125. Reims: Le Clou dans le Fer, 2011.

L'Égalité. April 28, 1880. http://gallica.bnf.fr/ark:/12148/bpt6k68307182/f3.item.r=l'egalite+journal;jsessionid=8EFF1ADF444E3A9C275C1E7AE689A61C.

———. May 5, 1880. http://gallica.bnf.fr/ark:/12148/bpt6k6830719g/f1.item.r=l'egalite+journal;jsessionid=8EFF1ADF444E3A9C275C1E7AE689A61C.

Elden, Stuart. "Peasant Revolts, Germanic Law and the Medieval Inquiry." Review of *Théories et institutions pénales: Cours au Collège de France, 1971–1972*, by Michel Foucault. *Berfrois*, June 2, 2015. http://www.berfrois.com/2015/06/foucaults-politics-of-truth-stuart-elden/.

Fanon, Frantz. *The Wretched of the Earth*. Translated by Richard Philcox. New York: Grove Press, 2004.

Fields, A. Belden. *Trotskyism and Maoism: Theory and Practice in France and the United States*. New York: Praeger, 1988.

Foucault, Michel. *Discipline and Punish: The Birth of the Prison*. Translated by Alan Sheridan. New York: Vintage Books, 1978.

———. Handwritten bibliography on Collège de France headed notepaper. BNF NAF28730 (13), Folder 3, Subfolder 3 "Biblio," 57. Fonds Michel Foucault. Bibliothèque nationale de France, Paris.

———. *Lectures on the Will to Know: Lectures at the Collège de France, 1970–1971 and Oedipal Knowledge*. Edited by Daniel Defert. Translated by Graham Burchell. New York: Palgrave Macmillan, 2013.

———. "Nul de nous n'est sûr d'échapper à la prison . . ." In *Le Group d'Information sur les Prisons: Archives d'une lutte, 1970–1972*, edited by Artières, Quéro, and Zancarini-Fournel, 43–44. Paris: Éditions de l'IMEC, 2003.

———. "On Popular Justice: A Discussion with Maoists." In *Power/Knowledge: Selected Interviews and Other Writings, 1972–1977*, edited by Colin Gordon, translated by Colin Gordon, Leo Marshall, John Mepham, and Kate Soper, 1–36. New York: Pantheon Books, 1980.

———. "Penal Theories and Institutions." In *Essential Works of Foucault, 1954–1984*, edited by Paul Rabinow. Vol. 1, *Ethics: Subjectivity and Truth*, edited by Paul Rabinow, translated by Robert Hurley and others, 17–21. New York: The New Press, 1997.

———. "La prison partout." In *Le Groupe d'Information sur les Prisons: Archives d'une lutte, 1970–1972*, edited by Artières, Quéro, and Zancarini-Fournel, 79. Paris: Éditions de l'IMEC, 2003.

———. "Revolutionary Action 'Until Now.'" In *Language, Counter-Memory, Practice: Selected Essays and Interviews*, edited by Donald F. Bouchard, translated by Donald F. Bouchard and Sherry Simon, 218–33. Ithaca, NY: Cornell University Press, 1977.

———. "La situation dans les prisons est intolérable . . ." In *Le Groupe d'Information sur les Prisons: Archives d'une lutte, 1970–1972*, by Artières, Quéro, and Zancarini-Fournel, 50–51. Paris: Éditions de l'IMEC, 2003.

———. *La société punitive: Cours au Collège de France (1972–1973)*. Edited by Bernard E. Harcourt. Paris: Gallimard/Seuil, 2013.

———. *"Society Must Be Defended": Lectures at the Collège de France, 1975–76*. Edited by Mauro Bertani and Alessandro Fontana. Translated by David Macey. New York: Picador, 2003.

———. *Surveiller et punir: naissance de la prison*. Paris: Gallimard, 1975.

———. *Théories et institutions pénales: Cours au Collège de France (1971–1972)*. Edited by Bernard E. Harcourt in collaboration with Elisabetta Basso and Claude-Olivier Doron and with the assistance of Daniel Defert. Paris: Seuil/Gallimard, 2015.

———. "Truth and Juridical Forms." In *Essential Works of Foucault, 1954–1984*, edited by Paul Rabinow. Vol. 3, *Power*, edited by James D. Faubion, translated by Robert Hurley and others, 1–89. New York: The New Press, 2000.

Foucault, Michel, Catharine von Bülow, and Daniel Defert. "The Masked Assassination." In *Warfare in the American Homeland: Policing and Prison in a Penal Democracy*, edited by Joy James, 140–58. Durham: Duke University Press, 2007.

Fromm, Erich. *The Working Class in Weimar Germany: A Psychological and Sociological Study*. Translated by Barbara Weinberger. Edited by Wolfgang Bonss. Cambridge, MA: Harvard University Press, 1984.

Glaberman, Martin. Introduction to *The American Worker*, by Paul Romano and Ria Stone, v–vi. Detroit: Bewick, 1972.

Golder, Ben. *Foucault and the Politics of Rights*. Stanford: Stanford University Press, 2015.

Groupe d'Information sur les Prisons (GIP). *L'assassinat de George Jackson*. Paris: Gallimard, 1971.

———. *Enquête dans une prison-modèle: Fleury-Mérogis*. Paris: Éditions Champ Libre, 1971.

———. "Enquête-intolérance." In *Le Groupe d'Information sur les Prisons: Archives d'une lutte, 1970–1972*, edited by Artières, Quéro, and Zancarini-Fournel, 53–54. Paris: Éditions de l'IMEC, 2003.

———. "Le GIP vient de lancer sa première enquête." In *Le Groupe d'Information sur les Prisons: Archives d'une lutte, 1970–1972*, edited by Artières, Quéro, and Zancarini-Fournel, 52. Paris: Éditions de l'IMEC, 2003.

———. "Nous venons discuter dans les files d'attente." In *Le Groupe d'Information sur les Prisons: Archives d'une lutte, 1970–1972*, edited by Artières, Quéro, and Zancarini-Fournel, 63–64. Paris: Éditions de l'IMEC, 2003.

———. "Quand l'information est une lutte." In *Le Groupe d'Information sur les Prisons: Archives d'une lutte, 1970–1972*, edited by Artières, Quéro, and Zancarini-Fournel, 72–73. Paris: Éditions de l'IMEC, 2003.

———. "Questionnaire aux détenus." In *Le Groupe d'Information sur les Prisons: Archives d'une lutte, 1970–1972*, edited by Artières, Quéro, and Zancarini-Fournel, 55–62. Paris: Éditions de l'IMEC, 2003.

Haider, Asad, and Salar Mohandesi. "Workers' Inquiry: A Genealogy." *Viewpoint Magazine*, September 27, 2013. https://viewpointmag.com/2013/09/27/workers-inquiry-a-genealogy/.

Hallward, Peter. *Badiou: A Subject to Truth*. Minneapolis: University of Minnesota Press, 2003.

Harvey, David. *A Companion to Marx's Capital*. New York: Verso, 2010.

Hastings-King, Stephen. *Looking for the Proletariat: Socialisme ou Barbarie and the Problem of Worker Writing*. Chicago: Haymarket Books, 2015.

Hoffman, Marcelo. "Foucault and the 'Lesson' of the Prisoner Support Movement." *New Political Science: A Journal of Politics and Culture* 34, no. 1 (March 2012): 21–36.

———. "Investigations from Marx to Foucault." In *Active Intolerance: Michel Foucault, the Prisons Information Group, and the Future of Abolition*, edited by Perry Zurn and Andrew Dilts, 169–85. New York: Palgrave Macmillan, 2016.

———. "Sources of Anxiety About the Party in Radical Political Theory." *Theoria: A Journal of Social and Political Theory* 63, no. 4 (December 2016): 18–36.

Høgsbjerg, Christian. "A 'Bohemian Freelancer'? C.L.R. James, His Early Relationship to Anarchism and the Intellectual Origins of Autonomism." In *Libertarian Socialism: Politics in Black and Red*, edited by Alex Prichard, Ruth Kinna, Saku Pinta, and David Berry, 143–66. New York: Palgrave Macmillan, 2012.

L'idiot liberte: Le torchon brûle. "Communique de presse." n.d. http://archivesautonomies.org/IMG/pdf/feminisme/torchonbrule/letorchonbrule-n000.pdf.

Information Group on Prisons (GIP). *See also* Groupe d'Information sur les Prisons.

———. *Investigation in 20 Prisons*. In *Foucault and Power: The Influence of Political Engagement on Theories of Power*, by Marcelo Hoffman, 155–204. New York: Bloomsbury Academic, 2014.

Jacquin, Jean-Baptiste. "A la prison de Fresnes, alerte sur le 'traitement inhumain' et 'dégradant' des détenus." *Le Monde*, December 14, 2016. http://www.lemonde.fr/police-justice/article/2016/12/14/la-controleure-des-prisons-alerte-sur-le-traitement-inhumain-des-detenus-a-fresnes_5048494_1653578.html.

James, C. L. R. *State Capitalism and World Revolution*. In collaboration with Raya Dunayevskaya and Grace Lee. Chicago: Charles H. Kerr, 1986.

Karl, Rebecca E. *Mao Zedong and China in the Twentieth-Century World: A Concise History*. Durham: Duke University Press, 2010.

Karlsen, Mads Peter, and Kaspar Villadsen. "Foucault, Maoism, Genealogy: The Influence of Political Militancy in Michel Foucault's Thought." *New Political Science: A Journal of Politics and Culture* 37, no. 1 (2015): 91–117.

Lagios, Thanasis. "Foucauldian Genealogy and Maoism." *foucaultblog*, February 6, 2016. doi: 10.13095/uzh.fsw.fb.130.

Lanzardo, Dario. "Marx et l'enquête ouvrière." In *Luttes ouvrières et capitalisme d'aujourd'hui*, by Quaderni Rossi, translated by Nicole Rouzet, 109–31. Paris: François Maspero, 1968.

Lawrence, Ken. Introduction to *A Workers' Inquiry*, by Karl Marx, 3. Tougaloo, MS: Freedom Information Service; Detroit: Bewick, 1973.

Le Dantec, Jean-Pierre. "D'où vient l'établissement?" *Les Temps Modernes*, nos. 684–85 (July–October 2015): 16–23.

Lenin, V. I. *Collected Works*. Vol. 3, *The Development of Capitalism in Russia*. Moscow: Progress Publishers, 1972.

———. "Questionnaire on the Situation of Workers in Enterprises." In *Marxism in Russia: Key Documents, 1879–1906*, edited by Neil Harding, 138–39. New York: Cambridge University Press, 1983.

———. *State and Revolution*. New York: International Publishers, 1943.

———. *What Is to Be Done? Burning Questions of Our Movement*. New York: International Publishers, 1969.

Lefort, Claude. "Proletarian Experience (1952)." Translated by Stephen Hastings-King. *Viewpoint Magazine*, September 26, 2013. https://viewpointmag.com/2013/09/26/proletarian-experience/.

Lih, Lars T. *Lenin*. London: Reaktion Books, 2011.

———. *Lenin Rediscovered: "What Is to Be Done?" in Context*. Chicago: Haymarket Books, 2008.

Linhart, Robert. *The Assembly Line*. Translated by Margaret Crosland. Amherst: University of Massachusetts Press, 1981.

Macey, David. *The Lives of Michel Foucault: A Biography*. New York: Pantheon Books, 1993.

Manceaux, Michèle. *Les maos en France*. Paris: Gallimard, 1972.

Mao Tsetung. *See also* Mao Zedong.

———. "On Contradiction." In *Selected Readings from the Works of Mao Tsetung*, 85–133. Peking: Foreign Languages Press, 1971.

———. "Oppose Book Worship." In *Selected Readings from the Works of Mao Tsetung*, 40–50. Peking: Foreign Languages Press, 1971.

———. "Preface to *Rural Surveys*." In *Selected Readings from the Works of Mao Tsetung*, 194–97. Peking: Foreign Languages Press, 1971.

———. "Report on an Investigation of the Peasant Movement in Hunan." In *Selected Readings from the Works of Mao Tsetung*, 23–39. Peking: Foreign Languages Press, 1971.

———. "Speech at the Chinese Communist Party's National Conference on Propaganda Work." In *Selected Readings from the Works of Mao Tsetung*, 480–98. Peking: Foreign Languages Press, 1971.

Mao Zedong. *See also* Mao Tsetung.

———. *Report from Xunwu*. Translated by Roger R. Thompson. Stanford: Stanford University Press, 1990.

Markun, Paulo. *Meu querido Vlado: A história de Vladimir Herzog e do sonho de uma geração*, 2nd ed. Rio de Janeiro: Objetiva, 2015.

Marx, Karl. *Capital: A Critique of Political Economy*. Vol. 1. Translated by Ben Fowkes. New York: Vintage Books, 1977.

———. "The Civil War in France." In *Marx: Later Political Writings*, edited and translated by Terrell Carver, 163–207. New York: Cambridge University Press, 2006.

———. "Enquête ouvrière." *La Revue socialiste*, April 20, 1880. http://gallica.bnf.fr/ark:/12148/bpt6k5817422b.item.r=Revue+Socialiste+1880.

———. "Marx's Enquête Ouvrière." In *Karl Marx: Selected Writings in Sociology & Social Philosophy*, edited by T. B. Bottomore and Maximilien Rubel, 204–12. New York: McGraw Hill, 1964.

———. "[Value, Price and Profit]." In *Collected Works*. Vol. 20, *Marx and Engels: 1864–68*, 101–49. Moscow: Progress Publishers, 1985.

———. *A Workers' Enquiry*. London: Utopia Press, 1933.

———. "A Workers' Inquiry." *New International: A Monthly Organ of Revolutionary Marxism* 12, no. 4 (1938): 379–81.

———. *A Workers' Inquiry*. Tougaloo, MS: Freedom Information Service; Detroit: Bewick, 1973.

———. "A Workers' Inquiry." Works of Karl Marx 1880. 1997. https://www.marxists.org/archive/marx/works/1880/04/20.htm.

———. "Workers' Questionnaire." In *Collected Works*. Vol. 24, *Marx and Engels: 1874–83*, 328–34. New York: International Publishers, 1989.

Marx, Karl, and Mao Tsetung. *Cadernos da prática 1: Inquérito operário e luta política*. Translated and edited by Amadeu Lopes Sabino and Sebastião Lima Rego. Lisbon: printed by the authors, 1971.

Montaldi, Danilo. "Introduction to L'Operaio Americano (1954)." Translated by Salar Mohandesi. *Viewpoint Magazine*, September 27, 2013. https://viewpointmag.com/2013/09/27/introduction-to-loperaio-americano-1954/.

Murray, Jennifer M. "The Shame of Servers: Inquiry and Agency in a Manhattan Cocktail Lounge." *ephemera: theory & politics in organization* 14, no. 3 (2014): 431–45. http://www.ephemerajournal.org/contribution/shame-servers-inquiry-and-agency-manhattan-cocktail-lounge.

Nail, Thomas. "Alain Badiou and the *Sans-Papiers*." *Angelaki: Journal of the Theoretical Humanities* 20, no. 4 (December 2015): 109–30.

Negri, Antonio. "Marx Is Still Marx: Interview with Rainer Ganahl." http://semiotexte.com/?p=660.

Organisation des prisonniers politiques (OPP). "Rapport sur les prisons." In *Le Groupe d'Information sur les Prisons: Archives d'une lutte, 1970–1972*, edited by Artières, Quéro, and Zancarini-Fournel, 34–36. Paris: Éditions de l'IMEC, 2003.

Panel on Responsible Conduct of Research (Government of Canada). "RCR Framework Interpretations." January 2015. http://www.rcr.ethics.gc.ca/eng/policy-politique/interpretations/inquiry-enquetes/.

Panzieri, Raniero. "Conception socialiste de l'enquête ouvrière." In *Luttes ouvrières et capitalisme d'aujourd'hui*, by Quaderni Rossi, translated by Nicole Rouzet, 109–16. Paris: François Maspero, 1968.

———. "Socialist Uses of Workers' Inquiry." Translated by Arianna Bove. *Transversal*. http://transform.eipcp.net/transversal/0406/panzieri/en.

Quaderni Rossi. Introduction to *Luttes ouvrières*. In *Luttes ouvrières et capitalisme d'aujourd'hui*, by Quaderni Rossi, translated by Nicole Rouzet, 7–39. Paris: François Maspero, 1968.

———. *Luttes ouvrières et capitalisme d'aujourd'hui*. Translated by Nicole Rouzet. Paris: François Maspero, 1968.

Rancière, Danielle. "Militer ensemble: Entretien avec Danielle Rancière." In *Michel Foucault*, edited by Philippe Artières, Jean-François Bert, Frédéric Gros, and Judith Revel, 53–56. Paris: Éditions de l'Herne, 2011.

Reid, Donald. "*Etablissement*: Working in the Factory to Make Revolution in France." *Radical History Review*, no. 88 (Winter 2004): 83–111.

La Revue Socialiste. "Enquête ouvrière." July 5, 1880. http://gallica.bnf.fr/ark:/12148/bpt6k58174319/f32.item.r=Revue+Socialiste+1880.

Rigaudias-Weiss, Hilde. *Les enquêtes ouvrières en France entre 1830 et 1848*. 1936. Reprint, New York: Arno Press, 1975.

———. *See also* Weiss, Hilde.

Robcis, Camille. "'China in Our Heads': Althusser, Maoism, and Structuralism." *Social Text 110* 30, no. 1 (2012): 51–69.

Romano, Paul. "Life in the Factory." In *The American Worker*, by Paul Romano and Ria Stone, 1–41. Detroit: Bewick, 1972.

Romano, Paul, and Ria Stone. *The American Worker*. Detroit: Bewick, 1972.

Ross, Kristin. *May '68 and its Afterlives*. Chicago: University of Chicago Press, 2002.

Rothstein, Andrew. Foreword to *A Workers' Enquiry*, by Karl Marx, 3–7. London: Utopia Press, 1933.

Shippen, Nichole Marie. *Decolonizing Time: Work, Leisure, and Freedom*. New York: Palgrave Macmillan, 2014.

Shukaitis, Stevphen, and David Graeber, eds. *Constituent Imagination: Militant Investigations // Collective Theorization*. With the assistance of Erika Biddle. Oakland: AK Press, 2007.

Simon, Henri. "Workers' Inquiry in Socialisme ou Barbarie." Translated by Asad Haider and Salar Mohandesi. *Viewpoint Magazine*, September 26, 2013. https://viewpointmag.com/2013/09/26/workers-inquiry-in-socialisme-ou-barbarie/.

Smith, Jason E. "From Établissement to Lip: On the Turns Taken by French Maoism." *Viewpoint Magazine*, September 25, 2013. https://viewpointmag.com/2013/09/25/from-etablissement-to-lip-on-the-turns-taken-by-french-maoism/.

Stone, Ria. "The Reconstruction of Society." In *The American Worker*, by Paul Romano and Ria Stone, 42–70. Detroit: Bewick, 1972.

Thiollent, Michel J. M. *Crítica metodológica, investigação social e enquete operária*. 4th ed. São Paulo: Polis, 1985.

Thompson, Roger R. Introduction to *Report from Xunwu*, by Mao Zedong, 3–41. Translated by Roger R. Thompson. Stanford: Stanford University Press, 1990.

Tout! April 23, 1971.

———. "Enquête . . ." April 23, 1971.

Touza, Sebastian, and Nate Holdren. Translator's Introduction to "Something More on Research Militancy: Footnotes on Procedures and (In)Decisions," by Colectivo Situaciones. In *Constituent Imagination: Militant Investigations // Collective Theorization*, edited by Stevphen Shukaitis and David Graeber with the assistance of Erika Biddle, 73–79. Oakland: AK Press, 2007.

Vieira, Priscila Piazentini. *A coragem da verdade e a ética do intelectual em Michel Foucault*. São Paulo: Intermeios, 2015.

Walker, Gavin. "On Marxism's Field of Operation: Badiou and the Critique of Political Economy." *Historical Materialism* 20, no. 3 (2012): 39–74.

Weiss, Hilde. "Karl Marx's 'Enquête Ouvrière.'" In *Interpretations of Marx*, edited by Tom Bottomore, 258–68. New York: Basil Blackwell, 1988.

———. *See also* Rigaudias-Weiss, Hilde.

Wolin, Richard. *The Wind From the East: French Intellectuals, the Cultural Revolution and the Legacy of the 1960s*. Princeton: Princeton University Press, 2010.

Woodcock, Jamie. "Smile Down the Phone: An Attempt at a Workers' Inquiry in a Call Center." *Viewpoint Magazine*, September 25, 2013. https://

viewpointmag.com/2013/09/25/smile-down-the-phone-an-attempt-at-a-workers-inquiry-in-a-call-center/.

———. "The Workers' Inquiry from Trotskyism to Operaismo: A Political Methodology for Investigating the Workplace." *ephemera: theory & politics in organization* 14, no. 3 (2014): 493–513. http://www.ephemerajournal.org/sites/default/files/pdfs/contribution/14-3woodcock.pdf.

Wright, Steve. *Storming Heaven: Class Composition and Struggle in Italian Autonomist Marxism*. Sterling, VA: Pluto Press, 2002.

Index

abnormality vs. normality, 89–90
Academy of Moral and Political Sciences, 30
administrative inquiries vs. workers' inquiries, 123, 124
Aisenberg, Andrew, 30
alienation of labor, 59–60
Alquati, Romano, 72
Althusser, Louis, 1–2, 87, 167n112
American Worker, The pamphlet (Johnson-Forest Tendency), 21, 54, 56–63
  division between mental and manual labor, 62–63
  influence of Marx's questionnaire, 60–61
  influence on *Quaderni Rossi*, 69
  influence on Socialisme ou Barbarie, 66
  narrative form vs. questionnaire form, 61–62
  purpose of, 57
  reasons for worker dissatisfaction, 58–60
  role in Marxist tradition, 56–57
antagonism vs. conflict, 76–78
anti-workers' inquiry, 138
Artières, Philippe, 123–24
Atelier, L', 125, 126, 127, 169n140
Badiou, Alain, 2, 6, 21, 22, 82–84
  critique of political economy, 157n13
  editorial work on *Le livre des paysans pauvres*, 86–87
  founding of UCFML, 84
  Peut-on penser la politique? 99
  "politics without party," 97–101
  "red years," 84, 91
  temporality of UCFML investigations, 90–91
bilan d'éxperience, 86
Blumenfeld, Jacob, 138, 139, 141
Boggs, Grace Lee, 2, 56
Bonss, Wolfgang, 5
Bosteels, Bruno, 83, 87
British Parliament, 29
bureaucracy
  creative expression vs., 58–59
  Trotsky's view of, 151n5
bureaucratic capitalism, 65
Buret, Eugène, 30

Cabet, Étienne, 125
Cahiers de Mai, 81, 121, 166n97
Capital (Marx), 28, 29, 30
capitalist exploitation, 73–76, 78–79
Carolingian Empire, 108
Casas-Cortés, Maribel, 136

Castoriadis, Cornelius, 64
Cavazzini, Andrea, 11
  consciousness-raising, 78
  Duroux interview, 89
  FIAT factory inquiries, 71–72
  reactivation of workers' inquiry, 70
  transformation of working class, 13, 134
Chaulieu, Pierre, 64
Chaulieu-Montal Tendency, 64, 153n58
Chinese Communist Party (CCP), 45
Chinese Cultural Revolution, 81, 84, 99
class composition, 68, 72
Cobarrubias, Sebastian, 136
Colectivo Situaciones, 7, 16, 135–36
Collected Works (Lenin), 39, 51
collective action, 40–41
collective political subjectivity of investigations, 16–19
Collège de France, 103, 104, 106, 119, 123
Communist Party of Great Britain, 38
conflict vs. antagonism, 76–78
consciousness-raising, *see also* mirror functions
  in *The American Worker*, 57–58
  Haider and Mohandesi literature on, 151n2
  by Johnson-Forest Tendency and Correspondence, 54
  in *Quaderni Rossi*, 68, 73–79
  in Socialisme ou Barbarie, 54, 65
Correspondence, 10, 21, 53–54, 55, 63–64
Correspondence, 63–64, 152n49
creative expression
  bureaucracy vs., 58–59
  in Marx's questionnaire, 34
Crítica metodológica, investigação social e enquete operária (Thiollent), 3
Critique of Political Economy (Marx), 73

De Martino, Ernesto, 70
De Palma, Dino, 71, 72
Defert, Daniel, 2, 103, 111, 113–15, 122, 156n2
Deng Xiaoping, 130
Development of Capitalism in Russia, The (Lenin), 42, 44, 87
Discipline and Punish (Foucault), 126
Dolci, Danilo, 70–71
Donzelot, Jacques, 122
Dunayevskaya, Raya, 2, 55, 63–64, 152n49
Duroux, Yves, 1, 11, 14, 17, 89, 139

economism, 38, 157n13
Égalité, L', 28, 36
Elden, Stuart, 124, 166n103, 168n120
Elle, 18–19
Engels, Friedrich, 77
enquête, 81, 155–56n1, *see also* inquiry
  English translations, 104–105, 161–62n1
  gap between theory and practice, 23, 105–106
  lessons from theory-practice gap, 127–31
  political effects of, 119–20
  practice of, 110–20
enquêtes ouvrières en France entre 1830 et 1848, Les (Rigaudias-Weiss), 124–26
Eskalera Karakola, 136
Esprit, 113
établissement, 11, 17, 82, 85–86, 88, 90, 92
exploitation, *see* capitalist exploitation

factory inspectors in England, 29
factory statistics in Russia, 43
Fanon, Frantz, 160n75

feminine precarity, 136
FIAT factory inquiries, see *Quaderni Rossi*
Fields, A. Belden, 88
First International Working Men's Association, 76
Fordism, 55, 65
Forest, Freddie, 55
Foucault, Michel, 2, *see also* Prisons Information Group (GIP)
  births of official inquiry and militant investigation, 133–34
  dialectical language, 167n112
  Discipline and Punish, 126
  English translations of enquête, 104–105
  founding of GIP, 7
  fusing of Marx and Mao, 103–104
  gap between theory and practice, 23, 105–106
  genealogy of inquiry, 18, 106–10, 157n7
  influence of workers' inquiries on, 120–27
  lessons from, 127–31
  Marx vs., 115
  practice of enquête, 110–20
  pre-Marxism in GIP investigations, 12, 104
  terminology, 22
  Théories et institutions pénales, 124, 127
Frankfurt Institute for Social Research, 5–6
French Communist Party (PCF), 85
French government inquiries into working class, 29–31
French Maoists' investigations, *see also* Union of Marxist-Leninist Communists of France (UCFML)
  "failure" of, 14
  framework, 11
  groups involved in, 87–90
  literature on, 21–22, 82–84
  Mao's influence on, 49, 81–82, 105, 156–57n7
  party vs. non-party form, 17–18
  role in Marxist tradition, 44
  UCFML investigations vs., 90–91
Fresnes prisoner abuse, 117–18, 165n92
Fromm, Erich, 5–6, 124

gap between theory and practice (Foucault), 23, 105–106
  influence of workers' inquiries on, 120–27
  lessons from, 127–31
Gautrat, Jacques, 67
genealogy of inquiry (Foucault), 18, 106–10, 157n7
General Confederation of Labor (CGT), 85
Glaberman, Martin, 62
Golder, Ben, 131
Guesde, Jules, 28
Guillaume, Philippe, 66

Haider, Asad, 34, 35, 55, 56, 60–61, 151n2
Hallward, Peter, 6, 98, 100
Harris, Keith, 169n149
Harvey, David, 29
Hastings-King, Stephen, 14, 64, 67–68
hierarchy destabilization, 17
Høgsbjerg, Christian, 56
Hunan investigation (Mao), 44–46

Il Mondo magico (De Martino), 70
illiteracy, 68
inquiry, *see also* enquête
  genealogy of, 18, 106–10, 157n7
  as judicial practice, 107–109, 118
  terminology, 4
"Inquiry: The Condition of Women" (*L'Atelier*), 126

"intolerance-investigations," 128
Investigation in 20 Prisons (GIP), 115–16, 117–18, 123
investigation in radical political struggles, *see also* French Maoists' investigations; Italian workerists' questionnaires; Lenin's questionnaire for Russian workers; Mao's investigations; Marx's questionnaire for French workers; recent militant investigations
adaptability of, 139
collective political subjectivity of, 16–19
contemporary shifts in, 24
"failure" of, 13–15, 139–40
fragmentary nature of analysis, 3–4
Lenin's critique of, 38–44
literature on, 26, 143–44n5
militant research vs., 7–8
political objectives of questionnaires, 15
sociological vs. political purposes, 5–7
sources in Marxism, 25–52
terminology, 4
timeline of Marxist investigation, 9–13
types of, 2
UCFML investigations vs., 91–92
value of studying, 8–9
investigations
combining with action, 86
as mirror functions, 31, 122, 159n42
types of, 1
Italian social context, 70–71
Italian Union of Labor, 78
Italian workerists' questionnaires, 10–11, 20–21, 54, 69–70, see also *Quaderni Rossi*

James, C. L. R., 2, 55, 56
Johnson, J. R., 55
Johnson-Forest Tendency, 10, 21, 53–54, 55, see also *American Worker, The* pamphlet (Johnson-Forest Tendency)
judicial practice, inquiry as, 107–109, 118

Karl, Rebecca E., 45
knowledge contents, 127–29, 130

Lanzardo, Dario, 2, 4, 18, 140, 141
analysis of Marx's questionnaire, 15, 121
completed Marx questionnaires, number of, 35
consciousness-raising, 54, 79
"Marx and Workers' Inquiry," 72–76
purpose of workers' inquiry, 78
success of Marx's questionnaire, 37
transformation of working class, 21
Lawrence, Ken, 31, 159n42
Lazarus, Sylvain, 84, 87, 90–91, 97
Le Dantec, Jean-Pierre, 87, 88
Lefort, Claude, 21, 54, 64, 66–67, 141
Lenin, V. I., 2, 3
Collected Works, 39, 51
criticism of Communards, 161n95
critique of workers' inquiries, 38–44, 119
Development of Capitalism in Russia, The, 42, 44, 87
politics and party, 98, 158n21
What Is to Be Done? 41
Lenin's questionnaire for Russian workers, 20
"failure" of, 27, 51–52, 141
formulation of, 25, 39, 51, 144n5
Mao's investigations vs., 47–48
Marx's questionnaire vs., 44
purpose of, 40–41

question types, 39–40
results of, 25–26
role in Marxist tradition, 10, 56
worker interview, 10, 20, 41–42, 66
Lévy, Benny, 85
Lih, Lars T., 40, 158n21
Linhart, Robert, 87, 88
literacy, social function of, 68
livre des paysans pauvres, Le: 5 années de travail maoïste dans une campagne française (UCFML), 22, 83–84, 85–86
editorial work, 86–87
Mao vs. UCFML understanding of peasants, 157n12
narrative form in, 92
peasant autonomy in, 96–97
"politics without party," 99–101
Long Live the Revolution (VLR), 89

Malon, Benoît, 28
manual labor, division with mental labor, 62–64
Mao Zedong, 2, 4, 91, 103–104, 167n112
"Oppose Book Worship," 47
"Preface to *Rural Surveys*," 49
Report from Xunwu, 46, 130
"Report on an Investigation of the Peasant Movement in Hunan," 45, 87
Maoism, 167n112
Mao's investigations, *see also* French Maoists' investigations
formulation of, 25, 51, 144n5
influence on French Maoists, 49, 81–82, 105, 156–57n7
influence on GIP investigations, 120
influence on *Quaderni Rossi*, 69–70
influence on recent investigations, 139
Lenin's questionnaire vs., 47–48
peasants, understanding of, 157n12
political knowledge gained from, 16
purpose of, 10, 47
results of, 25–26
right to speech and, 49
role in Marxist tradition, 44, 50, 56, 104
slogans of, 156n2
subjectivity and objectivity in, 44–50
success of, 20, 27, 50
Marks, Susan, 131
Markun, Paulo, 166n95
Martineau, Christine, 112, 122
Marx, Karl, 2, 3, 99, 161n95, 166n102
Capital, 28, 29, 30
Critique of Political Economy, 73
Foucault vs., 115
fusing with Mao, 103–104
"Marx and Workers' Inquiry" (Lanzardo), 72–76
Marxism, crisis of, 98
Marxism, investigations in, 2
heterogeneity, 20, 27–28
political effects of, 50–52
sources of, 25–52
timeline, 9–13
Marxism, sociology in, 77
Marxist-Leninist Communist Party of France (PCMLF), 84–85, 86
Marx's questionnaire for French workers
"creative expression," lack of, 34
English translations, 3, 37–38, 146–47n1
"failure" of, 14, 19–20, 26–27, 29–38, 116–17, 145n28
formulation of, 25, 51, 144n5
as framework for Italian workerists' questionnaires, 20–21, 54, 69–70

Marx's questionnaire for French workers *(continued)*
Fromm questionnaire vs., 5–6
influence on French Maoists, lack of, 81
influence on GIP investigations, 120–23
influence on recent investigations, 137–38, 139
influence on *The American Worker* pamphlet, 60–61
Lanzardo's interpretation of, 15
Lenin's questionnaire vs., 44
in "Marx and Workers' Inquiry" (Lanzardo), 73–76
publication in United States, 55, 60
purpose of, 31
question types, 32–34
responses received, 34–37
results of, 25–26
role in Marxist tradition, 9–10, 104
success of, 37
May, Todd, 169n149
mental labor, division with manual labor, 62–64
Michel, Natacha, 84, 97
militant investigations, *see* investigation in radical political struggles
militant research, investigations vs., 7–8
milk sales in UCFML investigation, 93–94, 95
Miller, Jacques-Alain, 111
Miller, Judith, 111
mirror functions, investigations as, 31, 122, 159n42, *see also* consciousness-raising
Mohandesi, Salar, 34, 35, 55, 56, 60–61, 151n2
Montal, Claude, 64
Montaldi, Danilo, 69
Mothé, Daniel, 67
Murray, Jennifer M., 137–38, 139, 141

Nail, Thomas, 97
narrative form vs. questionnaire form
in *The American Worker*, 61–62
in GIP investigations, 116
political effects of, 140–42
in *Quaderni Rossi*, 53–54, 68, 69, 79
in Socialisme ou Barbarie, 65–68
in UCFML investigations, 92
Nazism, 5
Negri, Antonio, 71, 78
neutrality, 169n144
New International, 34, 55, 60
non-party form vs. party form, 17–18
normality vs. abnormality, 89–90

objectivity in Mao's investigations, 44–50
Oedipus the King (Sophocles), 106–107, 118–19
"Oppose Book Worship" (Mao), 47
Organization of Political Prisoners (OPP), 111

pamphleteering, 38
Panel on Responsible Conduct of Research (PRCR), 4
Panzieri, Raniero, 2, 4
consciousness-raising, 54, 141
FIAT factory inquiries, 71
founding of *Quaderni Rossi*, 68, 70
physical displacements and spatial dislocation, 91
role of workers, 69
"Socialist uses of workers' inquiry," 76–78
Paris Commune, 36, 99, 161n95

party form
  critique of, 84
  non-party form vs., 17–18
  "politics without party," 97–101
  UCFML view of, 85, 91–92
"party of a new type," 85, 91, 97–101, 158n21
party-state, 99
Passeron, Jean-Claude, 7, 122
path maintenance in UCFML investigation, 94
peasants
  autonomy, 95–97, 160n75
  classification of, 42–43
  Hunan investigation, 44–46
  knowledge gained from/by, 52
  Mao vs. UCFML understanding of, 157n12
  revolt of the bare feet (Normandy), 163n40, 167n112
  UCFML investigation, 85–86, 92–95
  village locations in France, 160n57
  voice of, 159n52
  Xunwu investigation (Mao), 46–47
"perguntório," 166n95
Peut-on penser la politique? (Badiou), 99
physical displacements, 91–92
Piazza Statuto revolt, 78
political economy, critique of, 157n13
political effects
  of enquête, 119–20
  of GIP investigations, 119–20
  of investigations in Marxism, 50–52
  of questionnaire form vs. narrative form, 140–42
Political Organization (OP), 97–98
political purposes of investigation
  collective political subjectivity, 16–19
  in early Marxism, 50–52
  questionnaires, effects of, 15
  sociological purposes vs., 5–7
"Political Role of the Inquiry, The" (*Cahiers de Mai*), 121
"politics" vs. "the political," 99
"politics without party," 97–101
Populaire, Le, 125
popular knowledge, 8–9
power-knowledge form, 106–107, 109–10
Precarias a la Deriva, 136
"Preface to *Rural Surveys*" (Mao), 49
pre-Marxism in GIP investigations, 12, 104
principal contradiction, 167n112
prisoner abuse
  Fresnes prison, 117–18, 165n92
  Toul prison, 115, 164–65n77
Prisons Information Group (GIP), 7, 18, 88, 103
  hierarchy destabilization, 17
  influence of Mao's investigations, 120–23
  influence of Marx's questionnaire, 120–23
  "intolerance-investigations," 128
  Investigation in 20 Prisons, 115–18, 123
  investigations of, 22–23, 104–105
  origin of, 110–12
  political effects of investigation, 119–20
  pre-Marxism in investigations, 11–12, 104
  questionnaire distribution, 112–14
  responses received, 117–18
  success of investigation, 116–17
  UCFML vs., 112
  verifying questionnaire responses, 114–15
  voices of prisoners in, 169n144
"Proletarian Experience" (Lefort), 66

Proletarian Left (GP), 85
 arrest and imprisonment of, 86, 103
 cessation of, 91
 investigations of, 88–89
 origin of GIP, 105, 110–11
proletarian political leadership vs. peasant autonomy, 95–97
psychiatric hospital patients, survey of, 89–90

Quaderni Rossi, 21, 68–79, 122
 collective political subjectivity, 16–17
 conflict vs. antagonism, 76–78
 French translations, 81
 influence of *The American Worker* pamphlet, 69
 Marx's questionnaire as model for, 54, 69–70
 narrative form vs. questionnaire form, 53–54, 68, 69, 79
 reactivation of workers' inquiry, 10
 roots in Italian social context, 70–71
 sociological approach to inquiry, 7, 71–72, 77–78
 theorization of workers' inquiry, 72–76
Quéro, Laurent, 123–24
questionnaire form vs. narrative form
 in *The American Worker*, 61–62
 in GIP investigations, 116
 political effects of, 140–42
 in *Quaderni Rossi*, 53–54, 68, 69, 79
 in Socialisme ou Barbarie, 65–68
questionnaires, *see* investigation in radical political struggles; workers' inquiries

Rancière, Danielle, 2, 88, 112, 122
Read, Jason, 169n149
Reading Capital (Althusser), 2
recent militant investigations
 3Cups Counter-Cartographies Collective, 136–37
 Blumenfeld's anti-workers' inquiry, 138
 Colectivo Situaciones, 135–36
 influence of Marx's questionnaire, 137–38, 139
 Murray's inquiry of cocktail servers, 137–38
 Precarias a la Deriva, 136
 reasons for studying, 134–35
 Woodcock's inquiry of call center workers, 137
Red Aid (SR), 111
Report from Palermo (Dolci), 70
Report from Xunwu (Mao), 46, 130
"Report on an Investigation of the Peasant Movement in Hunan" (Mao), 45, 87
Revue socialiste, La, 28, 31, 35, 36, 37, 75
Rieser, Vittorio, 71, 72
Rigaudias-Weiss, Hilde, 12
 consciousness-raising, 31
 enquêtes ouvrières en France entre 1830 et 1848, Les, 124–26
 "failure" of Marx's questionnaire, 14, 30, 36
 gap between theory and practice, 23
 mirror functions, 159n42
 origin of workers' inquiries, 168n122
 plea for responses to Marx's questionnaire, 35
right to speech, 49
Romano, Paul, 56, 57–59, 62, 66
Ross, Kristin, 87, 166n97
Rothstein, Andrew, 32, 33

Salvadori, Edda, 71, 72
Sartre, Jean-Paul, 98
Séguier, Pierre, 167n112
shame, 138, 141
Simon, Henri, 65
Singer, Phil, 56
Smith, Jason E., 87
Social Democracy, 39, 40
social function of literacy, 68
Socialisme ou Barbarie, 10, 14, 53–54, 64–68, 169n140
Socialisme ou Barbarie, 65, 66, 69
"Socialist uses of workers' inquiry" (Panzieri), 76–78
sociological purposes of investigation
  political purposes vs., 5–7
  in *Quaderni Rossi*, 71–72, 77–78
Sophocles, 106–107, 118–19
spatial dislocation, 91–92
speech, right to, 49
Stalin, Joseph, 151n5
Stalinist Russia, 55
state capitalism, 55
stationary drift, 136–37
Stone, Ria, 56, 59–60, 62, 66
strikes, 40–41
subjectivity in Mao's investigations, 44–50
surplus knowledge, 123
surplus value, 123

test vs. inquiry, 108
Théories et institutions pénales (Foucault), 124, 127
theorization of workers' inquiry, 69, 72–76
Thiers, Adolphe, 161n95
Thiollent, Michel J. M., 6
  administrative inquiries vs. workers' inquiries, 124
  conflict vs. antagonism, 76
  consciousness-raising, 78–79
  Crítica metodológica, investigação social e enquete operária, 3
  "failure" of Marx's questionnaire, 28
  Lenin's critique of workers' inquiries, 38
  success of Marx's questionnaire, 37
  theory vs. practice, 69–70
Thompson, Roger R., 44, 46, 48, 130
3Cups Counter-Cartographies Collective, 136–37
Tito, Josip Broz, 153n58
Toscano, Alberto, 98
Toul prisoner abuse, 115, 164–65n77
Tout! 89
Tribune Ouvrière, 67, 169n140
Tronti, Mario, 78
Trotsky, Leon, 151n5
Trotskyist groups, 10, 20–21, 55, *see also* Correspondence; Johnson-Forest Tendency; Socialisme ou Barbarie
Trotskyist International Communist Party, 153n58
Trotskyist Workers' Party, 55

Undercover Boss, 130
Union of Marxist-Leninist Communist Youth (UJCML), 18, 87–88
Union of Marxist-Leninist Communists of France (UCFML), 18, 22
  établissement in investigations, 85–86
  French Maoists' investigations vs., 90–91
  GIP vs., 112
  historical context, 84–85
  investigation in radical political struggles vs., 91–92
  Le livre des paysans pauvres, 22, 83–87, 92, 96–97, 99–101, 157n12

Union of Marxist-Leninist Communists of France (UCFML) *(continued)*
peasants, understanding of, 157n12
"politics without party," 97–101
practical challenges to investigations, 92–95
proletarian political leadership vs. peasant autonomy, 95–97
University of North Carolina at Chapel Hill, 136–37

Victor, Pierre, 85
Vieira, Priscila Piazentini, 167n116
Villermé, Louis, 30

Weiss, *see* Rigaudias-Weiss, Hilde
What Is to Be Done? (Lenin), 41
Wolin, Richard, 89
Women's Liberation Movement (MLF), 19
Woodcock, Jamie, 56–57, 130, 137
workers' inquiries, *see also* investigation in radical political struggles
administrative inquiries vs., 123, 124
failure of, 125–26
influence on Foucault, 120–27
origin in France, 124–25, 168n122
"Workers' Inquiry, A" (Marx), *see* Marx's questionnaire for French workers
workers' newspapers, origin of, 152n49
working class
breakdown of, 134
transformation of, 13
Working Class in Weimar Germany: A Psychological and Sociological Study, The (Fromm), 5–6
Wright, Steve, 69, 70–71, 72

Xunwu investigation (Mao), 46–47

Zancarini-Fournel, Michelle, 123–24
Zemstvo, 42–43

www.ingramcontent.com/pod-product-compliance
Lightning Source LLC
LaVergne TN
LVHW040758070826
844660LV00025B/1188

* 9 7 8 1 4 3 8 4 7 2 6 2 1 *